BREAKING A RAINBOW, BUILDING A NATION

Breaking a Rainbow, Building a Nation

The Politics behind #MustFall Movements

Rekgotsofetse Chikane

PICADOR AFRICA

First published in 2018 by Picador Africa
An imprint of Pan Macmillan South Africa
Private Bag X19, Northlands
Johannesburg
2116

www.panmacmillan.co.za

ISBN 978 177010 590 4
e-ISBN 978 177010 5911

Editing by Alison Lowry
Editorial assistance by Katlego Tapala
Proofreading by Sean Fraser
Design and typesetting by Triple M Design, Johannesburg
Cover design by Alexander Papkok

This is my homage to the generations of youth before me,
those I fought alongside and those who will inevitably come after.
For the sacrifices you make for a country that will never thank you.

Contents

Chapter 1

Can Coconuts be Trusted with the Revolution?

It's probably best to start this book off by getting the elephant in the room out of the way.

Dinner-table discussions with my father can be fascinating. Who wouldn't take advantage of the knowledge of a man described as one of the 'fathers of democracy'?[1] He was the former director-general in the presidency in the era of Thabo Mbeki, former secretary-general of the South African Council of Churches, religious moral compass of the African National Congress, and one of the very rare ANC veterans who did what seemingly no other veteran would do at the time: he stood up against the Jacob Zuma regime.

My father has been my political school for as long as I can remember and, for most of my young life, he provided me with front-row tickets to a daily screening of How to Build a Democratic South Africa. A screening that included not only the director's comments but all the uncut footage that didn't make it into the public domain. Though not every screening is shown without criticism in my home, the experience has provided me with a wealth of insight into the hardships that the generation before me went through to give me the opportunities available to me today.

It's probably because of this that I find myself at odds with my father.

His work in building a 'rainbow nation' is at odds with my desire to break it. Where he seeks to build unity, I seek to fragment it. My dad believes that we can change through reform, while I believe we can only improve through revolution. A revolution that breaks apart the pretence that the negotiated settlement in 1994 created a society that provided equal opportunities for all. Looking at the state of the country, in 2018, to say that we all have equal opportunities couldn't be further from the truth. I want my legacy to be that I was part of a generation that sought to build a society whose genuine intent was to benefit those who were not only historically marginalised then but who are still marginalised today.

I don't remember the 1995 Rugby World Cup because I wasn't in the country at the time and, to be honest, I am grateful that I wasn't. It has been my experience that those who were present to experience the joys of winning the tournament and kick-starting the rainbow nation project are the most adept at forcing you to inhale their second-hand nostalgia. The 1995 World Cup was the moment when President Mandela forced an entire generation of South Africans to drink the Kool-Aid of the rainbow nation. In one lifetime-defining moment, Mandela slowly handed the trophy to François Pienaar – South Africa's national rugby captain – gently placed his left hand over Pienaar's right shoulder and whispered words of thanks for what the Springbok captain had done to bring the country together. At that moment Mandela created a reimagined country. However, what was instilled into this newly formed country was not the belief that we were all hands-on-deck to change the country, but rather a sense of unquestioning obedience towards the status quo. A status quo that entrenched the belief that we are all equal, but some are 'more' equal than others. A status quo that assumes the double consciousness that took hold in our country to be unassailable.

Renowned African-American sociologist WEB Du Bois – and the first African-American to earn a doctorate from Harvard University – described double consciousness as 'the sense of always looking at oneself through the eyes of others, of measuring one's soul by the tape of a world that looks on in amused contempt and pity'.[2] South Africa's particular double consciousness allows and encourages us to live in a state of unsustainable stasis. It creates a sense of acceptance that we can live in what is an institutionally corrupt country and still believe that we are democratic. It impresses upon us the belief that a mineral-rich state where poverty is fuelled and driven by a mineral-energy industrial complex are compatible ideals in a modern society.

We have told ourselves that it is normal for our country to exist in a state where being black is to be disadvantaged at birth, yet supposedly is filled with the opportunity to achieve a level of prosperity in the future. We live in a country that is oddly enamoured with the struggle between its two souls: one that embraces a post-apartheid society and one that under-stands this society as a post-1994 one.

Not many people in South Africa have fully understood what impelled the student protests that gripped the country in 2015 and 2016. In fact, not even students fully understood what drove them passionately to ques-tion the state of the country during that period and continues to drive them now. What I do know is that it was the realisation of this double consciousness that has kept us in stasis, that made us aware that the coun-try that was born in 1994, was still. It neither drove us forward nor did it drive us backwards. The protests that gripped the country in 2015 and 2016 were the first real nationally co-ordinated attempt by citizens of the country to resuscitate the urgency to change the status quo. A status quo which ensured that the dreams of millions of South Africans in 1994 were dreams deferred.

Young people across the country are beginning to look beyond the mirage created by this double consciousness and to reject the veil of igno-rance under which the architects of our democratic dispensation created the country. Young people are beginning the process of 'unlearning'. Not within the confines of a classroom – the same classroom that tried to instil in them the sense of being born free – but rather through a process of their everyday experiences. Young people are beginning to look beyond the mirage of the miracle of 1994 and understand that for South Africa to grow effectively then #EverythingMustFall.

Although I consider myself one of those who is looking beyond the mirage of 1994, the question that should be asked of me is whether I should be trusted with what happens next. I am part of the political elite in South Africa currently caught up in a game of snakes and ladders. Ladders that lead to prosperity and snakes that lead to despair. We are an elite group of young people who, unlike others, have had the opportunity to embrace the concept of being born free, yet have rejected it.

In delivering the 2015 Ruth First Lecture, activist, author and one of #FeesMustFall's fiercest intellectuals Panashe Chigumadzi described this elite, the 'coconuts', as:

> ... a particular category of 'born-free' black youth that were hailed as torchbearers for the 'Rainbow Nation'; the same category of black youth that is now part of the forefront of new student movements calling for Rhodes to fall at our universities and in South Africa.
>
> It is these very coconuts that have been increasingly disillusioned by and have pushed back against the notion of the Rainbow Nation. We were a conduit for the country's absolution from the real work of reconciliation as we were shipped off, Woolies skhaftins in tow, to the likes of Pretoria Girls High and Michaelhouse. Yet it is this very generation, supposedly robed in the privileges of democracy, that is now 'behaving badly' and 'militantly'. Instead of becoming the trusted go-betweens between black and white, we are turning to conceptions of blackness and mobilizing anger at the very concept of the Rainbow Nation. The fantasy of a 'colour-blind', 'post-race' South Africa has been projected onto us coconuts, but our lived experiences are far from free of racism.[3]

Fellow coconut Chigumadzi doesn't refer to coconuts in this context with the usual disdain that the term carries. She associates the term with agents who have rejected the weight of whiteness that their social reality seems to lay on their shoulders. Coconut Chigumadzi has chosen to self-identify as a coconut not because it attributes to her benefits within society, but because it gives her the freedom to refuse these opportunities. For her, this refusal to be co-opted into whiteness allows her to express a new form of radical anti-racist politics.

Day by day this form of politics is gathering new and more dynamic supporters across the political spectrum. It is a form of politics whose tactics are formed through experiential learning and unlearning. It lends itself to interrogating both the concepts and metaphors of nation-building and multi-culturalism in South Africa to make it easier to understand the rejection of the notion of a 'rainbow nation'. This rejection has a dialectical element to it: a decision to reject formed by the experience of being rejected by those from whom you sought acceptance.

The rainbow nation motif, in hindsight, was probably the most toxic way of bringing our nation together. The phrase was bestowed upon us by Archbishop Desmond Tutu, and the metaphor was used to describe how a nation historically divided had been united in its diversity. It became an artificial conch of righteousness but it belied the truth of the country's reality. The failure of the rainbow nation motif can be seen, ironically, in its strongest symbolic attribute: its imagery. The colours of the rainbow never intersect. They merely blend together at their fringe, creating white hues where they do. The image reinforces the belief that we must co-exist with one another yet ensure that our diversity runs infinitely parallel without ever truly integrating. The rainbow nation is simply an emotional ploy to garner support for a South Africa whose foundations are based on whiteness and, as such, perpetuates various forms of discrimination – often using our own democratic institutions to do so.

Using the idea of the rainbow nation we, as a society, have trapped ourselves in a false understanding of our social reality. We to and fro in a space where ignorance of those in your community is acceptable so long as you are at ease with sharing the community with them. We are not encouraged to feel uncomfortable in the face of difference. Instead, we are encouraged to ignore difference to make it easier for us to co-exist. The rainbow nation motif doesn't drive us together, it forces us apart. It prioritises the acknowledgement of our differences over the understanding of them. However, this 'easing' is primarily concerned with ensuring the comfort of white people. This comfort zone is predicated on the creation of white hues within the rainbow. Instances of integration in South Africa are often only accepted if they ensure that whiteness is made comfortable.

White hues are spaces that are centred on whiteness and permit the existence of others. Whether these are shopping malls in suburbs or rugby stadiums across the country, the barometer for integration is not how many white people are in black spaces, but how many black people are in white spaces and are not causing a revolt. White hues are not the result of arbitrary happenings within society, but of a constellation of micro-actions (or coercive micro-aggressions) which create a macro form of societal easing for white people. A societal easing that generates a host of white hues across the country where interactions of difference must take place within the comfort zone of whiteness.

To coconuts, however, whiteness engenders a belief that you must be the right kind of black person in the right kind of situation. Your expression of free will is dependent on the institutionalised norms which have been set by the white people around you. What differentiates coconuts from black people, in general, is that even when you leave the aforementioned situation, whiteness stays with you, hunched over your shoulder, directing your every action. For a coconut, whiteness never requires white people; it merely requires a chained and co-opted mind.

The rejection of the rainbow nation narrative and its consequences will be a strong theme through this book. As such, it is essential to understand that my use of this concept of rejection is reliant on a distinction between young people who are born-free, coconuts and those who are born-into-bondage. In what can be considered a myth turned truism, there is a belief that every young South African born after 1994 is born-free. That we all will be inherently – or by circumstance – able to climb a ladder in life that leads to prosperity because we are all apparently equal. Coconuts, born-frees and those born-into-bondage are all forced to internalise this truism, even though only one group can actualise it.

Born-frees are a generation of South Africans who are indentured to the rainbow nation motif. Their existence is meant not only to maintain this motif but unconditionally accept that the injustice of the past has primarily been erased due to the democratic dispensation achieved in 1994 and the process undertaken by the Truth and Reconciliation Commission in 1996. It is a wishful ideal that is imposed on young people who live in a post-1994/post-apartheid society. It's not enforced enthralment, but it is institutionalised into our society. We are, after all, Mandela's children and have been handed the torch to continue his legacy.

Thus to be born-free in South Africa is to accept the mirage that 'the seeming permanence of apartheid-constructed socio-political identities, and the socio-economic concentration of poverty among the black population as a consequence of apartheid policies' has been resolved, and in situations in which it hasn't, that you are able to overcome them.[4]

It is hopeful, as much as it is naive. However, only by accepting this mirage are you permitted to climb the ladder of prosperity. Any form of rejection is swiftly regarded as not following the ideals of building a rainbow nation. Stepping out of the boundary of the white hues that surround us without the permission to do so. The idea of 'permission' is important here because it infers that the *choice* to climb the ladder of prosperity doesn't exist (because it requires permission to do so). But if this permission needs you to believe in the mirage of the rainbow, are you truly able to climb the ladder of prosperity?

What makes coconuts especially fascinating and dangerous is that we are the only born-frees who, due to our proximity to whiteness, can reject the rainbow nation narrative yet still climb the ladder of prosperity. The ability for coconuts to have the actual choice to climb the ladder is pivotal when trying to understand the changing dynamics of politics among young South Africans. Coconuts such as me carry both the economic and social capital to create new forms of discourse within the mainstream narrative of South Africa. Our proximity to whiteness and whiteness's acceptance of us – so long as we behave – allows us not to fall victim to the rainbow nation but gives us the illusion of space to strive to build something different by rejecting it. Because we can exist in two worlds simultaneously, we are able to create new hues of interaction that were previously unimaginable or non-existent. Furthermore, we can bring to light injustices which the rainbow nation narrative placates and deems normal. Thus, while fee-related protests have existed for decades in universities such as the University of Fort Hare or Walter Sisulu University, it was only when the students with both economic and social capital from the more affluent and privileged universities joined the calls for reform of the fee system that the mainstream narrative of the country became interested in the cause.

For the majority of young South Africans, being born-free has never been an option. The majority are born-into-bondage. They are caught in a perpetual cycle of social, economic and political exclusion from which they are unable to break away through their own volition, regardless of their belief or non-belief in the rainbow nation. For millions of South Africans, the inability to find an occupation or the means to resist the trap of impoverishment means they are bound to a life that belies the dream of a rainbow nation.

In 2015, 62% of the 18.1 million children in South Africa lived below Statistics South Africa's upper-bound poverty line of R965 per person per month (adjusted from its 2011 level of R779 per person per month), with 70% of black children living in poor households. Only 4% of white children lived in similar conditions. In addition to this, 62% of South African children resided in a household with only one employed adult and with the other 31% living in a household with no adults working.[5] Towards the end of 2017, of the 20.2 million 15–34 year olds in South Africa, 38% (7.7 million) were Not in Employment, Education or Training (NEET),[6] with over 70% of total unemployment in South Africa between 2004 and 2014 consisting of 15–34 year olds.[7]

Statistics and numbers reflective of every sector will all reveal similar glaring inequalities as they weave a story about how South Africa has failed its young people. For this group of South Africans being born-free is a pipe dream. Their liberation is dependent on the liberation of a small contingent of black South Africans who are born-free, and specifically coconuts. Coconuts, who for better or worse, are the most likely grouping to lift all young people out of impoverishment. This is because of how whiteness embraces coconuts when compared to ordinary born-frees and those born-into-bondage.

Coconuts provide whiteness with its most fervent potential rival because of our proximity to it, yet we remain its primary ally within the broader discourse of race. To maintain our allegiance, whiteness interacts with us differently from how it interacts with those who are born-into-bondage. It functions and interacts with born-frees and coconuts in rather complex ways that commonly play out through engagements that promote social inclusion. The proverbial 'Gosh, Thembi, I really like you. You aren't like the other black people who are [*insert your own stereotypical black action*]'.

Whiteness in this way makes the born-frees and coconuts 'other blackness'. Instead of whiteness accepting us 'other blackness' into its fold as equals, it leaves us in a state of purgatory. Waiting at the gates of salvation, with 'white' Peter our proverbial white saviour acting as a gatekeeper.

For those who are born-into-bondage, the maintenance of whiteness is dependent on their complete physical and mental subordination. The embrace of whiteness in this sense offers no mirage of choice. The system that whiteness creates through the rainbow nation ensures that these individuals remain trapped as the sacrificial lambs within the system. Whiteness treats this group differently due to its sheer size and requires a more forceful tactic that doesn't rely on purgatorial stasis. It involves a set of values that reinforce subjugation as the norm. This set of values has existed in South Africa since 1652.

Through its control of the born-frees through acceptance, the coconuts through choice and the born-into-bondages through subjugation, whiteness co-opts all of us into maintaining its hegemony in our society.

To white South Africans, to be at ease is to enforce and preserve their whiteness. I remember a conversation I had with Dr Max Price, former vice-chancellor of the University of Cape Town, regarding the pervasiveness of institutional racism at the university. When he posed the question to me about how to identify institutional racism within the university, I answered by saying, 'It's that you don't. It's the reason why it is institutionalised.' You are not supposed to know why the rules of the game are as they are; your role is merely to play the game within their ambit.

I sometimes liken institutionalised forms of discrimination to driving down a dark road with a car driving towards you. You don't sit in the car constantly wondering whether the oncoming vehicle will be in the correct lane or not. You don't spend those moments doubting whether the person driving towards you understands the basic rules of the road. Staying in your lane is simply an institutionalised norm that you've bought into without question because, without it, our road system wouldn't function. We

9

have bought into these norms and values because we have been told that it is the right thing to do and that without them, our system of co-existence wouldn't work. But we never ask who determined whether that institutionalised norm was right.

The act of not questioning the enunciation of rightness is deeply embedded in a discussion of decolonisation and decolonial thought, but it isn't a discussion I wish to engage in just yet. For now, I simply want to state that institutionalised discrimination requires us never to ask who enunciates rightness because doing so would breed a level of uncertainty regarding which side of the road is the 'right' side to drive on. We would be so worried about trusting our fellow drivers on the road that we would not want to drive at all, and thus a collapse of the system would ensue.

Whiteness is similar in this regard. It's a collection of institutionalised norms that guide our day-to-day interactions because we have been socially programmed to believe that if we don't follow these 'rules of the game', then our system will fail to function. Once you introduce the aspect of power relations – that is, social positioning, race, class, gender, heteronormativity, epistemology, ontology, authority – this breeds institutionalised forms of discrimination.

It's the day-to-day discrimination of this form that permeates our society. Therefore, if whiteness's logic is to create perverse inequalities that benefit people who just happen to be white, it follows that white people would choose not to reject such a system because it would not be in their self-interest to do so. This choice, whether consciously or unconsciously made, is what marks a white person in South Africa today as a '1652' – a maintainer of the subjugation of the other by whiteness. 1652s are white people in South Africa, regardless of how progressive they may be, who through their existence maintain whiteness by (un)consciously supporting it or giving it credence. Whiteness preserves and enforces (and reinforces) itself using institutions and not people. The rejection of whiteness by white people is fascinating in many respects, yet simultaneously trivial. Hence, I am not inclined to discuss with white people how white people should be better at understanding their complicity, but I do understand that there are many who remain what we would describe within the various #MustFall movements as allies: those who support our effort but are not allowed be part of it.

It's on a point such as this that my father and I will disagree about how to build a better South Africa. Where he would be willing to design the country alongside whiteness, I would not let whiteness see the blueprints. I am the consequence of building a nation alongside whiteness, a consequence of the rainbow nation's white hue and its societal easing.

Societal easing is two-fold in nature. For coconuts, easing is the encroachment towards whiteness through purgatorial stasis and reinforced institutional subjugation. For 1652s, easing is the compliance with and maintaining of self-interest. Easing allows us to understand how the rainbow nation motif has been forced upon a generation of young people to sustain a neo-apartheid double consciousness; how it is one of the consequences of the post-apartheid project.

To reject co-option is to undo the easing of the rainbow nation motif and embrace a new politics of engagement. What is remarkable about this change in politics is its innateness. It's not a co-ordinated rejection guided by one central body. Rather, it is a process of self-emancipation, and it has begun to take root in various forms in South Africa.

A protest that took place at a school in Pretoria in August 2016 is a good illustration of this new politics of engagement. It is also a testament to this new form of politics. At issue, on the surface of it, was Pretoria High School for Girls' 'hair' rules as stipulated in the school's code of conduct. By drawing attention to school rules about hair, young womxn who attended the school were challenging a set of its institutional arrangements that perpetuated the alienation of blackness by whiteness under the guise of a code of conduct.

This 'code of conduct' can be best considered as an institutionally racist code that shames students for being black.[8] It's not that the code of conduct explicitly stated that the natural state of black womxn's hair should be shamed. Institutionalised racism doesn't work that way. It doesn't show itself to the world because it doesn't require that form of signalling for it to exist and permeate. It's what the document infers, what it doesn't say, that allows those with preconceived and dormant prejudices a 'protected' avenue in which they are (un)knowingly permitted to express these prejudices.

In the rule about hair, the code of conduct stated that 'all styles should be conservative, neat and in keeping with the school uniform. No eccentric/fashion styles will be allowed.' Although this statement may seem innocuous, it is anything but. In a report by a law firm which investigated the accusations made during the protest, it was found that 'the difficulties associated with different educators, who may be white or black, having different views on what constitutes untidy hair' would lead to incidences of uncertainty. Uncertainty importunately led to disciplinary action, both formal and informal, taken against black students whose hair, in the eyes and pervasiveness of whiteness, was deemed neither conservative nor neat. Uncertainty resulted in a black student whose hair was (subjectively) deemed unkempt by a white teacher being sent to have the bantu knots undone by a black teacher – a process that took over 80 minutes.[9] Because of its institutionalised nature, the racism at Pretoria High School for Girls extended far beyond the ambit of the school's code of conduct. Uncertainty around how to manage black womxn's hair didn't lead to uncertainty about the action that was taken. Decisions in the face of this uncertainty are based on norms and values already prevalent. Norms and values that privilege whiteness. Norms and values, as the law firm's report indicated, strip students of their dignity.

Consider once again the situation in which you find yourself on a dark road driving towards an oncoming vehicle. Now if you extend this example to any other situation at any other time of day you find that the norm of what side of the road is the normalised side of the road to be on holds consistently. Institutionalised norms, if allowed and left unchallenged, can and will reverberate throughout society. And they apply whether you are driving on a dark road, a highway, down an alley, a dirt road, in rural or urban spaces, the parking lots of shopping malls, petrol stations or wherever. Unless the situation demands a reassessing of the norm, your default position is to stay in the lane that has been normalised. Institutionalised forms of racism and discrimination are no different.

This, at least in my experience, seems to hold even if you are placed in a situation that demands a change in your norm. Even in such a case, you still feel uncomfortable with the change. Thus, at Pretoria High School for Girls, although on the surface the high school students' issues related to the code of conduct's limitation (and co-option) of black womxn's hairstyles in a manner different from 1652s in the school, this was not the crux of the argument. What underpinned the accusation was teachers calling students monkeys, or dirty kaffirs who belonged to schools in Mamelodi (a traditionally black township). They were also accusing the school of placating discussions around race. The staff even purportedly stated that 'black girls focus too much on politics and race and that's why they have no black achievers in education'.[10] This spoke to a broader issue facing students, beyond a simple code of conduct. The code of conduct was just one tool used to express these issues against black students.

That the matter spoke to a deeper issue in the school was amply demonstrated by how the same issues and similar accusations were raised by many other students at other schools (and universities) across the country. This commonality between students' experiences is a clear indicator of institutionalised forms of discrimination having taken root.

We exist in a society where a variety of economic narratives informed by preconceptions of a situation are sewn together in a bid to embed expectations within the populace, expectations which shift economic behaviour, even when these narratives are sometimes frivolous. When a racial narrative regarding discrimination is sewn together, the narrative is often dismissed as speculation.

Mixed-race educational spaces in South Africa are fertile ground for clashes of identity because they are part of the few spaces left in our society that allow for forced integration; spaces in which you are always within the hue of the rainbow. Besides shopping malls and sporting events, how many other spaces does South Africa have, really, where we are forced to engage, almost every day, with people of another race without the option of retreating to our racial comfort zones? These spaces allow some of South Africa's many unresolved racial tensions to play out in secret. When they are exposed, this is usually met with shock and disbelief. This is our historical and selective amnesia at work.

The stories we hear from students are powerful explanatory instruments. They help elucidate the current position of a born-free in South Africa because they all have one constant: the search for acceptance. One student protester at Pretoria High School for Girls inadvertently explained this constant by detailing how the effects of this form of discrimination were deeply rooted in identity politics in South Africa: 'This is about our identity as black people. We're tired of being told to be less than what we are so we can fit in.'[11]

To refuse/reject acceptance is a powerful political statement. Coconuts can jump-start the process of removing the whiteness that has gripped them. Even though whiteness may have helped to form who you are now, who you may be in the future, or even create a sense of belief that this whiteness is your best attribute, it still doesn't define you. To reject whiteness is to liberate your blackness.

Whether or not Pretoria High School for Girls intended to discriminate against its students is not important nor even relevant to this discussion. The critical point that requires a closer look can be illuminated by asking two questions of coconuts. Firstly, what explains the deep-rooted desire to embark on a form of renewed civil disobedience inspired by anti-racist politics? In the case of Pretoria High School for Girls, for example, unless the parents of the young womxn protesting had imbued them with untold forms of wisdom, what would explain their motivation for acting as they did? And secondly, should we be sceptical of the motives of the coconuts who are embarking on this form of politics?

The issue of the motives of coconuts and to an extent born-frees is what I believe will make or break any student-inspired revolution in the country. Essentially, why was a protest of students pertaining to identity politics able to garner more attention from the country and its citizens than the tragedy of a six-year-old boy who died by falling into a pit latrine in his primary school? Admittedly, this is an unfair and, to an extent, disingenuous comparison. However, I believe a juxtapositioning of these questions can do much to explain the waves of student protests in South Africa in recent times.

Both questions speak directly to the psyches of those who are coconuts and those who are not. The first question seeks to understand the renewed desire for mass co-ordinated civil disobedience through 'unconventional' tactics of disruption. And the second question seeks to understand how coconuts can reconcile their new form of politics within the double consciousness of a South Africa that wants to placate them by offering them opportunities and advantages that are not available to all.

The second question is of greater importance to me than the first. Where the first speaks of the danger coconuts pose to the dominance of whiteness, the second speaks to the danger this same group poses to the liberation of blackness.

Can coconuts be trusted with a revolution? Can they undergo a process of rejection that involves the removal of their complicity within a system that offers them opportunities for advancement, while simultaneously explicitly denouncing it, using the privileges the same system has vested in them?

The question of whether coconuts should be trusted has been missed by most political pundits. It is why many of these pundits failed to understand the nationwide university protests. It explains why vice-chancellors ran around like headless chickens in 2015 trying to understand the logic of #FeesMustFall and why they chose (and choose) to unleash private security and a trigger-happy police force on students as a form of engagement. Vice-Chancellor Adam Habib, at the University of Witwatersrand, was probably the most vocal of vice-chancellors regarding the role of coconuts, but his efforts to communicate this point were often drowned out at the time.

The student protests on university campuses of the last few years should be understood as the inevitable result of an elaborate nest of competing yet intertwined vested interests. It is a nest which, for instance, informed how neither university management teams, the Department of Higher Education nor students have been able to reconcile their differences about the role universities should play in South Africa. In addition, these obvious macro differences and contestations between national stakeholders were exacerbated by internal strife and angst among micro stakeholders within individual universities. It often surprised me how often an overzealous head of department or dean of faculty can halt an entire national

15

transformational agenda over somewhat fickle issues.

Understanding when and how coconuts work to protect their interest (proximity to whiteness) and at the same time reject their co-option into the rainbow nation and born-free mantra is central to understanding the changing dynamics of youth politics in South Africa.

So, if one believes that rejecting the born-free identity is possible, then what does the process of rejection entail? From personal experience – and to be honest I don't know how else to explain this in a manner that gets the point across – the process is shit, and it's taxing. It's a process that requires deep introspection about yourself and your place in society. Once it begins, however, it snowballs.

Some white friends become allies; most turn into enemies. Others simply treat you like a plague to be avoided. Your blackness becomes a regular site of interrogation both by yourself and by others. It's a process in which you must either acknowledge or fully come to terms with the fact that you have been marked as an 'other' – you are different, exotic, eccentric, angry, dangerous, erratic, irrational and emotional. The designation is not intended to describe you but rather to place a label on your existence. You are never truly free to be who you want to be. You can only be what whiteness wants you to be.

The process of rejecting your born-free identity makes you understand that you are only a subject within whiteness's own dialectical understanding of its own reality. It's a process in which you realise that you have no real voice. You are mute. You have no control over the process once it begins. It leaves you bare and exposed. Many describe the process as deeply violent at its core. They say it requires that you strip away what has made you who you are so that, hopefully, you can find out who you should be. Though I wouldn't personally describe the process so vividly, I will admit it takes quite a psychological toll on a person. My time in #RhodesMustFall probably best illuminated this for me, but there were earlier signals.

Every young black person in South Africa has that one clear moment in life when he or she realises that they are black. It's a surreal moment. For some it's joyous; for others it's innocuous. For most it's traumatic. I am not talking about looking in the mirror and noticing that your skin is different. This is not an arbitrary and mental genetic understanding of your racial profile. Such an understanding of race should be left to the prerogative of 1652s. This moment is different because it is the moment when you realise that you are the victim of a social construct of blackness that bears a heavy socio-historical weight. Some come to terms with it at an early age, while others come to the realisation during high school or university. My own moment came in the second grade during a game of cricket in which our teams were deliberately separated along racial lines; the typical blacks-versus-whites trope. All coconuts go through this at some point, either explicitly or implicitly. To be told to be on the black team is one thing, but to be on the black team that is significantly worse than the white team is another.

Segregating teams by superficial difference is an arbitrary separation usually done for convenience. We could easily have been separated along dark and light-coloured shirts or even differing hairstyles. Yet out of all the arbitrary forms of separation I could have experienced, the segregation by race in this instance led me to realise that for no fault of their own, the white team were still more advantaged than the black team. Whether this was due to those on the white team having been exposed to cricket for a longer period or maybe having a cricket net at home, it became evident that there were perceived differences in ability. These differences closely mirrored race.

Perception is extremely important. Perception doesn't rely on the truth. Perception seeks to understand trends around you to which a truth value is allocated. Whether these values are fallible or not, perception contributes to the building of your understanding of reality. Perceptions, in my second-grade example, such as: why did it seem as if everyone on the white team had all the necessary sporting equipment for the game and everyone on the black team didn't? Why was the white team's skill apparently significantly higher than the black team's? Why did some people on the white team have cricket nets in their homes and no one on the black team did? Why did it seem as if the white team had been to more Proteas cricket games than the black team? Why did I want to be on the white team so badly?

These were my thoughts in second grade, and they led me to realise my place in society relative to those in the white team. Perhaps it was an infantile realisation of my ability compared to my white colleagues at the time, but it was a realisation none the less.

Regardless of when you understand your positioning within society through this realisation, the real obstacle black students face is finding a space in which they can verbalise it. Internalising it is easier than expressing it because the latter necessitates an uncomfortable interaction with the dominant identity.

I went to Sacred Heart College – one of South Africa's multi-racial 'progressive' schools – for most of my basic education training. A Catholic school which often forgot it was Catholic. In fact, it could be argued that my school was probably one of the best in creating a multi-cultural space founded on achieving respect for your dignity regardless of your difference(s). Through what I believe must have been some form of social engineering, you could never really guess from looking at the school which culture, religion, race, creed or ethnicity was in the majority. Yet, even in this space, I was never comfortable about asserting my realisation of being a young black man in a white world and, in this case, in a white school. Even with all our diversity, everything was still in relation to the centre; a centre that espoused whiteness.

In the absence of a space to articulate my realisation and fully come to terms with it, I felt the need to be on the 'winning' team. The White Team. It was a need that continued to play itself out through my life. It usually took place in two ways, and both involved an adjustment of my identity through a change in my behaviour.

The first was the need and desire to be the right kind of black person in the right kind of situation. This usually manifested whenever I found myself in a white space, for example, Claremont in Cape Town, especially when I was a student at UCT. (For the uninitiated, Claremont, in Cape Town's Southern Suburbs, is an overwhelmingly white and unduly privileged space.) I felt the need to assimilate into the culture of Claremont to exist in it. It is a culture that I look back on with disdain and disgust. From clubs like Tiger Tiger or Stones, I was always confronted with whiteness, rape culture, patriarchy, ableism, sexism, racism, and so on.

Yet, at the time, I assimilated. I talked like the right kind of black person. Acted like the right kind of black. Danced in a manner foreign to me because of the fear that any other way of dancing would bring some form of social exclusion. I felt a need for a level of proximity to whiteness, yet at the same time I hated all that was around me. I had to become the right kind of black in the right kind of situation. I sought the appeasement of whiteness while simultaneously looking to distance myself from the 'others'. To survive exclusion, I had to conform and adjust towards the dominant identity, whether that be black or white. I changed my behaviour both consciously and unconsciously as a means of embracing whiteness and as a means of survival. The goal was never to gain the respect of my colleagues. The goal was to gain acceptance and admittance into their centre, even if the centre proved to be hollow.

The second way of adjusting my behaviour involved black spaces. Acceptance here is always a double-edged sword. On one side, you are constantly trying to be black enough for a space but not so black that you won't be able to identify with whiteness and, more importantly, that whiteness can still recognise you. To identify with whiteness gives you social leverage in society. But the critical aspect here is that within these black spaces do you seek to be black or an 'other'? Though the former might seem like an obvious choice, I argue that coconuts who don't embark on a process of rejection for the most part fall into the latter category. They prefer to identify as being an 'other' because it's a form of self-determination in our society that allows you to keep a semblance of your social leverage.

Your search for recognition as a unique black individual will always be constrained by the parameters of whiteness. You can't identify as someone the centre doesn't recognise as being in existence. Through the coconuts' logic, their existence should not place whiteness under threat but should instead ensure its superiority. Why else would we change our accent to sound *more* black (especially in black spaces) or as a way of ridiculing the way black people grasp the English language?

Striving to be the right kind of black person in the right kind of situation or trying to be black but not too black are methods by which you work to be on the winning team, whether you're in a white or black space. More importantly, these methods allow you to stay in the good graces of whiteness overall. You pick and choose the ladders to obtain upward mobility, while desperately avoiding the snakes that will send you sliding down. By rejecting whiteness, we are refusing to play this game. Instead, we are actively working towards sliding down the back of the snake.

Each of us rides this snake for different reasons. Some ride it because they have no choice, while others ride it because the life they previously experienced has been violently exposed to them to be a myth. To undergo this process of liberation is to simultaneously undergo a process of reconstruction. It's treacherous, and it is by no means easy. This reconstruction can mean that you'll lose everything – friends, family, job opportunities, studies, livelihoods. Friends are usually the first to go. They become the most natural symbol of one's own oppression. We usually don't bear the responsibility of ending the friendship ourselves. As soon as we begin to enunciate our blackness, whiteness responds by rejecting us. Removing us from Facebook, no longer inviting us to the sleepovers, the dinners, meeting the parents, drinks.

To be young, black and conscious in South Africa is to be in a state of constant and uncertain liberty. It's a state of mind in which you are juxtaposed between wanting the status quo to be maintained and yearning for and needing revolutionary change. This inner conflict, which has been created by a liberated mind, is the state of being a young black-conscious individual who has rejected the idea of being born-free in South Africa. You are free from the mirage of a country created by the imagination of those to whom it no longer belongs yet confined by the constraints that it must include them.

Whiteness seeks to remove us from its embrace because we threaten it. We place its position at the centre at risk when we dare to usurp it rather than simply remain constant in relation to it. Exerting my identity undermines the identity of whiteness. Yet exerting my identity calls into question my commitment to follow this feeling of emancipation from whiteness to its natural conclusion. It challenges whether or not I am willing to dismantle the system in which I exist to place myself in the centre at the expense of whiteness and the social leverage it has afforded me. This uncertainty of the coconut's commitment begs the question: as a coconut, are you willing to slide down the snake to join those who have been excluded from the born-free ladder and assist them in the revolution, the chimurenga?

Chapter 2

The Curious Case of 1652s and South Africa's Paradox

The student protests that specifically caught the nation's attention and intrigued the public in 2015 and 2016 were not something new, even though images of mass protests or disruptions in the media might have made them seem so. The country has encountered a series of these protests over the years, but none of them (excluding Marikana) resonated with society. But there is a significant change in youth politics today in that it is driven by the unravelling of the uncertainty of who we are as a country. If you want to understand the #MustFall movement, you need to come to grips with what it means to compromise your identity at the behest of a society that appears not to accept your reality. Whether this is implicit or explicit, our country is undergoing an identity crisis, and the process is causing social and economic reverberations.

My name is a political compromise. Whenever I am referred to as Kgotsi, it's a subtle reminder to me of what it means to give up a piece of yourself. Something as fundamental as understanding why my name is a political compromise can give insight into how and why youth politics in South Africa is changing and where the motivations that continue to drive student protest come from.

The name Kgotsi isn't even a name. It's a random combination of letters with no meaning, no history, no culture and no sense of something bigger than myself. It would be wrong to simply say it's a nickname. No. A nickname implies some form of negotiation. A negotiation in which some agreement is met in which both parties are satisfied. This negotiation may be jovial, considered or even confrontational, but in the end a nickname becomes your identifier. Kgotsi is emblematic of the power struggle in which an eight-year-old willingly gave up his identity in a bid to find acceptance among his peers. This same power struggle continues to play out within broader society. It is a struggle with a group of individuals in the country who can be best described as 1652s and, in particular, wypipo (a colloquial term students use for white people).

My full name is Rekgotsofetse Chikane. The name was given to me by mother as her own form of political commentary within our family. It means 'we are satisfied', and it signalled that I would be the last child she would bring into this world. But in 1999 that name was changed to Kgotsi, which is a wholly butchered version of the original with no connection to the political tale the original told. The moment I gave up my name was the moment I fell victim to the curiosity of 1652s. This is not a fate unique to me. Black South Africans experience these moments (where you find yourself compromising your identity because of your need to find approval from a 1652) in many ways. A good way to describe it is like seeing the world through a kaleidoscope of discrimination. Though the form of the discrimination may change and seem disorientating at times, the pattern is continually repeated and always recognisable. The emergence of #MustFall politics was the result of students rejecting the urge to appease the curiosity of 1652s and their desire to hold onto the belief of a rainbow nation.

The term 1652 is odd, and I have yet to come across someone who truly knows what it means. A term most likely born from the depths of 'Black Twitter', it is a phrase most commonly used to describe wypipo in South Africa and to connect the motives for their actions to our colonial history. Often used by black people as a funny and flippant expression of any encounter with white ignorance, '1652' resonates with me because its simplicity encapsulates so many of South Africa's complexities. It provides an avenue to explore a deeper understanding of what is at the heart of this conflict of identity in South Africa.

I would describe a 1652 as someone who is incapable of understanding the world outside the framework of someone who landed on the shores of South Africa alongside Jan van Riebeeck in 1652 and who has enjoyed the benefits of rainbowism. Not in the sense that they view the country as a piece of land to conquer, but rather that they consider the country a blank canvas on which they may freely impose their will. Consideration of what existed before is only relevant in so far as it helps in the construction of what they believe the world should be rather than what it ought to be. In conjunction, they believe that their actions are justified because they are working to bring to life the narrative of a rainbow nation. In order to understand why young people are becoming increasingly militant in their demands for change from 'the stubborn closure of private spaces, the evident inability and unwillingness of some South Africans to overcome historical social fault lines, and the persistence of stereotypes and racism',[1] you need to understand why we have become frustrated with 1652s and what they represent.

I can't remember the first time I heard the term 'rainbow nation', but I do remember the first time I understood what it meant and the hope that it gave to so many in the country. It was the day that President Nelson Mandela first came to my school – Sacred Heart College – when I was still in the second grade. It wasn't his only visit to the school; many of his grandchildren could be found scattered across the grades. Sacred Heart, at the time, was considered an oddity. While other schools struggled to adapt to the new democratic South Africa, Sacred Heart was one of the few schools that espoused multi-culturalism and racial diversity. After the end of apartheid, it quickly became a home for many 'political babies' across the political spectrum. Although it was a Catholic school, in one year there might be more Jewish students than Catholic; in another more Muslim students. It was a school that espoused tolerance, bringing together students from different socio-economic backgrounds, religious beliefs, ethnic groupings and political ideologies. Sacred Heart College was probably the case study at the time of how to implement the notion of a rainbow nation

24

in a classroom. So to have Madiba come to the school was an opportunity for both him and the school to see the rainbow nation metaphor in action.

I remember sitting in our sports centre among a sea of yellow-and-blue tracksuits filled with children waiting anxiously to get a glimpse of the man we knew little about but knew held some form of importance. For starry-eyed children in the 1990s, Mandela felt more like a friend than the president of the country, a friend whose sense of calm and joy was infectious. We sat row by row, uniformed by our uniform yet pluriversal in our differences, waiting for him to walk into the room. Even teachers, some of whom would have spent much of their lives fearing Mandela's spectre, stood on the sidelines barely able to contain their excitement.

Looking around the room and seeing the excitement from students, teachers and parents alike when Mandela walked in was, as I have said, probably the first time I understood what was meant by the rainbow nation and the hope it gives to people. For most of my young life, it was an unshakeable feeling. For many South Africans it remains so; the hope for a better and united country under one flag, united in our diversity. Yet here I am, almost two decades later, and I look back on the memory and think to myself how naive I was and how I was conned. I feel conned because if we truly lived in a rainbow nation, why should I have had to change my name from Rekgotsofetse to Kgotsi?

It often gets misconstrued that #RhodesMustFall began the day that Chumani Maxwele, on Monday, 9 March 2015, threw shit at a statue. But the anger on the University of Cape Town's campus had already been building for some time. A large meeting of students, an open debate, had taken place on the steps of Jameson Plaza, only a few metres away from that statue, on 24 February. The topic: had Nelson Mandela sold South Africa out during the Convention for a Democratic South Africa (CODESA) negotiations? The nature of the debate was visceral, with multiple competing sides, but at the heart of the discussion was the belief that white people were dealt a better hand than black people after 1994. You could trace this anger even further back, to a 2012 discussion on campus titled 'Is UCT Racist?' These discussions went beyond individual instances of racism at UCT to the broader institutionalised forms of discrimination.

The anger seen across Historically White Institutions (HWIs) in 2015 had been simmering for a decade and was a result of the growing unrest with a failing ideology within the country: rainbowism. It was this anger that permeated the student protests during 2015 and 2016 and which gripped the nation. I don't believe we have come to its boiling point yet. The militant nature of the protests should not, therefore, be a surprise to anyone.

There are numerous interpretations of 'rainbowism' but at its heart it is a political metaphor meant to give South Africa an international identity and a sense of purpose. It is used by politicians, civil society, sporting authorities and big business in a bid to make a fractured society whole again and reconfigure its national identity.[2] This off-the-cuff phrase 'rainbow nation' evolved into a fully fledged political mindset. It provides a heuristic tool – a mental shortcut – to disjoin within the psyche of South Africans the old from the new. It represents a racially harmonious society as opposed to the apartheid past, which found its logic in the dis-union of people.[3]

The notion of a rainbow nation provides a quick method of understanding the collective of complex socio-economic concepts such as non-racialism, non-sexism, human rights and dignity, multi-party democracy, the rule of law, and equality. It's a way to simplify our understanding of what our overarching goal as a society should be. Creating heuristics such as these is not new to societies. The United States of America employs the notion of the 'American Dream'; Tanzania under the leadership of Julius Nyerere utilised Ujamaa; Gandhi and India's independence movement invoked Swaraj. Heuristics are an easy and practical way to solve what are inherently complex notions within the human experience of society and render them in tangible accounts.

Dr Pumla Gqola, a vociferous academic focused on socio-economic power relations in South Africa, and on gender-based violence, and an ally of the student movements, saw through the façade of rainbowism. She described it back in 2001 as 'an authorising narrative of South Africa's identity that invokes a collective identity that stifles discussions of power differentials and emphasises difference while preventing the discussion that such difference evokes'.[4]

When sitting in student meetings or attending race dialogues/symposiums/imbizos in the lead-up to what would become #RhodesMustFall, I felt bombarded from all sides with the sense that it was more common to come across someone who had discussed the idea of racism than it was to come across someone who believed racism remained prevalent in society.

It is clear that South Africa has experienced progress regarding the interaction and integration of people in our public lives since 1994, but it is less evident that this takes place in our private spaces and in our ability to create a sense of closeness with others.

Academics often portray the country as being inept at discussing race. However, through the advent of democracy, ordinary citizens have been given the opportunity to bridge the gaps created in the past with our national public discourse remaining obsessed with race.[5] It is not that we are incapable of speaking about racial differences in the country; rather, we are incapable of recognising our own complicity in the perpetuation of racial difference.

Rainbowism creates an eagerness to discuss the differences between people but hesitates to recognise a person's own contribution towards the continued existence of racialised inequality. As a result, rainbowism is simply the search for unity between people, without the recognition of people.

Whether the architects of South Africa's democratic institutions and the subsequent use of the rainbow nation narrative were influenced by John Rawls's *A Theory of Justice*, I can't say, but I believe it must have lurked at the back of the minds of some. Rawls, a prominent political philosopher of the twentieth century, devised the notion that a just and fair society can only be built if one follows a procedure from behind what he describes as 'a veil of ignorance'. For Rawls, a just and fair society must be designed according to a procedure that will negate the effects of the specific decisions/contingencies/circumstances that might tempt its architects to exploit society's social and natural circumstances to their own advantage. Such a procedure can only take place if you are placed in a position where you are ignorant about what your place in this just and fair society is. It ensures that if I were to design a just world based on fairness, I would design it in such a manner that it would ensure that whenever someone finds themselves within this society, they will be treated 'equally as moral persons'.[6]

This *original position* is a key concept within Rawls's conception of a just and fair society. In your given generation you would need to be unaware of your class, social status, economic positioning, political situation, or level of intelligence. You would have to design the country's institutions as if you would have to live with them whoever you were. Significantly, Rawls does admit that even within this original position, you would still place emphasis over your family lines – a care for your immediate descendants – to ensure some level of just saving for subsequent generations. Therefore, the institutions you build should remain just for your children and grandchildren.

I use Rawls to highlight the mindset of our democracy's architects – and I include my father in this group – for two reasons. The first reason is because of how our democratic institutions bear an uncanny resemblance to the two basic principles of Rawls's conception of 'justice as fairness', namely: each person is to have equal basic liberties, and social and economic inequalities should be arranged so that they provide the greatest benefit to the least advantaged of our society. The second principle, commonly known as 'the difference principle', is at the core of why I believe there is a growing rejection of the narrative of the rainbow nation. Our basic democratic institutions were built with the difference principle in mind: the Bill of Rights, Chapter 9 institutions, Section 25, the use of proportional representation, and the growth of the welfare state. Because of our history, our democratic institutions had to be built on the notion of justice as fairness.

The second reason why Rawls is useful is that he provides the justification for the use of the rainbow nation narrative as a means of obtaining acceptance of the institutions that were designed. The narrative of the rainbow nation does not necessitate that a person must understand how all the democratic institutions function. Rather, it acts as a heuristic to understand a complex concept. It doesn't necessitate explaining how the negotiated settlement was only accomplished due to substantial compromises. It doesn't require a person to undergo a semester course about respecting the rule of law. The rainbow nation is a tool to allow people intrinsically to understand both the first and second principles of Rawls's justice as fairness argument without ever having to evaluate how this is the case.

The anguish and mistrust that many young South Africans have when it comes to the rainbow nation narrative are because it hides the fact that our democratic institutions have not provided the equality of opportunity that was envisioned. The narrative has become an intrinsic tool that negates us meaningfully questioning injustice because it intends to entrench the belief that any social or economic inequality is justified because our institutions protect those in our society who are the least advantaged. But when we look at our society, I would argue that this narrative is fallacious. It functions as a façade. Rainbowism benefits only 1652s.

The student protests of 2015 did not find national resonance among young people because we found joy in seeing someone throw shit at a statue. We didn't mobilise ourselves in the thousands because we were angered by a proposed 10.5% increase in university fees. We found national resonance because we exposed the façade of the rainbow nation, a façade that hid the truth behind the rainbow nation motif. The rainbow nation doesn't protect the least advantaged of the country, who bear the brunt of social and economic inequality; instead it justifies social and economic inequality because it provides the greatest benefit to 1652s. For 1652s, their behaviour as gatekeepers to the rainbow nation narrative is due to how the narrative justifies their privileged position in society. Students' anger towards 1652s and, by extension, the rainbow nation narrative, comes from their knowing this.

The 1652s' societal position within South Africa gives rise to a belief that they were present at the negotiating table. They designed the country's institutions not from Rawls's 'original position', but from a position where they could look through the veil of ignorance. The design not only benefited them; it would have inter-generational resonance. Their children would benefit from this newly formulated society at the expense of non-1652s and not even truly know why. Thus, even if you weren't present at the table, you are the beneficiary of the system created by those who were able to cheat it.

If you talk to students across the country, read through their demands, and sit in their mass meetings, you will see that very few have qualms about the country's notion of a bill of rights or the notion that we should be provided equal liberties. The glaring and most recurrent issue is how, despite these equal liberties, there still exists the justified belief that some are more equal than others. This belief is embodied in the socio-economic inequalities in the country.

The blame that is placed on 1652s is because they don't see the rainbow nation as a metaphor that provides them undue privilege. They don't believe that their efforts to create unity come at the expense of failing to recognise others. They are unable to fathom how their actions perpetuate a feeling of injustice within society. It's why I don't limit the tag of 1652s to only wypipo. I extend it to the beneficiaries of the political settlement reached in 1994 between the Afrikaner state and African nationalists. Neville Alexander was right when he predicted that the eventual settlement reached between the two groups would be to the detriment of the country's urban and rural poor.[7] Being a 1652 is not dependent on race, gender or, arguably, even class. Coconuts and wypipo alike reap the significant benefits of the way our society is structured.

Being associated as 1652 often comes not by choice but by circumstance. Similar to the lack of choice of being born a man or a woman, as Di Giacomo notes, 'membership of certain social groups from birth leads to a particular type of socialisation, i.e. learning and practising beliefs, values, symbols, and norms specific to those groups.'[8] Although these benefits are by no means equal, in our society's mindset, they remain institutionally justified. These categories all misconstrue both the longevity of inequality in the country and the solutions for rectifying inequality. They delimit the discussions towards social identities rather than psycho-social identities and the methodologies these identities utilise to maintain their dominance in society.

The inability for 1652s to realise their complicity in the perpetuation of disadvantage – colloquially, to be 'woke' – is what draws the ire of many young South Africans. 1652s place themselves as the protagonists of democracy. They wield the constitution like a battle-axe and use it to cut down anyone who expresses dissent. It's the weapon they use to cut through the essence of a black person's understanding of their own reality, spilling their lived experiences in crimson red onto the marble floors of democracy, only to be washed away before they stain and leave a stench of guilt. Yet, regardless of their intent or purpose, the standpoint of a 1652 remains just in their minds. They defend the constitution because it represents what they believe is a justly built society. A society that was built to favour them, regardless of whether they are conscious or unconscious of the disparities within it. It is these methodologies that 1652s utilise to maintain power and privilege rather than the physical attributes that identify them.

I admit that the above might be dramatic, but it speaks to the heart of how the rejection of the notion of a rainbow nation is not based on race alone, but on the entire complex make-up of our society. It explains how an organisation such as #FeesMustFall found itself as an umbrella for a multitude of political and non-political platforms. The rejection of the rainbow nation is not the rejection of the belief in equal liberties and freedoms. It is the rejection of the normalisation of injustice despite these liberties. It's the reason why so many students within the protest movements across the country become nauseous at the thought of having yet another discussion about race. It is why there was and continues to be a marked increase in the awareness of various other forms of discrimination (gender and sexuality, for example, which can lead to the silencing of womxn). The rejection of the rainbow nation makes the increase in social tensions regarding race, gender, class, ethnicity and nationality visible.

Mill warns that the use of Rawlsian thought to understand a society misconstrues one's ability to understand racially linked issues of injustice. Instead, it allows for one to design a country pre-emptively to address injustice rather than rectify the issues of injustice.[9]

Marikana, #RhodesMustFall, #FeesMustFall, the rise of the Economic Freedom Fighters, the death of Andries Tatane – all of these were indicative of a growing frustration with the current identity of the country and translated into a series of proxy wars with 1652s. For the miners who lost their lives at Marikana, their battle was against the fabled 'white monopoly capital' with the assistance of certain black bourgeoisie. #RhodesMustFall initially fought their war with the notion of institutionalised forms of racism at UCT before casting their gaze towards black men, ableists and the other multi-layered forms of hidden yet indentured privilege our society has maintained. #FeesMustFall focused on society's off-handed justification for the lack of equal opportunities within society, utilising fees as their political metaphor for the financial exclusion of the least advantaged from society. Finally, the EFF and the death of Andries Tatane represented a proxy war with arguably the largest beneficiaries of being 1652, the African National Congress's elite.

The proxy wars that take place across South Africa are between 1652s who view the socio-economic issues in the country as the unintended consequences of an inherently just and democratic society and a generation of South Africans living under 'freedom' who have realised the game is rigged in 1652s' favour. The emergence of terms such as 'Black Tax' and 'Black Pain' and the resurgence of Biko-ist understandings of race, the narrative of decolonisation and the call for 'economic freedom in our lifetime' all indicate our growing realisation of the undue burdens falling on the least advantaged in our society, burdens that should not be present in our conception of how a constitutional democracy should function.

These proxy wars are all around us, but they are often masked by the façade of the rainbow nation. Our inability to see through this façade limits our ability to understand that the purpose of these proxy wars is not to scorch the earth but to claim the right to plant seeds, the seeds of a new nation as a post-apartheid post-1994 society.

Throughout my time in student and youth politics, and navigating the world of private schools, gated communities, townships, rural and urban South Africa, I came to realise that the proxy nature of South Africa's unrest with the broader conception of fairness is due to our inability to recognise that even though we all generally understand the notion of the rainbow nation in the same way, we have vastly different conceptions of its implications. Furthermore, being a 1652 is not a permanent state; rather it ebbs and flows, depending on the situation and context. For the average white male in South Africa, these ebbs and flows are minimal and create situations and settings that are relatively constant and give them a perpetual sense of advantage. For a coconut, these ebbs and flows become most apparent when we must engage and disengage between our 'white' and 'black' realities. Our sense of advantage is not as perpetual as that of our white colleagues. Due to coconuts' ability to understand and experience the same national identity and simultaneously reap both the rewards and costs of this national identity creates a world in which we live in paradox.

As an illustration of this paradox, a simple thought experiment can be useful. (Thought experiments have a myriad uses; I find them especially useful as a method of illustration in a debate because they allow a person to place themselves in a position to shift their institutionalised forms of thinking. I think of them as thought-provoking metaphors of a person's everyday life decisions, metaphors used to illuminate untold stories and narratives in a way that allows you to be susceptible to changing your perspective.)

A wooden ship leaves a dock with a cargo of wood and one by one the crew replaces all its old decaying wooden parts with the new wood on board until the entire ship has been replaced by the new wood. When the boat reaches its destination, is the crew on the original ship, the one they sailed on when they left the dock, or are they on a new ship? This is known as Theseus's paradox. It asks a simple question. Is the ship new because its component parts are new or is it still the original ship because regardless of the change in parts over time, its form, function and shape have remained the same? The experiment juxtaposes two extremes regarding the nature of the identity of an object. The paradox offers a myriad thought experiments about the nature of identity. For instance, what if the crew had used different timber, different paint for the sails, and changed the captain – would it have remained the same ship?[10] Using this paradox, can one ask if South Africa is a post-apartheid society or a post-1994 society?

If a country seeking to transition from an apartheid state towards a more democratic state over time replaces all its old oppressive laws and institutions with an array of new democratic institutions, does it remain a post-apartheid state (a new state)? Or is it the same state (the original state) with new democratic institutions, a post-1994 state? Applying Theseus's paradox to nation-states has its various caveats and issues, but it

33

does provide a means to understand the difference between the conception and perception of South Africa and why this has led to the unease in the country that has bred the rejection of the rainbow nation narrative.

Before I go on to explain why I believe South Africa exists in a paradox, I would like to clarify three thoughts. The first is that a nation-state – and this really should go without saying – is far more complicated than a wooden ship. My post-apartheid versus post-1994 example emphasises a juxtaposition of old oppressive institutions and new democratic institutions, while Theseus's paradox emphasises a shift from old to new wood. I did not use the example to question whether South Africa's old oppressive laws can be equated to our new democratic institutions; rather, I wanted to equate the logic underpinning apartheid with the logic that works as the cornerstone of our current democracy. If the core logic of apartheid was separate development, determined by those with institutionalised power, why should it be different from our current conception of democracy?

Secondly, I use the idea of institutions quite liberally. By institutions, I mean both the physical institutions and the intangible institutions, the ones that constitute the 'rules that govern the game in a society'.[11] These rules can be formalised in the form of a constitution and enforced by the state, or they can be informal rules that govern a person's behaviour and conduct.

The third thought I want to clarify is that just as the ship's performance may improve if you replace the old decaying parts with new ones, or the crew's quarters seem more aesthetically appealing with new wood rather than old decaying wood, the ship is still a ship, and its function remains the same. In the case of South Africa, although the democratic institutions have improved social and economic conditions in the country, the form and function of the country have remained the same. It is our conception of the ship's component parts that provides the difference to its identity. An old nation with new parts (and thus a new identity) versus an old nation with new parts with the same old identity. Determining the identity of a country is a normative argument.

Post-apartheid conceptions of South Africa underline that the country has transitioned from apartheid towards democracy, with the transition emphasised as a defining moment in the country's history. The end of apartheid acts as a fulcrum point for the conception of society. As time passes and the country is increasingly democratised the fulcrum shifts. Increased weight and emphasis are placed on the conceptions of the state after the end of apartheid rather than conceptions of the state before the end of apartheid. The imposition of new institutions inclines thought towards understanding the current nature of the state with eyes fixed on the present, with the past influencing only through memory. If one does not have access to the memory of apartheid in its most visceral state, it augments the ability of a post-apartheid thinker to reconcile the past with the present. It is thus no coincidence that when post-apartheid thinkers become increasingly separated personally, spatially and temporally from the legacy of apartheid, there is a marked increase in their preference of understanding the country outside the framework and legacy of apartheid.

For post-apartheid thinkers, the country has become a new vessel to carry the hopes and ambitions of the country. It is not a view that is necessarily bad, but because of it, the harms of the past function as footnotes for the future, guiding perceptions of the country in so far as they relate to the topic currently under consideration. Apartheid becomes a cautionary tale of what can happen when a society neglects to maintain its humanity, rather than a case study that continues to reflect itself on the true character of the country.

Turning to the youth and students, it is not necessarily the act of being a post-apartheid thinker that angers student activists; rather it is their appeal to the end of apartheid as a foundation for their responses to current ills. It is this belief that the end of apartheid was the silver bullet that would end generations of institutionalised discrimination that adds to youth activists' frustration. Furthermore, it provides a foundation for 1652s to misconstrue Rawls's 'difference principle', which is a core propellant for the rainbow nation narrative.

Thus, when you ask a post-apartheid thinker, in particular a 1652, whether they feel a sense of responsibility for the injustice of the past, more often than not they will immediately embark on the three-pivot train of thought. The first pivot is how 1652s contextualise the problems of society solely within the current democratic dispensation. The second pivot is their ability to absolve themselves of guilt linked to past injustices. And the third is the insistence on pacifying activism against the critics of the current democratic state to preserve the rainbow nation motif – and, by extension, the status quo. Each pivot works like clockwork, functioning simultaneously and containing a cacophony of deafening hollow platitudes about race, analogous deference to Mandela, rainbowism and the constitution. The notion of South Africa being a post-apartheid state allows one to view the problems of the country as outcomes of the decisions made by society, rather than the consequence of one's individual actions.

The question of land illuminates the logic of post-apartheid thinkers best. At its heart, the question of land in South Africa is about the moral conception of the role of property rights in our society. The logic of land ownership is profoundly influenced by the need to separate yourself from the other. Whether this is farmland, a gated community in Sandton, or Cape Town's Sea Point area, our moral conception of property rights is based on providing ourselves with a justification for separating ourselves from those we consider the other. This is not a mindset of our own doing. It is a lasting remnant of the apartheid structuring of our society. One only needs to look at the metro railway system in Johannesburg to see how the society into which we are born is structured to differentiate between citizens and the other.

For a post-apartheid thinker, the question of land is answered first by contextualising the morality of the question within the post-apartheid context and the constitution. While the constitution acknowledges the injustice of the past, it distances the individual from the responsibility of mending this injustice. It relies on the state to take on the role. The moral conception of property rights regarding land in South Africa is therefore determined by the constitution rather than societal debate and discussion. This is not uncommon for a constitution, and certainly there is value in an approach that places the rule of law above all other convictions. However, the concept of the rule of law should not be beyond reproach or off limits in debate.

After contextualising, post-apartheid thinkers will acknowledge the injustice of past land dispossession but will absolve themselves of any guilt with regard to said injustice. For a post-apartheid thinker, guilt does not function as an overriding motivating force that encourages someone to take on a more active role in society. Regardless of the context, discussions about land generally degenerate to one side claiming reparations in some form and the other arguing that there is no justification for land to be given up 'freely'. The latter argument usually devolves into a monologue about the economic implications of land. The ANC elite and government often fall into this mode of thinking, deferring responsibility to some other force rather than admitting their own failure as a state to resolve the issue. The nuances of this debate are for another conversation. For now, I am highlighting how people distance themselves from the guilt of the past even as they find themselves benefiting from it.

Lastly, post-apartheid thinkers will use the constitution and our democratic state as reasons to pacify activism, especially youth activism. Since the end of apartheid, the notion of the rainbow nation has been indoctrinated in young people. We have been brainwashed into the belief that Mandela's sacrifice should not be placed under question. We have been brainwashed into the belief that because we didn't experience apartheid, we cannot criticise how the country overcame it. The constitution, though a magnificent document, is given too much praise for the words written on its pages. Constitutions only work when the principles they espouse are already present in society. My criticism of the constitution is not with the document's words, but with our unquestioned belief that people espouse its values.

The three steps I've mentioned can be applied to a multitude of situations for post-apartheid thinkers. The students' fee-related protests are just one example. The crisis of fees is simplified to a post-apartheid view of higher education, attributing the crisis to decreasing subsidies given to universities rather than to the systematic impoverishment of the sector and to its deep links to colonial forms of academia. The responsibility for the crisis of fees is then deferred onto either students or university administrators, absolving the state and university vice-chancellors of guilt. The discontent among students regarding fees has always fallen on deaf ears, especially the ears of the privileged students on campuses. Pacification takes place when student concerns are arbitrarily dismissed when challenged by arguments focused on returning to class and they are forcefully dismissed through the justification of the presence of Public Order Police on campuses or the use of private security.

A constitution means nothing if people do not already have constitutional values and respect for the rule of law. Post-apartheid thinkers put the words of the constitution ahead of the values it wishes to bestow upon citizens. They are unable to extrapolate the values of the constitution across space and time because they locate the problems in society within the context of the post-apartheid state. Challenging post-apartheid thinkers' view on land, as I have shown, devolves in their minds into what is set down in the constitution and what constitutes the rule of law, instead of prompting them to question the values of the constitution and our conceptions of the rule of law.

Post-1994 conceptions of South Africa (as opposed to post-apartheid ones) don't place the change from an apartheid state to a democratic state as the defining identity of the country. The understanding of post-1994 thinkers is that the state is the same apartheid state, only with democratic institutions. The end of apartheid doesn't act as a fulcrum for the conception of society. The year 1994 is just a marker on an ever-changing society but whose basic identity of separate development among racialised and gendered groups has remained the same. Post-1994 thinkers don't view apartheid as a unique structure within the South African psyche. They view it as the logical conclusion of a society that embraced the notion of colonialism. As such, the year 1994 sits alongside other years such as 1948, 1910, 1889, 1880, 1879, among others, as markers of a larger endemic problem. The problem is in the DNA of our society.

Post-1994 thinkers emphasise that even with renewed institutions the country remains the same, by and large, in both form and function. They conceptualise the state without giving preference to the end of apartheid and the country's new institutions. They see the constitution as a particular manifestation of society's overall values. This is not to say that they necessarily agree with these values themselves. The constitution, therefore, becomes a contested document, which contestation is based on values and the conception of the rule of law, rather than on the *presence* of the rule of law.

Apart from the Pan-African Student Movement of Azania (PASMA), who believe that the Truth and Reconciliation Commission is a better marker of South Africa's changing identity than 1994, many of the student protesters locate themselves within the logic of post-1994 thinking. From #RhodesMustFall to #FeesMustFall, most if not all place no emphasis on the end of apartheid in their conceptualising of the nature of the country's problems. Neither do they use it as a means of carving out solutions to these problems. The end of apartheid holds no significant impact on the consciousness of the #MustFall movement. It is just another date on a long list of false positives that promised that South Africa's present would be better than its past.

To try to understand the logic that drives the movements can be jarring for someone who has not come across this form of thinking, and in part it explains the immediate opposition to the values and ideas of the #MustFall movements.

#RhodesMustFall's work to highlight institutionalised forms of dis-crimination at UCT never came at the expense of having to use the end of apartheid as a significant point of reference. This was why the movement instinctively rejected opponents' using the end of apartheid as the core of their opposition towards the movement.

For post-1994 thinkers, the injustice of the past mirrors the injustice of the present. They don't look at the state as new. They acknowledge the presence of new democratic institutions in the same way as they might acknowledge the new wood that makes up Theseus's ship. For many students, to claim the country is new is to say that the notion of hierarchical and separate development in South Africa has been abandoned. Post-1994 thinkers don't claim this. They contextualise both the solutions and prob-lems of society beyond 1994, and they contrast them to earlier forms of the South African state.

Post-apartheid thinking functions as the backbone of the political ideol-ogy of the rainbow nation. If there is anxiety among 1652s, this is the result of the challenge to this backbone by post-1994 thinking, which rejects the rainbow nation narrative as just another tactic used to perpetuate subjuga-tion and separate development.

* * *

From the moment when Nelson Mandela stepped into my school that year in second grade, I understood what was meant by living in a rainbow nation.

The rainbow nation demands that I become forgiving of my white friends and the actions of their parents. It demands a level of acquiescence towards the day-to-day feeling of being 'less than' to ensure a brighter tomorrow. It requires me to participate in interpersonal interactions with people who are different, but it does not necessitate a sense of closeness or recognition. It provides the physical space to interact with others – parks, sports stadiums, shopping malls and so on – but it doesn't necessitate such interaction in my private spaces.

The rainbow nation preaches unity but practises difference. University residence spaces are a useful example of the fleeting power of the rainbow nation. I remember my own experience of this when I walked into my first university, UCT. The residence I was in provided a multitude of events and activities designed to encourage integration. It pushed for togetherness regardless of race, class or ethnicity. Our dining hall became the barometer for the house committees' social interventions. At the beginning of the academic year the dining hall was a melting pot of cultures and races, with the walls echoing the sounds of young people, who were often from quite homogenous backgrounds, being placed in a heterogeneous and pluriversal space. The dream of the rainbow ran through the room, with tables exhibiting an array of diversity. Yet, as time passed, we regressed. We moved back to more familiar bonds across race, class and ethnicity.

What drives this segregation is catnip for social scientists. While most focus on what weakens the bonds of social interaction across lines of difference, I focus on what no longer strengthens them.

This story of the failure of integration has many plot lines and all of them lead to the same general conclusion. A breakdown. Yes, exceptions exist, but I don't believe these exceptions are worthy of serious discussion because, usually, they fail to provide an adequate blueprint for a brighter tomorrow. These exceptions exist on a foundation where the rejection of the rainbow nation finds its greatest cracks. As someone who has grown up learning to navigate these exceptions to the rule, while also trying to exist in a more homogenous world, I can see both sides of the coin. But I do not idolise the exception as some form of the norm.

The expectation that I will embrace the rainbow has created the expectation among my white friends, acquaintances and colleagues that they will be both implicitly and explicitly forgiven for the racial transgressions of the past. The rainbow nation requires a skewed social compact in our society, which disproportionately demands more from black people than from wypipo. Furthermore, it provides a justification for wypipo's heightened level of privilege. Post-apartheid thinking, they would say, mitigates the need to admit any guilt regarding the advantages bestowed upon them as a result of the structure of our society. The rainbow nation narrative pushes for reconciliation over restitution. It entrenches among wypipo the thinking that their privilege was earned either on merit or as happenstance of circumstances – circumstances which, as a result of a situation they had no control over, allows them to believe that they should not and cannot be held responsible for the injustice of these circumstances from which, simultaneously, they benefit.

This is the curious case of 1652s in South Africa.

Chapter 3

Learning to Fight
the Status Quo

On 17 March 2013, the ANC made a decision that would alter the nature of youth politics in South Africa. This was the decision to not only disband their Youth League (ANCYL) executive but the entire organisation, and it impacted profoundly on the way, I believe, young people viewed not only the party but youth politics in South Africa. This is not to say that all young people subscribed to the ANCYL, but its absence created a vacuum in the political discourse. This vacuum would eventually have to be filled. The ANC attempted to replace the organisation with an alternative which embraced the mantra of defending the status quo at all costs, but this was a far cry from the organisation that had sought, without fear or favour, 'Economic Freedom in Our Lifetime' (EFIL).

Sitting in my cubicle office in the Steve Biko Building – the home of the Student Representative Council (SRC) – at UCT, I saw the news during my morning trawl through news sites. As a member of the Youth League at the time, the announcement came as a shock. I felt a deep apprehension. Questions raced through my mind as I wondered what would happen next. What did this mean for the future of the party in general and how would I fit into the new organisation? I remember thinking to myself that this party, and what it had become, was no longer the party of old. How could it be, if it could so easily discard one of its last revolutionary institutions?

The significance of the announcement was not because of the importance of the ANCYL in South Africa, but more because of what the organisation represented at the time. For all its faults, the ANCYL brought to the fore-front of the imagination of society the discourse required to understand how we fight my generation's current and most immediate enemy. With its disbandment, the ANC fired the first shot against my generation's stand against our most pressing enemy. The reverberations from this shot would be seismic.

There is a common trope associated with young people in South Africa. This is that with the end of apartheid we didn't have an enemy to mobilise against. This trope (also described as 'youth apathy') is supposed to explain the lack of youth activism in formalised politics. It is a trope that pos-its young people as idle bystanders in the political discourse. I first came across the phrase during my first year at UCT in 2011 as the rationale for why voter turnout was so low for SRC elections that year. In what turned out to be a fierce election between the South African Students Congress (SASCO), a traditional ally of the ANC, and the Democratic Alliance Student Organisation (DASO), the university wing of the official opposi-tion party, the Democratic Alliance (DA), one might have expected that students would turn out in their droves to play out national politics on a more localised level. We should have been the proverbial microcosm of society and of the Western Cape. Yet voter turnout was paltry at best. Frustrating as it seemed at the time, as the years went on, leading up to the genesis of #RhodesMustFall, my response to the notion of youth apa-thy was that young people were not apathetic; we simply hadn't interested young people in the right way yet.

To label young people as apathetic is to provide yourself with a scape-goat for your own failure to understand their motives and rationale for mobilising and becoming active citizens. As seen through the emergence of the #MustFall formations within informal politics through the stu-dent movements and the continued growth of political parties such as the Economic Freedom Fighters (EFF), young people are primed to take their place in the political environment of South Africa. But our interest needed to be piqued by a better understanding of who and what we are fighting for.

The rise of #MustFall politics allowed our generation to identify the enemy. It also provided a platform for the discourse required to understand how to defeat the enemy regardless of one's own political inclination. Ironically, this once hidden enemy had been merrily lurking in our society in plain sight. After many discussions with various student leaders, I came to describe the enemy as 'systemic economic oppression' – which phrase during a discussion with Shaeera Kalla, who was the president of WITS's SRC at the beginning of #FeesMustFall and one of its more public personalities, quickly corrected to 'the status quo'. During our discussions, which were always frank and honest, something which speaks as much to Shaeera's character as it does to mine, we always seemed to come to the same understanding: that our country, for all its good, when you really sat down and thought about it, just didn't make sense.

Our country doesn't make sense.

Whether this is because of income inequality, racial segregation, both in an economic and political sense, systemic corruption or political immaturity – it doesn't make sense.

We are living in a completely unsustainable situation, and yet, in spite of all its ills, the country continues to churn its wheels. The 'status quo' is the belief that our current reality is normal. It feeds on the belief that because the state hasn't collapsed, South Africa's current incarnation is better than its past incarnations. Our democratic freedoms have blinded us to so many of the ills that plague our country. It was by taking the notion of 'economic freedom in our lifetime' that my generation turned a spotlight on the status quo and defined it as our enemy. But more importantly, that notion provided us with the discourse necessary to mobilise against it.

The disbandment of the ANCYL was the first full-frontal attack on the goal of economic freedom in our lifetime. EFIL was popularised by the ANCYL in the late 2000s, and it was the first organised response by young people across political lines towards ending systemic economic oppression. The emergence of the EFF, #RhodesMustFall and #FeesMustFall can all find their roots within the depths of the defence of the idea of 'economic freedom in our lifetime'.

My generation has often been described as dormant and seemingly indifferent to the systemic economic oppression rampaging through the country. Yet, even though we were primed to be the generation that enjoyed the fruits of democracy without the scars of its past, here we are, angry that the fruit tastes bittersweet. I am part of a generation that never faced the abuses of the apartheid system in its rawest legalised and normalised forms. I think about one story my father told me when I was growing up about how his father was once pulled over and beaten by a group of white men for having the audacity to overtake them. Or how my family was arbitrarily dispossessed of their land in Bushbuckridge not once but twice, arbitrary acts that forced my grandfather eventually to move to Johannesburg to find work. He would ultimately leave his wife and children behind to join the apartheid government's infamous migrant labour system. My dad often tells me that he still finds it bizarre to walk into a bathroom and find a white man there. Such an interaction would not have been deemed acceptable in the past, yet here I am, not only sharing a bathroom with white people but spending weekends away with them as well.

For my generation, these rawest forms of discrimination remain present across the country but are not accepted in the same manner as they were in the past. That being said, we face a different type of discrimination. It can be difficult to describe or pinpoint, yet you can always feel it in the air. We might not be dealing with an enemy that manifests itself as 'Europeans Only' benches; we face an enemy that has the same ideals as the apartheid system only now it wears a very different mask.

Though not brazen in its assault on one's humanity, it remains almost equally effective in achieving its objective: the systematic oppression of black people.

Even as a young black male who finds himself firmly among the political elite, I can feel the enemy every day. Walking through the streets of Parkhurst – a suburb in Johannesburg that perfectly represents how even with the end of apartheid as a system, its legacy continues – I was always reminded that I didn't truly belong there. In fact, I often wonder if one had to take a picture of this 'pristine' Johannesburg suburb during apartheid, how much it would differ from a picture of the suburb now. Not much at all, would be my guess. Whenever I walked out of the neighbourhood in the morning on my way to the nearest main road to catch a taxi to campus, I was always reminded how I was not the norm in that space, whether it be by the stream of black mothers walking into Parkhurst ready to take care of children who were not theirs, or the dog park that displayed that the role of the black man in this neighbourhood was to take care of the garden, walk the dogs and pick up their shit. The mere idea of a young black man living in Parkhurst was an affront to the sensibilities of the area.

Parkhurst, like so many other neighbourhoods of its kind, is a prime example of how black people are allowed to come and enjoy the cafés and restaurants of its main road but are never actually expected to live there.

Although I remain firmly in the sight of the enemy, as a coconut I have been privileged enough to be shielded from its more violent aspects. For the life of me, I can't even begin to imagine the horrors that await black unemployed and poverty-stricken women in the many townships in South Africa. Many of them have to contend with abusive men, who themselves are products of a broken system. For them, the enemy is both visceral and vicious in its violence towards them. For them, death and danger remain hidden in plain sight on every street.

The status quo, which was shifted into the shadows in favour of the rainbow-building project, was put firmly back in the spotlight through the resistance by young people both individually and collectively. This resistance comes as a result of the combination of racial and gendered inequality, entrenched youth unemployment and racialised systemic poverty.

In 2015, 30.4 million South Africans lived in poverty, with our poverty headcount increasing to 55.5% (from 53.2% in 2011).[1] According to Sharlene Swartz in *Another Country: Everyday Social Restitution*, '60% of Black South Africans live below the poverty line compared to 4% of White South Africans, who also have an average household income that is six times that of Black South Africans'.[2] Youth unemployment in 2017 sat at 38.6%, with '58% of unemployed people aged between 15 and 34'.[3] In addition to this, in 2017, 32.4% of young people aged 15–24 and 46% of 25–34-year-olds in 2016 were Not in Employment, Education or Training, with females making up the majority of this cohort.[4]

South Africa's youth unemployment is in a chronic state. Those who are NEET are particularly susceptible to a variety of social ills while simultaneously being denied the opportunity to improve their skills through education or gaining the necessary work experience to progress within the labour market.[5] The Gini coefficient – an index between 0 and 1 that measures the income inequality within a population – of South Africa is one of the highest in the world at 0.68. What makes South Africa's inequality even more precarious is its racial composition, with black South Africans having a Gini coefficient of 0.65 and white South Africans 0.51.[6]

Statistics seem still to belie the reality of many South Africans. Whether one wants to blame the ANC, white monopoly capital, imperial forces or the constitution for the ills of the country, the reality remains that we as South Africans have not only failed in our responsibility to the most disenfranchised in the country, but we have given up thinking about how to change our current circumstances. There is no question that the country has seen many gains over the past two and half decades. We have witnessed the expansion of public housing, health-care provision, educational services, and increased access to services such as water and electricity. In the face of an Aids epidemic, we can even claim an increase in life expectancy, a further indication of some of the many victories South Africans should be pleased about. So it is bizarre to think that my generation has inherited some of the exact same problems that plagued the country during apartheid. With all the gains South Africa has made since 1994, why do we still not only fall victim to systemic economic oppression but have both rationalised and institutionalised its presence? Often our efforts to change our society will lead to equal attempts to keep our society the same. If one were to think of South Africa's current social make-up as being in the form of an equilibrium, whose resting point is the maintenance of systemic racial and gendered inequality, entrenched youth unemployment and racialised systemic poverty, then efforts to change this equilibrium are merely seen as positive and negative amplifiers which cancel each other out. Our society since 1994 has maintained the endemic nature of all three of their wicked problems. That South Africa has genuinely advanced since the end of apartheid is a myth.

47

Efforts to change the equilibrium are generally countered by an equal reaction to maintain it. The countering forces have been institutionalised in ways that make this seem rational. For example, how does one achieve real economic growth of 5%, characterised by a resource boom, yet simultaneously maintain world-leading levels of unemployment?[7] Why is it that growth for the country finds itself facing a countering balancing force of an uneven distribution of its benefits?

During South Africa's arguably most substantial period of sustained economic growth, 1995–2007, the country achieved an average annualised growth rate of 3% (1995–2003) and 5% (2004–2007), which led to the reduction of headcount poverty in South Africa. Despite this growth, for a variety of reasons income inequality and unemployment both increased.[8] Between 1995 and 2005 real incomes (including wages, salaries and unearned income) of African households decreased by 1.8%, while white households increased by 40.5%.[9] As Bhorat explains, although extreme poverty in South Africa has declined, South Africa's inability to translate growth into the reduction of the national poverty line is largely due to the unequal nature of our society. He goes on to state that the exclusivity of South Africa's growth to a racial minority within the country is further emphasised by an unemployment rate that has averaged 23.7% over two decades.[10]

These countering forces which bring the country back to its equilibrium point are not isolated to economic issues; they include the social and symbolic.

#RhodesMustFall was the reaction to a combination of instances where moments of headway made towards transforming UCT were negated by the institutional culture of the university wanting to bring it back to equilibrium. Transformation at the university became a frustrating back-and-forth process. For every step forward, the university, through various interventions, naturally worked to push us backwards. As some would intimate during the first iteration of #FeesMustFall, we had to learn that for every revolutionary force, there is a counter-revolutionary one sharpening its knives around the corner.

We are plagued with countless examples of how progress is mitigated by the rationale or institutions that seem set on maintaining the status quo. Take land restitution, for example. Where a successful claim has been made and land is to be restored, the more immediately enticing choice of the recipient of monetary remuneration for lost land (remuneration that is far below the market value of the land) is all too frequently made.[11] Every Sandton needs an Alexandra. Every mine in South Africa requires a migrant labour system. Every suburban house needs a domestic worker.

For all the gains that have been made by South Africa's social welfare programmes, one of the downsides, as Barchiesi explains, has been the dampening effect of 'generalising, institutionalising and perpetuating social precariousness'.[12] South Africa's social welfare system does not represent an exceptionally generous system in the same vein as, for example, some Scandinavian countries. When taken at an individual level, our programme provides no guarantee of a life out of poverty. Families that rely on grants are usually compelled to seek labour in whatever low-wage, insecure and exploitative opportunity presents itself.

We have, for some reason, accepted all of this as normal. As everyday life. We only take notice of the injustice when people die en masse – for example, as in the cases of the Marikana Massacre or the Life Esidimeni scandal. But even then we rationalise the violence perpetrated against South Africans (and against black women especially) as a natural occurrence that should be noted, but not treated.

The #RUReferenceList protest at the University Currently Known as Rhodes (UCKR) was a particularly interesting #MustFall protest, which sought to highlight this point. At its heart, the movement aimed to change how we view the innocence of accused perpetrators of sexual violence. The intention was to show how 'innocent until proven guilty', for all its well-established, good intentions, served actively to normalise sexual violence on campus. It protected and to an extent entrenched a culture of rape at the university. The protest was designed to highlight the need to interrogate this doctrine and its intended and unintended consequences by publicly announcing a list of accused rapists on campus. By placing these names in public, the plan was to bypass 'innocent until proven guilty', not to suggest replacing it with 'guilty until proven innocent'. The intention was not to allow the presumption of innocence to deny the preservation of the humanity of the accuser. The general response to the protest was predictable. Here we had a classic example of trying to return the campus to the status quo. This same status quo, however, was what students were going to some lengths to show had failed countless women on campus. Though the #RUReferenceList protest had its individual detractors leading the charge against its cause, the movement's most prominent opponent was the entrenched attitudes of ordinary citizens when it comes to sexual assault in this country. This belief, unfortunately, belies the truth.

Whether through the university administration, police in Grahamstown, or the protesters' own parents, our inability to imagine a new and different South Africa has the effect of dampening the efforts of those who are attempting to change these imaginations into realities. These countering forces have become an everyday facet of our society, subconsciously embedding itself into our psyche to justify its nature. The inequalities that visualise themselves as competing dualities in South Africa have not critically changed from their apartheid roots. Yet so many will confidently state that in achieving political freedom, we also achieved victory against the apartheid system. It is this constant return to equilibrium that creates the illusion that my generation has been dormant. It creates, for example, the illusion that the #FeesMustFall movement started on 15 October 2015 on the campus of Wits University. This, we know, is a fallacy. What made 2015 and 2016 different from previous iterations of #FMF in the decade before, however, was that the movement had no natural countering force to temper the impact it would have on South Africa's point of equilibrium.

It is difficult to state accurately why #FMF didn't have a natural countering force. I think the only way to really determine why would be by doing an extensive qualitative study of the protests through the experiences of students and of society. That should give us a true understanding of why youth politics in South Africa is currently heading in the direction it is now. Regardless, I would like to suggest a few answers of my own to this question. Based on my time in #RhodesMustFall, witnessing the events of #FeesMustFall and my work on youth politics in South Africa, I believe some of these reasons are obvious while others are more hidden.

This, then, is my attempt at beginning the process of better understanding changing youth politics in South Africa.

The language of 'economic freedom in our lifetime' enabled young people to identify the status quo as a clear enemy of youth advancement in South Africa. The ANCYL in 2010 presented a discussion document at its National General Council meeting which declared that the political programme of young activists across the country would be to achieve 'Youth Action for Economic Freedom in Our Lifetime'.[13] From that point onwards economic freedom became synonymous with youth-focused political action. The translation of political freedom to economic freedom is at the heart of mobilising young people against the maintenance of the status quo.

Whether one has socialist or capitalist tendencies, young people across the board would agree that achieving economic prosperity is at the heart of many of their activities. The notion of EFIL simply instils the belief that one must rid society of often arbitrary conditions that prevent one's own economic advancement. Although poverty, unemployment and inequality were not new in South Africa, the call of economic freedom gave language and discourse to the problem and allowed for co-ordinated mobilisation. It re-orientated how many of us viewed the opportunities available to black South Africans for upward social mobility, and it created a discourse that conceptualised what it meant to be free in South Africa.

Throughout the fight against apartheid and until the very last moment, economic freedom was never put aside in favour of political freedom. When Mandela called for 'Freedom in Our Lifetime' in 1956, even he understood that political freedom in a country that has been historically unevenly economically demarcated along racial lines would be fruitless.[14] The achievement of the vote was not the end game for the liberation movements; the upliftment of black South Africans from the economic and social subjugation of an oppressive system was the goal. Thus, the achievement of the vote alone cannot be considered a true victory in a country that has experienced the full fury of systemic economic oppression. It should be seen as an important gain towards an even higher goal. To understand what drives the student movements it is important to understand that the call of EFIL has usurped the belief that achieving a rainbow nation was all that was needed to be a better nation.

The second reason for the lack of a countervailing force against the emergence of new forms of youth activism, characterised as #MustFall politics, is due to the political vacuum that was created through the disbandment of the ANCYL. Its dissolution was the first major attack on the notion of EFIL and the spirit of the ANCYL. The spirit of the ANCYL speaks to the spirit among South African youth characterised by antagonism, disruption and respectful disrespect of those who hold the title of elder in our country. It is a spirit that views itself as the vanguard of the elimination of oppression, of taking the responsibility to determine the right course of action – a right usually reserved for the elders within the revolution – and declaring themselves the guardians of the liberation struggle purely on the basis of their youth.[15]

At its core, the ANCYL embraced this spirit. In its founding manifesto in 1944 it stated:

> *The Congress Youth League must be the brains-trust and power-station of the spirit of African nationalism; the spirit of African self-determination; the spirit that is so discernible in the thinking of our Youth. It must be an organisation where young African men and women will meet and exchange ideas in an atmosphere pervaded by a common hatred of oppression. At this power-station, the league will be a co-ordinating agency for all youthful forces employed in rousing popular political consciousness and fighting oppression and reaction. It will educate the people politically by concentrating its energies on the African homefront to make all sections of our people Congress minded and nation-conscious.[16]*

This spirit is the ability to create self-aware generations who chafe against the restraint and moderation of their elders, distancing themselves from their parents and speaking of themselves as 'we, the youth of South Africa'. It takes an antagonistic stance against those we consider elders.[17] It is a spirit that inspired Anton Lembede, the first president of the African National Congress.[18] It fuelled the writings of Bantu Stephen Biko, the son of Black Consciousness,[19] and Robert Sobukwe, founder of the Pan-Africanist Congress and the man who dared to defy the ANC.

We have countless examples of the spirit of resistance against the moderation of our elders. The martyrs within the coloured communities in Cape Town during the 1985 schools boycott elicit a comparison to the generation of #FeesMustFall through the much-vaunted slogan of 'Freedom Now, Education Later'. This was a generation filled with sacrifice. Historic figures such as Ashley Kriel, the 20-year-old anti-apartheid activist murdered by the apartheid regime, are symbolic of the sacrifice of that generation.

The political void created by the disbandment of the ANCYL saw new organisations, in formal and informal politics, move to take on its spirit. The emergence of the EFF, for instance, was a direct result of the disbandment. During the initial stages of the EFF's formation, as Malaika Wa Azania (author of *Memoirs of a Born Free* and a fierce and unapologetic writer and community organiser) explains: 'Most of those supporting EFF are former and current members of the ANC who are tired of giving support to an organisation that fails to deliver even the most basic of services, such as sanitation and free education.'[20] Early surveys of youth response to the EFF mainly indicated that many of the policies proposed by the organisation resonated with young people.[21]

Through a combination of its enigmatic leader, Julius Malema, and its populist policies, young people flocked to the organisation in droves. The new party made a successful debut on the political scene when it contested the 2014 general election and won 6% of the vote. It also brought a different form of politics to the chambers of parliament. Performative in nature and characterised by their overt disruption of parliamentary proceedings, their refusal to wear formal clothing in favour of their now signature red overalls, the EFF brought with it a level of entertainment that grabbed the attention of thousands of young minds. The EFF understood that the notion of youth apathy was simply an excuse for not knowing how to engage with young people. Throughout my time at UCT I never imagined that I would walk into the food court to find students across the board sitting and watching events unfold on the parliamentary channel on TV, but this was what I witnessed. This fascination with national politics and sessions of parliament can almost exclusively be attributed to the EFF. Protests such as #PayBackTheMoney had the youth of the country engaged and attentive.

The EFF follows the logic incorporated within the notion of EFIL that one cannot simply accept the status quo because the rules of engagement preclude you from changing it. Of the three branches of government, parliament has probably been the least capable of holding the other branches to account. In recent years, however, this has begun to change, with the EFF leading the charge to alter the status quo in parliament itself. The EFF brought young people and their interests back into formal politics, ironically, yet fittingly so, through the spirit associated with the original ANCYL. Being part of a generation of youth who are the direct beneficiaries of the sacrifices of the youth of old, it sometimes fills me with unease that people view us as flaccid.

The 1985 student boycotts were driven by believing that one could use the crisis that emanated from the educational system at a local level as a means of advancing national liberation. This is not a unique position. In fact, it is common in our history. South Africa's educational institutions don't function within a socio-economic vacuum, but they are the battleground for many of the social tensions that persist. Socio-economic conditions generally have a direct effect on educational institutions and, in response, these institutions will influence the socio-economic climate of the nation.

Claims that the explosion of #MustFall politics was simply a populist response to the prevailing economic and political climate in South Africa are patently false. This is far removed from the reality of students' motivations. This view is to see the emergence of #FeesMustFall as distinct from the protests that took place at Pretoria High School for Girls about the school's code of conduct. It is to see the motivation of Black Twitter and its reaction to incidents such as Penny Sparrow's social media posts equating black people with monkeys as distinct from shifts to remove Afrikaans as the language of instruction at universities and high schools such as Hoërskool Overvaal.

Populism is 'quintessentially mercurial' and difficult to define.[22] Thus I would hesitate simply to equate the outburst of youth politics with populism. Hurt and Kuisma, in 'Undermining the "Rainbow Nation"? The Economic Freedom Fighters and Left-Wing Populism in South Africa', describe populism as carrying two characteristics. Firstly, it is used as both a thin ideology that is driven by the juxtaposition of 'pure people' and 'corrupt elites' and the belief that the nation's political life should be driven by the people. It is a form of politics that seeks direct rather than a representative democracy. And secondly, it is a form of politics based on a nationalist ontology.[23]

The motivations for many #MustFall political movements are not characterised by the above, but by a realisation that South Africa's society is abnormal, with most intangible benefits still skewed towards the minority.

The emergence of coconuts within #MustFall politics is probably one of the strongest inhibitors against attempts to temper the achievement of economic freedom. To be a coconut and involved in politics in South Africa is in fact a fascinating experience. For instance, to be a coconut and a supporter of the ANC is to represent both the best of the organisation and its inherent faults. We pay our tithes to the broad church but never attend service. We are the rebel pastor's children whose loyalty to the movement is only as strong as our sense of disagreement with it. Devoted to the cause, but unwilling to bring ourselves into the depths of the organisation, coconuts represent a generation of supporters the organisation has never encountered before. We hold no historical attachment to the organisation but remain endowed with its oral and written history, which have been passed down to us by members of our families and friends. Born free, yet enslaved to the ANC's awe, we revel in our association with the old guard of Tambo and Hani, deifying the lives of heroes we never knew. Yet often we find ourselves secretly praying for the return of Jesus Christ – the moment when former President Zuma prophesied the ANC would finally lose an election – hoping he will bring revolutionary change to the organisation.

Coconuts in politics represent the love-hate relationship so many in South Africa exhibit towards the ANC. Added to this is the fact that our long-term future is influenced more by inaction now than any other generation ahead of us. We are the new generation of 'clever blacks' – a term often reserved for the black elite of the country who, by questioning the ANC, are deemed to have turned their backs on the organisation. We are filled with anger and distrust of the state, underpinned by a love of party that is often never flinching. Coupled with these conflicting emotions are a constant sense of disappointment and fatigue with the state and the ANC, and the active pursuit of a non-partisan commitment to its abolition. Coconuts' discontent with the ANC stems largely from the organisation's lack of urgency in tackling the status quo. And while its stranglehold on our political imagination may remain as tight as ever, we refuse to sit on the sidelines of change. Instead, we have taken on the responsibility to lead the fight.

It was the insistence of coconuts to push for change that saw #MustFall movements gather the type of momentum we see running through our universities. Coconuts, who sit on the precipice of achieving economic freedom yet are often denied the illustrious goal due to arbitrary barriers created by a variety of countering forces, have both the social and political capital to maintain a charge against this injustice. More so than those in the country who aren't coconuts. We are the remedy. We are the counter-force to stand against attempts to retain the status quo because the status quo works directly against our own self-interests.

We are not only learning who our enemy is, but we are learning how to fight the enemy. Coconuts nationwide have begun to realise that to simply march on the streets of South Africa will not succeed in changing the status quo. Marches of this kind never really garner the attention of the country. But, like a young Mandela who decided to embark on a more militant approach to the struggle, in attacking the 1652s we have begun to realise that the only way of gaining the full attention of the country is to target them where it hurts the most. Using our proximity to the 1652s, we began to learn how best to disrupt the way they conceptualise and rationalise the country and, as a result, their complicity in the maintenance of the status quo, the educational and economic prospects of their children and their reliance on the country's democratic institutions to mask the injustices of the past.

56

Chapter 4

Fighting a Perpetual Sense of Survival

I often wonder how white people gain a sense of the mood of the country. When I stop to think about the nature of the discussions I imagine take place within many white communities, I wonder where their reference point lies for assessing how most black people feel. Do they believe that the discussions they have among themselves are representative of the country as a whole? If their views run in contradiction with the predominant view of black South Africans, do they sit back and think, 'I was so wrong about this.' Or do they think, 'These people don't know what they are talking about.'

From the moment in the second grade I realised there was a difference between myself and white friends, I wondered how, with no access to my world, they would understand my point of view. My best guess for where white people get a feel for the pulse of the nation is when they tune in to drive-time talk radio in the afternoon. Or maybe it's the proverbial drinking holes of Tasha-esque restaurants in Sandton or Rosebank. Perhaps it's office banter, considering that offices, like so many other 'integrated' spaces in South Africa, are apparently valuable for obtaining a seemingly diverse set of opinions. As many learned through the emergence of #RhodesMustFall, 'integrated' public spaces are poor barometers for gauging the feeling and mood of the country. In general, white people lack the ability to eavesdrop on the psyche of black people, while black people within integrated spaces are forced to internalise the white psyche.

This is not to say that all black people find themselves in one WhatsApp group discussing their feelings about the state of the nation, but how do white people get to understand the pulse of the country without removing themselves from either the echo chamber of talk radio or integrated spaces that curate the black experience? The emergence of a movement like #RhodesMustFall, in a similar sense to Biko's Black Consciousness movement, wouldn't and shouldn't have surprised white people if they'd been able to understand the mood of a room filled with blackness.

The best way to understand how a university functions is to think of it as an organisation that plays to a musical score. Every inch of the institution, from students, academics and administrators to the Senate and Council, functions together to create a symphony. The vice-chancellor is the conductor. Every facet of the university is an instrument playing to the score that represents the culture of the institution. From research on nanotechnology to the vendor in the food court, every aspect functions to a rhythm that is predetermined and played on a loop.

Think of the score with a rhythm set at a 7-count:1, 2, 3, 4, 5, 6, 7. Each part of the orchestra can play a different tune from the others, but in the main you are not allowed to deviate from the rhythm set by the score. This is because tune, like many other parameters of music, such as tone, articulation and the dynamic, is subjective and malleable. For some, being out of tune is a jarring experience, whereas for others it is barely noticeable.

Differences within a university are only acceptable when diverse opinions and departmental idiosyncrasies follow the beat of the score. Thus, the job of the vice-chancellor, as the conductor, is to ensure that the various parameters and the idiosyncrasies the university naturally creates remain faithful to the score. Departments, faculties and students alike are forced to alter their rhythms.

In the decade leading up to #RhodesMustFall, UCT had gone through a variety of moments in which its rhythm was challenged and altered. Rather than a 1 through 7 beat count, debates about the admissions policy would alter to a 1, 2, 1, 2, 3, 4, 5 rhythm. The emergence of the Black Academic Caucus (BAC) would seek to alter the rhythm to a 1, 2, 3, 4, 1, 2, 3 beat. But despite attempts to alter the rhythm, none was able to change the overall score or its beat count. While changes might be perceived to be a sign of difference, the reality never really altered. Nevertheless, the accumulation of these rhythm-altering moments – almost as if each one of the moments added its own weight – brought the score closer to its crescendo. In the days leading up to #RhodesMustFall UCT's score became increasingly imperceptible, with its conductor, Vice-Chancellor Max Price, desperately working to rectify the situation.

#RhodesMustFall at its core agitated for the change of UCT's score. A score that made black students feel invisible on campus. Motivated by the growing notion of #MustFall politics in South Africa's discourse, its purpose was to determine how to inculcate a tradition among students that would not accept a life played to a score they'd had no say in creating. The emergence of #RMF gave students a vehicle with which they could purposefully disrupt the university's rhythm to such an extent that it would change its score.

If you knew what you were looking for, you had to have known that #RhodesMustFall was inevitable. The need for a change in the score of the university was a result of the crisis created by an institutional culture that felt designed to isolate, alienate and 'other' groups of people en masse who failed to fit the normative identity of UCT, namely, that of the 1652s.

Throughout my time in universities, both in South Africa and in Oxford, I went through all three processes, sometimes all at the same time. Isolation was the feeling that others wouldn't understand how the institution treated me. It is what I imagine the feeling of being abandoned on a desert island might be like – alone and having to deal with an environment that is foreign and treacherous. Alienation was the process in which I was made to realise that I was somehow different from the 'normal' culture on campus. Lastly, othering was a result of being completely excluded from truly joining the dominant culture because of my difference.

#MustFall politics finds its purpose in helping individuals rationalise the crisis created within an individual through the process of isolation, alienation and othering by attempting to remove the influence such an institution has on an individual's cognitive dissonance.

UCT had created the environment for the perfect storm, but it was wholly underprepared for the consequences of its actions. The rise in black consciousness on campus was neither a matter of happenstance nor was it an eventuality. Its emergence was a result of the culture that UCT inculcated in its ivy-clad buildings. When I look back at how UCT tried to justify its actions, I realise that it did so, ironically, under the guise of trying to preserve the dignity of black students.

The demographic structure of previously advantaged universities is probably the most direct contributor to the unrest seen among students, academic staff and workers on campus in recent years. Race, like a variety of physical features that differentiate humans, is an arbitrary signifier of difference. Race is the result of the slightest and most miniscule of genetic difference between us. Yet race still matters because of what it represents in a society such as ours. Those who dismiss its significance are merely being naive. Race maintains a strong socialising influence in the way people understand others who are perceived to be different. You can't discard the issue of race in the same way that you might discard the size of your nose as a differentiator between individuals – no matter how much you might want to.

The demographic structure of our universities often informs and to an extent sets the default tone of the score everyone follows. It determines the starting point of everyone's experience of the university and ensures that any deviations from its central mantra are quickly returned to the norm. Even as far back as 2004, UCT fully understood that black students felt out of place in the institution; black students were given the burden of finding their relevance while white students took their relevance for granted.[1] It only took me a couple weeks into my first year at UCT to realise the extent to which the structures of the institution would allow for meaningful transformation to take place and the realisation of what my place, as a black student, was supposed to be.

When I first walked into Kopano Residence at UCT, I immediately noticed that the residence's series of blocks, each three storeys tall with corridors filled with single bedrooms, was wholly reliant on the dining hall – a room large enough to seat 300-plus people at once – as the fulcrum that held the residence together. Its high ceilings, long Game of Thrones-esque tables and west-facing, sun-drenched cascading windows helped create a space that screamed for the integration of its occupants. Kopano, like its name suggests, was seemingly designed to encourage integration and camaraderie among its residents and yet, three weeks in, try as it might, it became as segregated as any other space in the institution. Besides the odd exception (which shouldn't be ignored) of cross-racial interaction, within a couple of weeks Kopano's dining hall went from tables that were largely diverse to tables separated by race, class and ethnicity. What struck me the most was that the further you got from the main door of the dining hall, the darker the skin tone of the hall's inhabitants. It was almost as if the white students, uncomfortable with the notion of sharing a space with black students, were making sure they were close to the exit.

This was not exclusively a Kopano problem. The same pattern played – and plays – out at many university residences and in public spaces across the country. It's not only racial difference that segregates. Ethnicity and language do too. For instance, Leo Marquard Hall at UCT is notorious for not just its racial segregation, but the self-segregation of its black community as well. It wasn't too difficult to detect that that dining hall had Xhosa-only tables, with language and culture used to not only self-identify but to find mutual acquaintances. Finding commonality is a normal aspect of human relations, especially when one's commonality is physical appearance.

For all their faults, residences such as Kopano and Leo Marquard do work hard to foster a bond among all who live there. However, efforts to integrate at a micro-level are largely fruitless when the overarching structural nature of the institution remains built against such integration or is built on a foundation in which a lack of knowledge of the other simultaneously creates a lack of trust. In his introductory remarks in *Viewpoints*, in a powerful and beautiful take of a pre-#RhodesMustFall UCT, former UCT Vice-Chancellor Njabulo Ndebele eloquently explained this dilemma facing students:

The easiest congregations may occur between 'birds of a feather'. But in an institution under pressure to 'transform', such congregations are seldom allowed to rest. Who has to make the move and respond to the question 'Who are you?' Will the white group, members of the majority campus population, move to join a black group, members of a minority group, and risk being shunned, or accused of imposing and patronising behaviour? Or will it be the other way round, as black students risk being seen as seeking proximity to their 'superior' colleagues?[2]

Ndebele's remarks could be applied to most spaces across the country, whether they be schools, workplaces or stadiums. These small interventions at integration mean nothing if the overarching structure of authority is not on board, whether implicitly or explicitly, with your plans. How do we integrate when we can barely find the words to ask, 'Who are you?'

As a predominantly white, male institution, UCT's macro-structure mirrors some of South Africa's broader ills. This is not a slight against the institution, but just a statement of its demographic make-up. In 2015, of UCT's 1 286 academic staff, just under 23% (296) were black (all inclusive), and there wasn't a single black African female professor. If you were to ask a student how many black lecturers they'd had since they started at UCT, most would say one (two, if you were lucky). Of the 27 809 students enrolled in 2015, only 43% were black (all inclusive). This figure seems slowly but surely to be adjusting with subsequent years of enrolment. Though the population of white students sat at 29% in 2015, the university has admitted that this figure might be distorted as more students elect to not self-declare their race.[3]

The Professional, Administrative, Support and Service (PASS) staff demographics create a mirror image of racialised income distribution in South Africa, with top management being almost exclusively white, and support staff almost exclusively black.[4] For service staff at UCT's lowest pay grade, the opposite is true. Once again, it is a scenario that is not new to many South Africans, but it is particularly acute at an institution like UCT. White people are the core drivers of the institution while black people are simply the workers or tourists within. The Others.

So why does representation matter? Why would the racial and gendered demographics of the institution matter if the institution remains one of high academic calibre? This is a question regularly posed to students when they bring up issues of transformation in universities. For me, the question of why we need a representative demography on campus (not necessarily a one-to-one equivalent with national or provincial demographics) is less important than the question of what the unintended consequences are of maintaining such a sustained situation. Or, in other words, the unintended consequences of keeping students perpetually in survival mode.

If you are white and reading this book, you – more than most – should understand the fear of being othered, alone and unrepresented. Take a moment to imagine yourself living in a black township. Not in an empathetic manner; instead, I want you to imagine how your everyday life would play out in a black township. Don't try to imagine yourself in the shoes of a black person in a township; imagine, instead, that you are the only white person living there. Resist the temptation of seeing yourself within this experience as a form of pseudo-township tour, because township tours are designed to provide you, a white person, whether local or international, the vehicle to explore the curated black experience.

Imagine being dropped into a space that was not curated for you. You are left in a black township and told to survive this space for the next four years with only intermittent opportunities to go back home. Travelling to work on taxis every morning, none of your friends living anywhere near you, buying groceries at the local spaza shop, trying to navigate the space with only English – a language that is foreign to most of the people around you – as your language of communication. Your housing situation is not ensured, and neither is your stream of income. But your success within this space is equated to your success in life. You can barely speak Sesotho, isiZulu or isiXhosa, yet there is an expectation that one of these languages should be your home language. You have never encountered any of the norms or traditions of the space, and those who have been designated to help you, although they may fully acknowledge that you are displaced, are either ill-equipped to assist in your transition or, because of your difference, respond to you with pity. For those who have been given the job of helping you acclimatise: their job is to get you out of the township, rather than help you survive the township. You have a few white friends scattered around the area, and you can find solace among them, but none of them can really help you change your situation because they are experiencing the same struggle as you are. Here the dominant culture is black and your only option to survive this space is to assimilate.

Now consider this: this is the life of a black student in a white institution. This is a student in a perpetual state of survival.

Chapter 5

Challenging the Score and Setting the Stage for #RhodesMustFall

Many of you who are reading this book are probably doing so to better understand what motivated students to mobilise as they did. It is all well and good to tell you about the philosophy guiding the #MustFall movement but describing specific events that motivated the need to find this philosophy is as important. The emergence of #RhodesMustFall at UCT was the culmination of factors at the university, and society at large, which set in motion a series of incidents that necessitated the emergence of a structure for students to express themselves in a world where they felt silenced.

Although this chapter will not exhaust all the reasons for the emergence of #RhodesMustFall, I would like to highlight here three important fault lines. These fault lines informed many of the vital alliances required to form #RhodesMustFall. The detractors of attempts to change the university often maintained the view that they were helping black students on campus. But what they couldn't see was that they were giving them a lifejacket when what they really wanted was to get out of the water. Oddly, the first of these fault lines was not even caused by the actions of students, but by one of their most vocal and hubristic critics, Prof David Benatar, and the Philosophy Department, both of whom were among the most vocal and traditional opponents of student activism at UCT.

Prof Benatar is an interesting individual, to say the least. During my time at Oxford, I sometimes came across academics who would attest that Benatar was a wily old philosopher and not often liked. He was always in search of the best argument rather than the proverbial 'right' argument. Benatar's approach to most contentious debates was to place scientific truth and deductive reasoning over value judgements. The privileging of logic over 'emotion' is not a form of argumentation I disagree with. In fact, it's a form of reasoning I would hope most people subscribe to. However, unlike Benatar, I am not naive enough to believe that my deductive reasoning is not laced with value judgements, by which I mean a series of implicit systems of understanding of the world that inform the way we structure our understanding of it. This is the area where the ontological meets the epistemological.

In his inaugural lecture in 2007, Prof Benatar argued, through an ethical assessment, that the more weight one places on race within an affirmative action policy, the more unjustified such a policy becomes. His anti-affirmative action arguments were not new, something Dr Pumla Gobodo-Madikizela alluded to in her response.[1] It wasn't Prof Benatar's line of reasoning, however, that fired the first salvo at the university's rhythm, but a premise that would completely alter race discussions at the university for the next decade. This premise was: 'Race should not be used as a proxy for disadvantage.' Though not a complete reflection of his argument, Benatar said that those who opposed a race-based admissions policy did so because they wanted 'South Africa to get beyond this unscientific and harmful racial thinking'. Its use, he claimed, was a betrayal of the non-racialism to which the country was supposed to subscribe.[2]

Although this notion had been present at the university before, in his articulation of the point in delivering his inaugural lecture – which reverberated throughout the university and also garnered national attention – Benatar brought it to the general population of 1652s in South Africa and formed their opinion of UCT. It elicited a fury of responses from a variety of academics inside the institution as well as from the public. Arguably, it changed the discourse on campus when it came to race. The previous race-based admissions policy, which Benatar was attacking, managed the ebb and flow of transformation, gently nudging it along in a manner that would not disturb the core functions of the university. It was slow, but seemingly effective in its gradual pursuit of change. Yet such change was frowned upon because of its means, rather than its ends.

UCT's admissions policy debate brought to the forefront the question of the purpose of a South African university post-1994. After Benatar's assertions – although to be fair, he was not alone in these – the university's admissions policy, which until then had used race as a proxy for disadvantaged, begged the larger question of the means available to South Africa when it came to transformation. Benatar's focus at the time was primarily on UCT's affirmative action policy with regard to employment equity, but there was no clearly identifiable opponent (or natural defender) for where the logic of his argument led. As it happened, its primary opponents were university lecturers – a group who at the time had not yet found a collective voice to defend their position and, to an extent, their future employment.

For the casual observer, the admissions policy debate was simply an extension of society's broader issues with affirmative action. But UCT was different. For those who chose to look carefully and listen to the conversations, the debate represented the first full-frontal attack on coconuts' access to the university. As Vice-Chancellor Max Price explained it years later, in 2014, there was a noticeable increase of black students coming from 'good schools and achieving marks high enough to be admitted in straight competition with white students, without any affirmative action intervention.'[3] He suggested that race had increasingly become irrelevant from the perspective of an admissions process that depended on self-identified racial classification.

In 2015, UCT had 1 292 South African undergraduates who had not declared their race.[4] Previous debates around transformation had focused on changing apartheid-era institutions that dodged the bullet of change in 1994. These debates took on recognisable forms. The most obvious of these was the transformation of sports teams, like the Springbok rugby team, for example. What made UCT's proxy war different was that it was an attack on coconuts entering the institution. It was, to all intents and purposes, the first institutional attempt to disaggregate the black populace along class

67

as a mode of transformation. The central argument was that black high-school matriculants from 'good' schools were not disadvantaged, and thus should not be given an advantage within the admissions cycle over their white contemporaries.

Opponents of UCT's admissions policy cited a variety of reasons for its inadequacy, such as race is an arbitrary biological distinguisher of difference, let alone ability; utilising race as a proxy for disadvantage further segregates South Africans; the use of apartheid classifiers of race is an archaic system that will not lead to restitution; the admissions policy denied top-performing white students entrance into a university such as UCT.

The most prominent argument, however, was that the current admissions policy at UCT benefited the emerging black middle class who had, in the university's eyes, overcome the disadvantages of South Africa's schooling system. In their eyes, UCT had become a form of a 'tax haven' for the black elite to sneak in through the back door. Masking their argument through the resolve that the black elite was taking positions from more deserving black students, opponents to the admissions policy argued for a system that relied less on race and more on a variety of socio-economic indicators of disadvantage.

The university had no clear defender of the old admissions policy when the debate first began, and so initially the defence of the policy suffered from carrying the weight of an incoherent smorgasbord of responses. As Crain Soudien explained, there were three general camps of thought regarding the defence of the admissions policy: those who thought that race remained the best indicator of 'disadvantaged'; those who considered race as a problematic indicator but believed that of all the alternatives available none could take into consideration the nuances of race; and, lastly, those who understood race as a social construct and thought to reimagine it as being positive rather than negative.[5] The first two arguments, within the structural pursuit of the rainbow nation and the festival of negatives, became a rather weak defence of the admissions policy and was often more about political rhetoric than focused on the nature of the university itself. Only the last-mentioned camp – those who understood race as a social construct and thought to reimagine it as positive – understood the role the admissions policy played in changing the institution's score.

The problem with conceptualising the initial defences of the admissions policy was that those whom the policy would most directly affect were still in matric – that is, not yet students eligible (or not) for university – and therefore, to some extent, they were ambivalent about the impact the debate would have on them. With only a few willing to take a stand, academics could easily turn a blind eye if they needed to. Thus the responsibility was largely left to students already attending university to ensure that the advantage that had benefited them was maintained to benefit others. In hindsight, allowing the SRC to take on this defence of the admissions policy only further exacerbated arguments focused on the political rhetoric of race at the expense of seeing race on campus as a positive construct rather than one that impeded the notion of non-racialism.

This was best demonstrated during an admissions policy debate UCT held in 2010.[6] The debate was chaired by Judge Dennis Davis and included SRC president at that time, Sizwe Mpofu-Walsh (almost as if fate would have it, he was both a matriculant of St John's and a fellow coconut), Prof Benatar, Dr Max Price, Archbishop Ndungane and academic luminary Prof Neville Alexander. Watching the debate again many years later, the biggest thing that strikes me now is how willing the opponents of the admissions policy were to defend the dignity of the coconuts, and how those who found themselves as proponents believed that the dignity of black students, in general, would be protected by it. Those opposing argued that, in shifting admission criteria away from race, thereby removing the advantage the current policy afforded to privileged black students, they would be protecting these students' dignity. Those defending using race as a factor in admitting students to university argued, on the other hand, that the dignity of all black students, not just the dignity of coconuts, would be preserved.

Surprisingly, the argument for understanding racial difference (while fully acknowledging that race was a social construct and not of any biological importance) as a positive step towards better understanding race relations in South Africa remained absent. Surprising, because it would be this notion of the instrumental benefit of race that would drive the emergence of #RhodesMustFall. The notion that as a society we can accept these differences among ourselves not as negatives but as gateways to understanding ourselves, as well as others, in a manner that creates racial diversity without the loss of racial dignity. It's an argument that posits that one cannot ignore the long-lasting effects of South Africa's legacy of racial classification and that we should thus 'work with the grain' regarding race issues rather than reinvent the wheel.

The debate completely ignored this conception of race. It focused instead on the use of race as a proxy for disadvantage, with both camps hoping to dismiss the other's moral equivalence and each trying to outdo the other in showing who cared for the nature and future of black students the most. A true understanding of the nature of the black student within the university was not part of the discussion at all. This oversight would be corrected just a few years later.

As the admissions policy debate continued over the next few years, it primarily focused on three effects a socio-economically informed policy might have. The first was whether the new policy would slow the rate of increase of black students by limiting access to the institution. The second was how the policy would create greater class diversification in the university. The third asked whether the policy would provide relief to previously maligned white students. It should be made clear that the admissions policy debate did not intend to find the socio-economically disadvantaged white students in the country and bring them into the institution. The debate boiled down to how the institution might create a level of fairness for both white and black students on the margins who might be pipped to the line by more privileged black students.

Students, the primary 'on the ground' defenders of the race-based policy, fought through a variety of institutional structures while the parents of those marginally maligned white students took their fight to talk radio and op-eds. This was a clear display of a revolution meeting its natural counter-revolution. Submissions to the Howie Commission on the admissions policy, which was convened in 2012 to discern whether UCT should draft and implement a new policy, had a total of 86 submissions, with academics accounting for 35.3% of these, students for 15%, and PASS staff making 8.8%. The rest of the submissions consisted of alumni, parents of students, non-governmental organisations and members of parliament, among others.[7]

The Howie Commission is significant in that it was evidence of the university shifting the discourse about race on campus from a question of increasing representation to how to transform the university in a way that didn't jeopardise the quality of the institution or the dignity of its black students. The change in discourse was meant to maintain the central score of the university – which was under threat as a result of the increased representation of black students – under the guise that the reason for the change was to protect black students' dignity.

The second fault line was created by an unexpected yet long-awaited ally. While in the main black students advocated for an admissions policy that would change demographics of the student body in their favour, the formation of the Black Academic Caucus strengthened their cause. In banding together, black academics highlighted how they were regarded at the university and sought to escalate their role – as a group rather than individually – in the transformation discourse. Black academics usually fought institutional battles within their silos of influence. Their efforts were mostly unco-ordinated, and even when they tried to co-ordinate them, they were never really able to hold the alliance for a significant period of time.

In a similar vein to Benatar's butterfly effect on the institution's notion of race, UCT's own vice-chancellor, Max Price, would set in motion the formation of the most robust alliance of black academics in UCT's history, an alliance that would quickly become his biggest detractor. In 2014, in response to an article by Prof Xolela Mangcu published in the *Sunday Times* about the downgrading of race in UCT's admissions policy and the generally lamentable progress in transforming the academic demographics of the institution,[8] Dr Price said that slow transformation in academia in South Africa was a national university sector problem and not uniquely UCT's. He detailed a variety of ways in which UCT had tried to mitigate the problem. These included earmarking black academics who showed potential to become professors and setting up special programmes to accelerate

71

the advancement of black academics. Price ended his argument by stating: 'What UCT has achieved in quality and global excellence is not a trade-off against transformation, but rather the consequence of the right sort of transformation, one which taps into the much larger and more diverse pool of talent now available to us, and builds that talent slowly and incrementally, takes no shortcuts, does not compromise on quality in the short term but takes a long-term view.'[9]

Price's view of academic transformation was familiar in that it followed the same pattern of debates about academic transformation that were taking place at universities across the country. These debates were nearly always framed within a discourse of quantity versus quality. In a similar vein to the broader racial undertones of the admissions policy, this discourse posits, hubristically, that increased representation within academia is negatively correlated with the quality of the institution. It is a discourse informed by the notion that black academics should only be included in academia if they can meet a bar of quality. This is not a bar, it must be said, that is set before white academics.

Although I have quoted Max Price's 2014 assertion here, this is not a problem unique to the University of Cape Town. It is endemic across HWIs. In 2015 (2013) 40% (32%) of permanent academic staff at the University of the Witwatersrand were black, 27% (20%) at the University Currently Known as Rhodes, 21% (18%) at Stellenbosch University, and 25% (2016) at the University of Pretoria. On a national level, while 50% of permanent academic staff were black, this number was primarily driven upwards by HBIs which, on average, in 2013, accounted for above 80% of their academic staff being black.[10]

Underpinning Dr Price's argument was a central premise about the primary inhibitor of black academic advancement (which I first heard when I was a student leader at UCT), namely, that it takes 20 years to turn a PhD student into a professor. Therefore, this was saying that since apartheid only ended in 1994, the pool of black professors would generally be small and not yet of adequate quality. The premise is dishonest. It is used as a guise to justify the slow rate of change in universities. It is also laced with racist undertones and a level of historical erasure that continues the logic of the form of transformation at play being intended to protect academics rather than to suppress their advancement.

Price's premise was false for three reasons. Firstly, it assumed there were no qualified black academics before 1994; secondly, it implicitly argued that all white academics teaching at UCT had embarked on this 20-year journey to achieve their positions; and, finally, it suggested that meritocracy and tenure are mutually beneficial ideals that co-exist within a university in a manner that is not discriminatory. As the Council on Higher Education (CHE) explained in a 2016 review, the 'unwillingness to make systematic attempts to address the issue [of the transformation of academic staff] arises, almost inevitably, from the fact that there is little incentive to do so and potentially much cost in the form of internal resistance and conflict.'[11]

There are several reasons why achieving academic equity proceeds at a slow pace. Among these are the national policy environment, institutional behaviour, economic supply-and-demand factors, and institutional autonomy.[12] Considering that universities – arguably among the most value-filled institutions in our society, with collegial governance, institutional autonomy and academic freedom frequently being defining elements of their scores – are often dogmatic in their approach to understanding their institutional identity, it is no surprise that change within academic staffing would be slow.[13]

This situation is further exacerbated with the delineation between academic managers and managed academics. The influence in universities of managerialism and the seepage of practices associated with New Public Management made their appearance in the 1990s.[14] The rise in 'managerial ideology' led to the 'creation of a class of managerial elites completely removed from their academic colleagues and no longer accountable to them'.[15] Academic managers usually hold a professorial position in the university reflecting a level of entrenched power, authority and patronage, and they take on a variety of managerial roles. They can be characterised by how they act, that is, with the mentality of having a legitimate right to manage other academics as subordinates in the interest of organisational efficiency and improved productivity. They are instrumental in maintaining the institution's central character.[16] Managed academics, on the other hand, draw on their professional, normative ideological beliefs to create distinct autonomous professional identities. They are among those who challenge the managerialism orthodoxy by suggesting alternative non-economic-orientated visions of the institution and its importance.[17]

A combination of UCT's institutional inertia and the institution's continued disregard for the managed 'black' academic created by the predominantly white academic managers was what eventually led to the creation of the Black Academic Caucus – the first cohesive and organised response by a black collective of academic staff to UCT's academic hiring procedures. The BAC's basic argument was designed to dismantle the quantity-versus-quality dichotomy within the discourse of employment equity. This group would also become an integral component of the #RhodesMustFall movement.

They responded to Vice-Chancellor Price's assertions about academic transformation by penning an open letter. In it, they stated that they sought to reframe the complex matter of transformation by drawing on their personal experiences of being black academics at UCT. The open letter began the first real form of discussion about employment equity to focus on non-exclusionary ways of discussing quality and standards and creating models of transformation that did not presuppose a lack of quality among black academics, but the enabling of the human resources already present and available.[18]

The position taken by the BAC espoused the understanding that the inclusion of black academics within the higher echelons of academia at the university would exhibit a positive change in conceptions about race within academia, and that their exclusion from these hiring practices was symbolic of the institution's unchanging score. Thus, BAC became a natural ally to the student motivations for institutional change. The revolt against UCT was not student led; it was a joint venture between academics and students. This alliance set the stage for the last piece of the student movement puzzle and the third fault line: the employment of outsourced workers on campus.

The advent of outsourcing at universities in South Africa came during the 1990s. The practice can be attributed to the government embarking on a neo-liberal developmental programme. With the announcement of the Growth, Employment and Redistribution programme (GEAR) implemented by Mandela's government of national unity in 1996, the strategy for the development of higher education institutions required that expenditures needed to be contained 'through reductions in subsidisation of the more expensive parts of the system and greater private sector involvement in higher education'.[19] The announcement set in motion a series of decisions in the sector with the focus on fiscal austerity and demonstrated a shift to market-driven interventions. These decisions evolved, in universities' financial planning, into the commodification of the academic practice.[20]

Under the leadership of Dr Mamphela Ramphele, UCT embarked on a 'process of rationalising and merging faculties and departments, the implementation of cost-centre financial systems, and shrinkage in academic staff'.[21] The focus of the restructuring was to exhibit a level of cost-cutting that involved the pruning of 'non-core' activities while expanding what the university deemed to be its more marketable functions. Non-core activities included residence cleaning, campus cleaning and maintenance, gardening, grounds maintenance, and security and catering services.[22] The cost-cutting process resulted in the retrenchment of 267 workers and with it the loss of almost all the benefits and parts of the wages of those who remained. As noted by Mathekga, 'Before outsourcing, UCT cleaning workers used to earn between R11 and R14 per hour. After outsourcing, workers' hourly rate was R6 per hour.'[23]

The logic of outsourcing was immediately met with fierce opposition from workers and students on campus, who believed that restructuring should not come at the expense of its most vulnerable groups. Several cases of mistreatment of workers were cited by students as they accused the university of paying the outsourced workers less than when they were directly working for the university. Eventually, the National Education and Health Workers Union (NEHAWU) lodged a legal complaint about the outsourcing of workers, which complaint made its way to the Constitutional Court, a case they would eventually win on appeal.

UCT's response was to impose an outsourcing code of conduct. This was intended to ensure and regulate the humane treatment of outsourced workers on campus by their employers, ensure that workers would be remunerated significantly above market rate, and change the behaviour of companies in how they treated their workers.[24] The implementation of the code of conduct was generally poor, however, and the mistreatment of workers continued. The university subsequently initiated an Implementation Protocol which detailed the procedures the university should follow in cases of a breach of the code by employers.[25]

The issue of outsourcing brought something else into focus at the university. A fierce debate ensued about what the institution considered 'core' and 'non-core' responsibilities, and why there was a need for a dichotomy at all. A university simply can't function without its support staff, and the support staff wouldn't be employed without the university. The relationship between the proverbial non-core and core activities, in many students' and workers' eyes, was mutually beneficial, not mutually exclusive. Seeing the relationship as mutually beneficial was wholly informed by the need to ensure that workers, the majority of whom were black, would not be the cannon fodder for the university's strategy to be more market driven.

SASCO became the student movement most concerned with the plight of workers on campus, a role it shared with the UCT Workers Solidarity Committee and the UCT Left Students Forum. The attachment to the cause was due to the often-cited emotional attachment that students, in particular black students, had to workers on campus, who they viewed as their mothers and fathers. The entire system of outsourcing represented just one of the ways our society justified the exploitation of workers on campus. The alliance forged between workers and students became a constant, with both groupings supporting each other.

* * *

I don't think there is anything particularly life-affirming about finding yourself sitting in the offices of the South African Human Rights Commission. Whether you are a respondent, a witness or the accused, just being there signifies that something has gone astray in your life. Yet there I was, on 19 August 2013, at the top of Adderley Street in Cape Town, only a few metres away from the gates of parliament where, unbeknown to me at the time, another significant day in my life – and in others' lives – would play out just two years later.

On this day in 2013, however, I was there in my capacity as deputy president of Internal Affairs for the SRC at UCT. I waited patiently to speak to the commissioners present about my thoughts concerning yet another race issue that had arisen at the university, and one that had drawn international attention. Somehow UCT appeared to have become the melting pot for South Africa's racial and economic contradictions.

The issue at hand was an opinion piece published by *Varsity* – UCT's student-run newspaper – on 2 April 2013, titled 'Is Love Colour-blind?' The piece was written by Qamran Tabo. Qamran, for reasons known only to her, decided to try her hand at understanding people's sexual preferences through the filter of race. Although one could follow her logic (which went about trying to show how society unfairly portrays white people as more attractive than black people and we should realise this and look beyond race as a barometer of attractiveness), it was her use of a straw poll of 60 people as her base that angered students the most. The results of the poll – which were displayed in an editorially moronic pie chart with the heading 'UCT Votes on Most Attractive Race' – indicated that UCT students found black students the least attractive racial grouping at the university.

Why this moment is important to note and is relevant to the broader discussion of youth politics is not because of the article itself, or that it landed me at the SAHRC, but the response to it by white students. It can be described in two words: distant and disinterested. I don't want to engage in a discussion of 'not all white people ...' here. My point is that this was (and is) an endemic response to issues on campus that affect black people in the main. Extending this argument to issues of gender-based discrimination and violence, which also affect black students in the main, these are also seemingly ignored by white males and females. One can extend this disengagement more broadly to the fight for ending outsourcing, reduction of fees, the increase of financial aid, housing issues, and academic exclusion.

These are all issues which disproportionately affect black students at UCT. For the most part, they are met by white students with a sense of distance and a level of disinterest. Black students, meanwhile, who often didn't have the luxury of waiting to see an issue play out, were forced to fight and vocalise their issues.

This is what I mean when I talk about the score of the university. It is the way it rationalises and balances racial tension.

The example of the piece in *Varsity* is a relatively small incident, but there are countless others. The proposed shutdown of the Centre of African Studies was one, as were the persistence of outsourcing, the admissions policy, the failure to meet employment equity targets, black students sleeping in lecture theatres, black students dealing with racially derogatory comments both on and off campus, and the growing number of black students being academically excluded. It is an extraordinarily tiring process, being constantly required to try to find recognition within a space that is built to not even be cognisant of you.

What precipitated the need for #RhodesMustFall was the realisation that the fight to change the university's score on your own would be like running the 4 x 400 metre relay on your own. It was the realisation that if we didn't attempt to change the score as a collective, those who believed themselves to be our defenders would dictate to us what protecting our dignity meant. It was the realisation that you could exist within a university without the university being cognisant of you. #RhodesMustFall was the realisation that the status quo at UCT generated a logic which, even when black rage threatened to change the university's score, saw the university working to return itself to equilibrium.

It constantly astounds me that it required an act of throwing shit at a statue to help some of the brightest minds on the continent and in the world begin to see all the problems that existed not only at the University of Cape Town but across all South Africa's HWIs. That we had to reduce ourselves to such an act to galvanise a belief that this low point should never be reached again is just astonishing.

#MustFall politics is primarily concerned with the creation rather than the destruction of the social infrastructure in South Africa and many of its institutions. Whether it be fees, issues of representation or the toxic prevalence of rape culture, #MustFall politics, using disruption as its method, seeks to create a new social infrastructure to address many of the systemic and endemic problems in the country. Old institutions, cultures, mindsets and belief systems simply fail to see some of the world's greatest social ills even when they are right in front of them. #MustFall politics wanted to manufacture a crisis to restart the process of social restructuring which began in 1994 but which over the past decade and a half had stalled. As a result, #MustFall politics set its sights on the future overall betterment of South Africa through institutional change as opposed to piecemeal attempts to change the current state of the country.

Chapter 6

Why #RhodesMustFall had to Die

There is something of a Christ-like feel to #RhodesMustFall. Born from a sense of unjust prosecution, the movement went on to preach a message of love that was predicated on the notion of self-love. It might sound odd for me to say this, but #RhodesMustFall borrowed heavily from biblical motifs. The question it asked of all its followers was: how can you love others if you do not know how to love yourself? This was the message that spread across the country and inspired many of the student movements that followed #RMF.

Many of these movements could be seen as disciples of sorts, although each with their own unique characteristics and personalities.

For instance, #TransformWits could be seen as the John the Baptist – the biblical figure who heralded the coming of Jesus and baptised him – of the #MustFall movements. Formed the year before #RhodesMustFall, it formulated a Transformation Memorandum that proposed the need to revisit past debates about the role and responsibilities of university academics to interrogate South Africa's post-1994 academy. It spent much of its time preaching its gospel to all who wanted to hear its message.[1]

At Stellenbosch University, #OpenStellenbosch became a more reluctant disciple of #RMF. It sought to mobilise similarly but would not close its doors to white students (which #RMF would eventually do). #BlackStudentsMovement at the University Currently Known as Rhodes became the ideological anchor for the majority of the #MustFall movements, providing them with some of their most fervent authors. #MustFall politics spread across the country: there was #ReformPukke at North-West University, #SteynMustFall at the University of the Free State, #AfrikaansMustFall and #TuksUprising at the University of Pretoria, and even a #RhodesMustFallOxford, which found its home at the heart of empire, Oxford University. All espoused similar beliefs to those of #RhodesMustFall.[2]

Yet, like any martyr, there is a fine line between being seen as a hero or as a villain. #RMF often struggled to tread this line and at times chose to be the villain in society's eyes. With Fanon, Biko and Sobukwe in tow, they always considered their actions to be just. There was a logic to the madness and a level of madness that informed the logic. The establishment of a military wing, for example, was intended to provide an avenue for the expression of ideological violence without the need to bring such actions to the determination of a plenary. In the same vein, the creation of an arts and drama wing of the movement was meant to enable the idea of ideological disruption using music, art installations and live performances; it introduced the notion of 'actor-visits'.

Most remember #RhodesMustFall for either its villainous side – the burning of paintings on UCT's campus and the bombing of the vice-chancellor's office – or its more heroic element – the renaming of Bremner Building to Azania House and the triumphant removal of Rhodes's statue. The coin was the same. Hero and villain were just displayed on different sides and people's opinion of the movement often seamlessly switched between them.

#RMF was the villain in many people's eyes because, in agitating for change by increasing racial divisions on campus, it was the physical and symbolic antithesis of the narrative of the rainbow nation. Opponents of the movement saw it as an unorganised, unwieldy group of university students causing disruption for the sake of disruption with the purpose of creating a myopic utopia: Azania. Yet the creation of Azania was an act of heroism for many students and became embedded in the minds of the many young South Africans who yearn for a change from the rainbowism adage that continues to dominate our public sphere.

The story of #RhodesMustFall is difficult to tell because of the emotions it elicits among its detractors and its defenders. I am not here to decipher the intricacies of the movement or reveal its dark inner secrets. But I do want to tell you why #RMF had to die. It had to die so that young people, both in South Africa and abroad, would no longer live for themselves but for the message that #RMF espoused: to build a nation, we must break the rainbow.

#RMF became a space where black students at UCT could learn how to love and re-love themselves as black people within a white society.

A standard retort to this thought usually follows in the form of this question: 'What is a white society?' Some see this as an easy question to answer, while others, and I include myself here, acknowledge that it is incredibly complex. My simple understanding of it, within the context of the alliance that coconuts and 1652s have with each other, is that a white society privileges certain forms of living above others. This form of thinking doesn't take on a racial profile, but it has a racial bias. As a personal admirer of Du Bois, I prefer his understanding of the dominance of whiteness within a society. As he explains it, whiteness provided a level of compensation towards white people in the nineteenth and twentieth centuries by ensuring that the value of whiteness was dependent on the devaluation of the black existence/experience.[3] As a result, the benefits of being white were not only monetary. They included other areas of societal living such as culture, religion and social relations. When conceptualised within this framework and including the belief that the apartheid system didn't simply end at the end of 1994 but was designed to legalise this form of discrimination, then one begins to build a better understanding of what a white society looks like.

You do not need to look deeply into UCT to understand how prevalent whiteness was (and remains). To see yourself outside of this dynamic was difficult. How to see yourself within the university without the filter of the 1652 was a difficult task. Those who became adept at this skill became the disciples of #RhodesMustFall, which was tasked with the goal of spreading its word to all who would listen. Its purpose was to create a world that would love black people as they would love themselves. But if black people don't know how to love themselves, how do they expect others to love them? It was this conundrum, or rather this paradox, that gave rise to #RMF. The movement came from an urgent need to make sense of a society built on contradiction.

#RMF created a new site of struggle for the expression of a post-1994 conception of society. As noted in earlier chapters, previous struggles had found expression within the confines of political emancipation, with economic emancipation relegated to a long-term project dictated by 1652s. #RMF was not primarily concerned with material emancipation; it allowed for the realisation that the strongest countering force to economic emancipation being attained was within the incorporeal – that which does not consist of matter. Finding importance within the symbolic was not a matter of happenstance or the expression of intellectual naivety. It was the realisation that one cannot mobilise a society to fight something one does not have the language to describe. Without #RhodesMustFall, you could never imagine #FeesMustFall. Its focus on the incorporeal at UCT, in the beginning, allowed #RMF to highlight the musical score of the institution and force it to change, not through external pressure but internally, through the university's own realisation of its faults. The process required exposing the university's social institutions as morally and ethically contradictory.

To UCT's credit, the process of removing the statue of Cecil John Rhodes from its position of prominence at the base of Jameson Steps, the hallmark image of the university, had already started in 2014. Speaking at an event at the Baxter Theatre regarding transformation, Max Price announced that he didn't believe the statue of Rhodes – and in particular its location – was still appropriate.[4] What Price was alluding to was that the statue lacked a sense of historical context, but more importantly, that where it was situated on campus further elevated its status and exaggerated its skewed historicity.

Commissioned during the early 1930s by the Rhodes National South African Memorial Committee and sculpted by Marion Walgate, the statue was unveiled on 7 March 1934 by George Villiers, the Governor-General of the Union of South Africa.[5] The statue showed Rhodes serenely seated at the base of Jameson Steps, embodying the fulcrum that held not only the symmetric architecture of the university but its institutional culture too. Njabulo Ndebele explained it thus:

> To appreciate the bold magnificence of this symmetry, you have to imagine a centre line which begins some two to three hundred metres down the hill below Solomon's framed foreground, at a spot known as the Japonica Walk. The line cuts upward through the white structure known as Summer House, 'built about 1760 by the Dutch' and 'reconstructed by Herbert Baker in 1894'. A point of architectural serenity amid the din of the M3 highway traffic just above it, the Summer House stands at the upper edge of the Middle Campus.
>
> The line then hops over the highway to the lawn of the rugby fields, the lowest point of the wide-angle picture frame's foreground. Standing at the edge of these green lawns, the Summer House behind you, you can see clearly the line of symmetry cutting through Rhodes's statue, giving it a place of honour you may never have imagined. Rhodes is placed firmly at the centre of the space between the third and fourth pillars of Jameson Hall. It is a marvel!
>
> The line then ascends to Jameson Hall, to cut perfectly into two halves the pediment, a perfect, flat, isosceles triangle resting on the entablature just above the pillars. It cuts through the pediment's vertex angle, lining its tip with the flagpole at the centre of the Hall's summit. Then, finally, it leaps like a laser beam across the fynbos and the end of Newlands Forest, to head straight for the forehead tip of Devil's Peak.
>
> But from where he sits in a panelled armchair about one hundred metres in front of Jameson Hall, Rhodes has his back to the splendour behind him. It is with a great sense of himself that he seems to feel the presence of everything behind him without having to validate it with his eyes. It is there, on his land.
>
> Leaning on his right hand, his right elbow on his right thigh, Rhodes contemplates the wide vista in front of him, below him, facing east. He takes it all in, in a leisurely if thoughtful pose. His left hand, hanging

casually over the left armrest and side panel of his chair, holds a scroll
loosely. The manner of his clutch is in his gaze. He seems to have sus-
pended reading momentarily to ponder. He will get back to it, when he
needs to.[6]

One can only wonder what Walgate intended to show Rhodes contemplating. I believe that the engraving of an imperialist poem about Cape Town by Rudyard Kipling would have captured Rhodes's thoughts perfectly:

I DREAM MY DREAM
BY ROCK AND HEATH AND PINE
OF EMPIRE TO THE NORTHWARD
AY, ONE LAND
FROM LION'S HEAD TO LINE.
– Rudyard Kipling[7]

If we had simply allowed UCT to remove the statue on their own terms – a process which without our intervention would have taken years – the change would have happened within the context of the score of the university. It would have been a change made under the guise of transformation. A change that would deny the institution the opportunity to reimagine itself and those who walk through its halls. A change that would limit the way students and academics understand what transformation truly means by limiting it to the removal of a statue – a statue that meant so much more when it was unveiled than the bronze it was made from.

If we had just wanted the statue of Rhodes gone, we would have removed it ourselves. This was a debate that often came up during #RhodesMustFall's first occupation. A debate, I should note, that did not begin with #RMF. One of the earliest recordings of protests regarding Rhodes's statue was during the 1950s, when Afrikaans nationalist students, angered by the symbolic reminder of Rhodes, who to them was the aggressor during the Second Anglo-Boer War and had placed thousands of Afrikaners in concentration camps, pushed for its removal.[8] The debate continued for the next 60 years, with recorded protests throughout that time. In 2014 the statue was vandalised with the words 'Remember Marikana' graffitied on its pedestal by a group dubbed the Tokoloshes, who claimed responsibility in a statement that read: 'In honour of all black UCT students whose land was stolen from their ancestors and whose natural resources were privatised by one Cecil John Rhodes.' The Tokoloshes reminded us that colonialism and the massacre at Marikana were not only interconnected but part of a long history of dispossession, exploitation and murder of blacks (and especially poor blacks).[9]

During the student occupation of Bremner (at that stage it had not taken on the moniker Azania House) I remember receiving an urgent call one night to return and attend an ongoing plenary session. The plenary had resolved to remove the statue of Rhodes ourselves and had begun a discussion about the logistics of the operation. Some proclaimed that we should bring a hammer and jackhammer while others were in the process of organising a bulldozer. The room was filled with a sense of hyperbole, which is often the result of the group-think that manifests when one succumbs to the cabin fever of an occupation. It was why I avoided remaining in Bremner for more than two days at a time. Through a co-ordinated effort of a few, we were able to dispel the notion by reminding all those in attendance that if we were to remove the statue ourselves we would be labelled anarchists and our long-term plans would be put in immediate jeopardy. More importantly, we would be confirming that #RhodesMustFall was only about a statue. #RMF was much more than that. This was very clear in the movement's mission statement. The statue of Rhodes, it said, was the 'perfect embodiment of black alienation and disempowerment at the hands of UCT's institutional culture and was the natural starting point of this movement. The removal of the statue will not be the end of this movement, but rather the beginning of the decolonisation of the university.'

To force the university to remove the statue of Rhodes of their own accord but under our terms would indicate not only to us but to society at large that we could change the score of an institution – *decolonise* it – without having to follow the logic of it. The logic of UCT before this moment often unconsciously followed the argument that excluded black people without realising it was doing so – 'an othering prior to acknowledgement'[10] – and ensured that the institution remained incognisant of the lives of black people on campus. It was a logic whose first proclamation when faced with the threat of #RMF, was 'But it's only a statue.'

#RhodesMustFall didn't want UCT as an institution to understand the plight of black students on campus but to change its score to become cognisant of black people on campus. To make the invisible visible. To give language to the feeling of exclusion. But, as is the case with any messianic figure, #RMF's martyrdom necessitated that it made itself the threat to the well-being of others, not in a physical or violent sense, but by threatening the privileges enjoyed by 1652s on campus. Yet, ironically so, its persecution by those who wanted #RMF to fail only gave rise to the eventual dismantling of what they sought to preserve in their society.

#RhodesMustFall imparted a message that called for universal moral equality between people that was reliant on the creation, by all of society, of a moral equivalence of the worst-off within our society, blacks, and those who benefited from their impoverishment. In a similar vein to John Rawls's determination of 'justice as fairness',[11] #RMF believed that inequality could only be just if it provided the greatest benefit to the worst off.

At least, that was what it used to be. #RhodesMustFall fell into the dilemma of knowing what it could achieve but understanding that it would fall short of what it ought achieve. This was why #RMF had to die. Its life was far from meaningless, but its death was necessary. Before the movement died to liberate the minds of others and illuminated how the score of UCT was not only endemic to the institution but society at large, it became a villain. In-fighting, disorganisation and competing egos all played a part in tarnishing its image. The burning of portraits at the beginning of 2016 at the time of the #ShackvilleProtests – which I will talk about in more detail in a later chapter – and the subsequent petrol bombing of student buses and the vice-chancellor's office led many people to look at #RMF as a group of anarchists incapable of engaging in debate or discussion. Even our most fervent supporters began to believe that #RMF could only rely on violence as a form of communication. It was an unfortunate turn of events, inspired by a moment of rage and anguish. But before and after the #ShackvilleProtests #RMF underwent many trials and much tribulation, requiring both individual and collective introspection. We made mistakes, they made mistakes and I made mistakes. But we learned from them and sharpened our responses as a result. However, regardless of our efforts, #RhodesMustFall had to die.

South Africa loves martyrs. We love to heap praise on individuals as icons of change. Mandela, Biko, Sisulu, Hani. The names roll off the tongue. But ideas seem to fall on deaf ears. #RhodesMustFall had to die because we needed its ideas to live beyond its existence and not die with the individuals who were there to create and maintain it. #RMF died in a similar fashion to Christ: its death was violent and it split opinion among the masses. For some, it became an idea that would be passed on to others through the emergence of Fallism and to others it was the justified end to a group of criminals.

I am not a disciple of #RhodesMustFall, but I would like to tell its story. I do this not for personal fame, but so future generations can understand the roots of why this movement eventually fell under its own hubris.

Chapter 7

How UCT Stopped Buying what Mandela was Selling

O n 24 February 2015, The Collective – previously known as the Anarchist Collective – a student society on campus which hosted discussions intended to provoke debate, organised an event on Jameson Plaza, the social hub of the university. Overlooking the Cape Flats, with the iconic Jameson Hall behind it, the plaza is a key location. At any given moment during meridian, the hour between morning and afternoon classes, there are hundreds of students roaming along the plaza, using the space to socialise with friends or using the break to join the human high-way moving from one side of campus to the other. There is generally a vibrant atmosphere on the plaza, which is also often the scene of a variety of promotional events hosted by corporates seeking to break into the UCT student market.

The Collective chose to hold this event during meridian and on the plaza because of the sheer magnitude of the students present. The topic on the day was the legacy of Nelson Mandela and the event was titled: 'FreeTalk – Nelson Mandela: Saviour or Sellout?'

For many in South Africa and abroad, Nelson Mandela remains a giant of our time. He not only helped liberate South Africa but demonstrated a passion for reconciliation that was infectious. His place in history has been firmly cemented by his advocates, with his detractors often margin-alised or ostracised. During my time at Oxford, on a variety of occasions, I found myself the *de facto* spokesperson for the legacy of Mandela because of my nationality and possibly my skin colour. A black South African in Oxford is still quite a sight, not only for the British, but South Africans as well. There was an implicit assumption that my politics would align with Mandela's by the mere fact that I was South African. At the end of the first of my college's BOPs (Big Organised Party – a series of college-based parties held on a bi-monthly basis) I was introduced to a tradition dating back to the early 1980s. At the end of every BOP, students would sit on each other's shoulders and dance to 'Free Nelson Mandela' by The Special AKA. It was a tradition meant to showcase the progressive nature of the college by highlighting that it had fought and would continue to fight against injustice in the world. It was a tradition, like many other traditions at Oxford, in which I refused to participate. What struck me the most was how most of the British undergraduates at Oxford knew more about the story of Mandela than they did about the history of South Africa, let alone the current state of the country. For them, Madiba remained a symbol of hope against adversity, but for many of us at UCT, he remained one of our fiercest gatekeepers to achieving true economic freedom.

We, as 'born frees', had begun to question the role of Nelson Mandela and consider whether he was complicit in the way our country developed after the fall of apartheid. Admittedly, it is an unfair exercise, but it was an exercise we were not going to shy away from either. In the main, our antagonism against Madiba was not due to his efforts to reconcile, but how his legacy of unifying a racially segregated country was used to beat out the notion of the racial difference between people. Our issue was not with the man himself, but the role his legacy played in stifling tough conversations about race. A legacy that we believed was predicated on a need to sell the black majority short during the negotiations to appease the white minor-ity in the country. The deal that was struck still reverberates through the country today.

The discussion that took place on Jameson Plaza was fascinating. Tough questions about race relations on campus were asked and the concept of unearned privilege was put on the table. But, almost like clockwork, just as the discussion began to reach its breakthrough crescendo, it was brought back down by the appeal of 'What would Mandela do?'

The moment came when Keenan Hendricks, a prominent student leader at the time, exclaimed: 'Just because I can now sit next to a white person in a classroom doesn't mean we're free, it doesn't mean we're equal – and that's the biggest façade we've been painted in South Africa.'[1] In response to Keenan, a white student argued that 'the oppressor today doesn't take on colour. The oppressor today, he's Black, he's White, he's Indian. He's every colour you can imagine and he is in a specific point in politics, in corporations, and he is oppressing all people and I have a problem that it is always the race card.'[2] It was at this point that a black student, dismayed by the comments he was making, began to walk away while publicly voicing her frustration about them. Her disdain for the white student's comment was not *that* it was made, but rather *how* it was made. He had uttered the words with a level of authority that made it seem to many of us that *we* were the real enemies of progress. That somehow we stood on the wrong side of history and that we should be put back on track because we refused to accept the idea that colour didn't matter.

This is a tactic regularly used in race-related discussions in this country. Throughout my time working in youth development in South Africa and student politics at UCT, I became accustomed to hearing this self-declared authority from white students. It almost always comes in the form of a response to a comment or remark by a black student rather than as its own proposition, and it proceeds to direct the conversation towards what I describe as a 'rainbow conclusion'. The conversation usually follows these steps:

Step 1: Black student voices a race-related frustration.

Step 2: White student, uncomfortable with the comment, seeks to sympathise with/reject (because within these discussions there really is no difference) the black student but will seek to raise the conversation above race. The usual rhetoric that is associated with this step is either 'We should be united through our differences' or 'We shouldn't look at race, we are all human' or some form of derivative of the two.

Step 3: Black student reaffirms his/her position regarding their experience.

At the Jammie Plaza discussion Step 3 was showcased by a black student who, in response to a white student's earlier comment in which he'd said he had played no part in oppressing black people and only learned about it in a textbook, had replied: 'Even though I agree with you that it's not your fault because you are a born free, you are saying that you learned about apartheid from a textbook – but, like, black people and people of colour learn from living in a shack. And that's the difference. At the end of the day, you could be the type of person that says, "I don't believe in an oppressor," but the thing that is still oppressing you is your race.'

Step 4: Receiving support from other black colleagues.

This step was shown by Keenan again, who replied to the white student, saying: 'I think this is indicative of exactly why some of us are saying Nelson Mandela is a sell-out: we have this culture of people not confronting their own privilege and the privileged position they are in now because of what happened before.'[3]

Step 5: The failure to reach a resolution.

Even this conversation fell victim to Step 5 when the last speaker stated: 'Although right now we're all here together, most of us are going to go away to all our friends who probably look like us; who probably speak like us. And if we don't change that, then how are we going to change the economy – when we can't even change the way we think about other people?'[4]

It is this last comment that is indicative of the way race discussions are often handled in the country. Our failure to find a resolution that moves beyond the notion of the status quo and the rainbow nation hampers our ability to engage with racial difference and the consequences that that has on our society.

The outcome of the discussion that day is not of any real importance. What *was* significant was that among the students present, many of them would form the core of student leaders who would lead the #RhodesMustFall movement only a few weeks later. Many of these same student leaders had previously been at odds with one another over certain political differences, but it was at this meeting that a revision of historical differences between political opponents on campus began.

Unlike most universities across South Africa, where SRC elections are run with either only independents or only political parties, UCT employs a hybrid election which combines independent candidates and political parties who run for individual positions. The system at Wits is similar, but their SRC elections are wholly dominated by political organisations. UCT is different in that it tends to lean towards a more balanced system between parties and independents.

There had been a growing desire at UCT for a black-conscious political organisation on campus in the years leading up to #RMF considering the numerous incidents over the years, for example, the university's process to finalise its new admissions policy during 2013/2014. It was SASCO that led the charge against the university, but without having control of the SRC, their ability institutionally to challenge the policy was limited. Also, SASCO was not altogether trusted on campus because of its allegiance to the African National Congress, which at the time was an unpopular party to the majority white students on campus. There was a fear that SASCO would place party politics ahead of student issues.

In its place, a group of independents stepped in. They called themselves BLVCK and were led by Jessica Breakey, Athenkosi Sophitshi, Kgabo Senyatsi and Lungisa Ntobela. BLVCK, who got their inspiration from the definition of black as the absence of colour, positioned themselves as an SRC candidate focused on creating a united campus actively working to improve its future.[5] What was most interesting about BLVCK was its focus on the psychological well-being and stability of students. Although their manifesto would not mention this explicitly, through various SRC question and answer sessions, it became clear that their focus was not on the psychological well-being of all students, but of black students. BLVCK went on to win four seats in the 2013/2014 SRC elections, with three of its candidates placing in the top five and Jessica Breakey (the only white candidate) taking the top spot with a record number of votes. None would lead the SRC, however, owing to the unholy alliance between SASCO (four seats) and DASO (five seats) that year – desperate times, I guess, called for desperate measures – but BLVCK's victory was evidence that independent students could speak on the plight of black students without needing SASCO. This was unprecedented. In the past, independent students generally shied away from such a philosophical commitment as understanding the experiences of black students on campus. Black consciousness at the time didn't win you an election. The establishment of BLVCK would be an important first step towards the formalisation of #RhodesMustFall. It paved the road for other organisations.

The rise of Aluta during the following elections combined the independent energy and ability to speak on the plight of black students on campus with the organisational strength and populism of a political party. Aluta was formed by a group of branch executive members of SASCO who broke away from SASCO because of a range of disagreements between themselves and the provincial executive of the organisation. It was a break that would split SASCO across the province, with Aluta competing in SRC elections at the University of the Western Cape and at the Cape Peninsula University of Technology. The organisation was led by three primary figures, all of whom would become the closest approximation to the idea of 'founders' of #RhodesMustFall (though this is not an exclusive group): Ramabina Mahapa, who would become SRC president and official middleman between management and protesters, Alexandra Hotz, who became an influential mobiliser, and Kealeboga Ramaru, who would became #RMF's linchpin. All had ties to SASCO, but for a variety of reasons had grown disillusioned with the organisation and had left. This was a move that would not be unique to them.

The emergence of Aluta is important in understanding the genealogy of #RhodesMustFall for three reasons. The first is that it provided a black-conscious political student organisation on campus as an alternative to SASCO without subscribing to the latter's broader political ties to the ANC. At the time, organisations such as the Pan-African Student Movement of Azania (PASMA) had only been a footnote at UCT and the Economic Freedom Fighters Student Command (EFFSC) had not even been conceived. Similarly to BLVCK, Aluta believed in uniting diverse people from different walks of life, even though its electoral rhetoric was underpinned by an ideology of black consciousness and Pan-Africanism. Secondly, the organisation actively campaigned on the principle that it respected individual affiliations to other organisations if students were placed above political difference. Lastly, it explicitly sought to delegitimise the notion of the SRC by claiming that the SRC was the mouthpiece of management and an agent of management's mandate.[6] This rhetoric was not new to many universities in the country, but certainly Aluta was an anomaly at UCT. All three of Aluta's leaders would find their own expression within #RMF in its infancy.

Aluta's stance on the legitimacy of the SRC was one they would regret. They performed dismally in the elections, running 11 candidates but winning only 3 of the 17 available seats, while DASO won 10 of the 17.[7] That election, however, was probably the clearest indicator that the expressly pro-black organisations over the previous two years that threatened to change the score of the institution had to be met by their own natural countering force: elections. Regardless of the result of the 2014/2015 elections, over the course of the following year Aluta employed a series of Machiavellian tactics to usurp DASO as the majority party on the SRC and in so doing opened the doors for #RhodesMustFall to enter the university's governance system. It is commonly thought that #RMF simply bullied their way into university negotiations. But it was through Aluta that they already had their foot in the door.

Though the rise of black consciousness was finally beginning to infiltrate

95

student governance, its failure to garner electoral support at UCT gave rise to doubt. Was the university community ready for such an ideology to take root or even seep in? SASCO and DASO embraced, first and foremost, non-racialism as their strategy to attract both white and black voters at UCT and they would use proxy terms to refer to black students. SASCO, a historical derivation and watered-down version of Steve Biko's South African Student Organisation (SASO), used the proxy 'working class' for black students, while DASO used the term 'poor'. Neither organisation would actively campaign on defending the rights of black students on campus. Though both BLVCK and Aluta began this trend, it would be a group of four students at Leo Marquard Hall who would bring it to the forefront of our imagination.

In late 2013, in the dining hall of Leo Marquard men's residence, Masixole Mlandu, Sechaba Nkitseng and Siyabonga Njica sat discussing how, due to the limitations of the ANC, South Africa had failed to liberate the black populace of the country from the yoke of white people and their economic, social and cultural supremacy. The conversation focused on how black people who accepted the Charterist notions of the ANC had abandoned the struggle to liberate themselves. Discussions like these were taking place in student dining halls across the country, but there was a different element and outcome to this one. A house committee member, Tokologo Phetla, who aspired to something more, promised to give Masixole and company the funding and a formal space to further their dining-hall discussions if they helped him become head student of Leo Marquard. With his help, this small group started a series of imbizos, the purpose of which was to create a space for young people to discuss a variety of issues about Africa, and South Africa in particular.

The first imbizo was held in Leo Marquard Hall on 28 March 2014 and, according to Sechaba, 'centred on African consciousness as we try to redefine what it means to be African while developing a new mandate and identity for South Africa'. The event was a resounding success and the group of four men soon expanded to five, with the inclusion of Athabile Nonxuba. These five would go on to host the imbizos for the next two years, laying the foundation for what eventually would become #RhodesMustFall.

The conversations, modest at first, began to grow in notoriety as the topics of discussion swayed from reconciliation to what it meant to be black, problematising residence culture, land dispossession and restitution, and whether black consciousness was still relevant in South Africa. The imbizos included documentary screenings, art exhibitions and poetry recitals. Masixole described these meetings as 'black coffee conversations'; during one of my interviews with him, he explained how these imbizos were not only attended by students but workers in residence as well. For Masixole, and many of those who participated in the imbizos, this is what they believed to be the prototype of #RhodesMustFall. It would be the combination of music, art and dialogue among black students about issues that affected them that would become the pillars on which #RMF would stand.

Attendance varied in number from a handful to over a hundred for poetry slams. The imbizos outgrew Leo Marquard residence and began to be hosted at a variety of locations across the university. These events helped sow the seeds of change by creating a completely non-partisan space to talk about the politics of being a black student on campus. Similar to the event on Jameson Plaza which The Collective had held, the Marquard imbizos sought to bring the born-free out of its conception of the country as a post-apartheid society and into thinking of South Africa as a post-1994 society. Or, as Athabile Nonxuba would no doubt argue with me, a post-TRC South Africa. The difference between The Collective's debate and the Marquard imbizos was that the imbizos eliminated Step 2: the appeasement of white students who felt uncomfortable talking about race. The elimination of this step allowed for conversations to not be a dialogue between blackness and whiteness, but an inner monologue on issues of identity.

It is ironic to reflect that it was the legacy of Mandela that brought together the key figures within #RhodesMustFall. The Collective's event brought together DASO and SASCO activists, leading independents from BLVCK and Aluta, non-political students who were looking for a sounding board for their views, and some of the organisers of the Marquard imbizos. That event triggered the aligning of views of many of these stakeholders who had in the past been at loggerheads. The event provided the fuse that lit the fire of #RMF.

The next time these students would stand together was at a mass meeting of students just two weeks later. The topic this time: the statue of Cecil John Rhodes.

Chapter 8

Shit, Statues and #RhodesMustFall

Chumani Maxwele, for some, will be remembered as the man who threw shit on a statue. For others, though a small contingent of his following, he will be remembered for being detained by the South African Police Service for disrespecting President Jacob Zuma by giving the middle finger to the president's motorcade and uttering the words 'Fuck you, Zuma, you are disrupting traffic'.[1] Others see him as his apparent embodiment of the sexism, misogyny, anti-womxn, anti-LGBTQI, chauvinism and the emergence of 'Big Man' politics within the student movement.[2]

I believe Chumani was the person who gave life to #RhodesMustFall. I am not alone in this, but whether one agrees with my claim or not, Chumani Maxwele gave rise to the belief that only radical action would get the attention of students on campus. Though protests had taken place at UCT before, none had ever been as visceral as Chumani's. Standing shirtless in front of the statue of Rhodes, which he had desecrated with human faeces, wearing his now iconic pink construction helmet and blowing on his whistle to gain the attention of passersby, Chumani held up a sign that read: 'White Arrogance @ UCT'. Simple in its messaging yet complex and powerful in its delivery, Chumani's protest was soon joined by Athabile Nonxuba, Masixole Mlandu and Siyabonga Njica, the instigators of the Marquard imbizos. The use of human excrement as a form of protest (something that had become increasingly prominent in the Western Cape) quickly drew national attention.

On campus, the 'poo protest' sparked a discussion that was primarily concerned with whether throwing poo at a statue was an adequate form of expressing one's frustration. Even I fell victim to the allure of this debate, although my focus was on how the symbolism of your action is taken away by the real-world implication of who cleans that crap. It took me a day or so to realise that complaining about the mode of protest diverted attention from the reason for the protest. It was a common countering force on campus: your complaint was only valid if the way you made your complaint was considered appropriate. And those who set the terms of what was appropriate were the ones most likely not to believe your complaint was valid. This is a cycle often fallen into regardless of how many times you experience it. This countering force, intended to bring the university back to equilibrium and playing to its score, was challenged over the week following the throwing of the excrement. It would culminate in the first meeting of #RhodesMustFall.

The group comprised those who had organised the Marquard imbizos, with the inclusion of Chumani Maxwele and Wandile Kasibe, a PhD student at UCT who would become an important voice in the movement (although not one without controversy). Most of this group had been present at the initial protest with Chumani and had stood side by side with him. The view was that Chumani's actions could be the catalyst to evolve the Marquard imbizos into a movement. Setting themselves different tasks, the purpose of the group was to use the protest as the rationale to bring together a variety of stakeholders.

The second meeting was an event held by the student-run newspaper *Vernac News* on 11 March 2015 to launch its second edition. *Vernac News* had announced itself on campus the previous year, being the first student newspaper to privilege indigenous languages over English. In its first edition, the editor, Taariq Amod, explained that the inspiration for the paper was the result of trying to answer the question 'What is African about UCT?'[3] The reception to the paper was resoundingly positive, with students often commenting that they'd never believed they could see them-selves in a student newspaper, especially after *Varsity*'s *faux pas* the year before with the opinion piece 'Is Love Colour-blind?' It seems quite poetic that the week Chumani threw poo at a statue *Vernac* would launch its sec-ond edition at a seminar seeking directly to answer the question Taariq posed. The seminar involved students and critical academics from the Black Academic Caucus and primed many responses of the mass meeting that was to be hosted the following day.

The mass meeting that was held on 12 March 2014 was the culmination of the variety of efforts on campus to restructure the debate away from a discussion about the mode of protest towards a discussion about finally dealing with its cause. When putting the mass meeting together with the help of Ru Slayen (soon to be a prominent thinker of #RhodesMustFall and *de facto* statement writer), Jessica Breakey from BLVCK, Muhammed 'Todd' Abdulla (from The Collective) and the SRC, I didn't think it would be that significant. I was expecting 50 or so people to attend, but then … there I was on Jameson Plaza – standing in front of thousands.

The mass meeting became a sounding board for many of the grievances students had with the university. From political parties to independents, there was a general call for the university to refrain from charging Chumani and focus on the real issue on the table: institutionalised racism. Student after student, one after the other, came up to the microphone. Regardless of race, gender or sexuality, the majority who spoke voiced their displeasure about the lack of transformation. One could sense the anger emanating from each speaker. Some denounced the exclusionary culture of the uni-versity, while others led the crowd in singing a rendition of 'Thina Sizwe'. It was on that day that I met Masixole and Athabile, my first interaction with PASMA in a more formalised manner; till this day they claim that I hijacked their programme of action with the mass meeting. Their response to the singing of 'Thina Sizwe' was to lead their own rendition of 'Cape to Cairo', a traditional song of the South African Pan-African movement.

Regardless of the politicking, the general feeling on Jameson Plaza that day was one of excitement. It is hard to describe the exhilaration I felt. The only real university-wide political gathering that had taken place on

Jameson Plaza before that mass meeting had been the 'We Say Enough' march against gender-based violence in 2013. That march had been organised in response to the gruesome rape and murder of Anene Booysen, a teenager from Bredasdorp.

As the chair of the mass meeting, I thought keeping the discussion open to all races would be beneficial for the overall process we were embarking on. The whole idea of the mass meeting was for it to be an open dialogue among students about transformation on campus. But, as was expected, almost like clockwork when one allows all races equal expression in an inter-race dialogue, it inevitably led to Step 2. In this case, it came from a white male student in the form of the denouncement of race as the issue of contention and the elevation of racial unity among all those present. He felt that the discussion at the time had lost most students on campus because of its antagonistic approach to white students who, he believed, played no part in the anguish being expressed by black students. His comments were met with the usual derision, with students quickly asking me to take the microphone away from him. I was reluctant to do that because I thought it would detract from the open nature of the discussion. I found myself stuck on both sides of the same coin.

On the one hand, I had students who were baying for the blood of this white student and on the other I had students agreeing with his assertions. Eventually, I ceded to the cries from the crowd and ushered the individual away from the students, who angrily jeered him as he went. At that point, it seemed inevitable that Step 3 would come into play and, predictably, as always, the discussion would lead to nothing. But something different happened that afternoon. Something that would change UCT.

After ushering the student away and appeasing the crowd by allowing PASMA a bit more airtime than they needed, much to the derision of Kealeboga Ramaru, who was still associated with Aluta at the time, and being keenly aware of the growing influence the men from PASMA and the Marquard imbizos were having on the crowd, the next white student I allowed to speak met a very different crowd reaction than that of her predecessor. She came up to the microphone to dismiss the claim for racial unity. It was a call one didn't often hear from a white student at UCT and she clearly piqued the interest of the students. They sat listening to her, more attentive than they had been the whole afternoon. As she continued, she spoke about the need to better understand the experiences of black students on campus and pay attention to the stories they told of discrimination and unfair treatment. She went on to elaborate, drawing many nods of reluctant agreement from other white students. It was almost as if all those who derided the race-centric approach to past speakers had put aside their differences to listen to their fellow white student wax lyrical about the lived experience of black students. It was at this moment that a shout came from the crowd. 'Who are you to talk about the lived experience of black bodies on campus?'

It was at this moment that #RhodesMustFall was born.

The Step 1 through 4 approach to race dialogues on campus was smashed apart in a solitary instance. Rejecting the white student's authority or right to talk about the black experience provided a new avenue for challenging the score of the university. That one sentence was a small yet multi-layered protest in and of itself. A protest not only against the steering of the conversation by white bodies, but a protest against allowing a white student to even speak about the experience of black students.

By refusing to allow a white student to not only tell her how she felt as a black student on campus but to dictate how black students should react resonated profoundly amongst the hundreds of students listening attentively. This was the moment that a core group of black students realised that if they didn't own this moment in history, it would be owned by someone else or something else.

So, when Kealeboga announced that students, staff and workers should meet after the mass meeting to discuss what was going to happen next, the large contingent who followed her didn't only do so to continue the discussion but to protect the discussion from the influence of whiteness and keep it away from the glare of the 1652.

The next two weeks saw a series of protests on UCT's Upper Campus. Though not exclusively held under the #RhodesMustFall banner at the time, all were linked to the removal of the statue. The first publicly prominent protest was led by a group of students under the moniker Black Monday, who in attempting symbolically to show comparisons between Nazism and Rhodes, displayed swastikas across the pillars of Jameson Hall. This protest was widely denounced by student leaders who considered it distasteful and strategically naive, but it would find pockets of support nevertheless.

One thing the protest action did bring to light was the ease with which we are able to denounce Nazism as morally reprehensible yet find moral equivalence between Cecil Rhodes's genocidal and warmongering inclinations and South Africa's development. Though I disagreed with Black Monday's actions, they helped set the tone of questioning the manner we engage in debates and challenge many of the preconceived ideas and beliefs that we brought into these debates. In fact, in hindsight, Black Monday's actions were probably the most prophetic foreshadowing of student protest culture in the years to come. A glimpse into how students and university staff would react to unhinged radicalism on campus.

The first protest under the moniker of #RhodesMustFall targeted the ABSA Cape Epic, an internationally televised mountain bike race, the first leg of which was traditionally hosted at UCT. With our makeshift banner in hand, a remnant of Aluta's campaign the previous year for SRC and still heavily daubed with many of its slogans but now also displaying 'Rhodes Must Fall', we marched onto Upper Campus. Leading the march were Chumani, Ramabina and myself, with other figures such as Alexandra Hotz and Kealeboga Ramaru and a host of other vocal women who would form the heart of #RMF not far behind. I didn't know it then, but this man first, women second approach to the protest would become the tinder that would eventually spark the beginning of the end for #RMF. We sang and wrapped the statue in black plastic bags, tape and rope while looking down at the ABSA Cape Epic cyclists, who stared back at us bemused. One cyclist confronted us and when he tried to remove the plastic from the statue, he got into a physical altercation with Chumani. I didn't pay too much attention to the scuffle at the time, but it was a precursor for the Chumani we would see throughout the protest – passionate and motivated, but extremely short-tempered and prone to violence.

I should note that at this point you are probably thinking to yourself: who were these students who seemed to believe they could speak on behalf of all students? Why should the frustration of the few affect the many? I think the answer to this doesn't reside in trying to find a democratic aspect of the protests because #RhodesMustFall was far from democratic. Rather, I would say that it is better to understand why the protesters were motivated by the belief that they were acting as the proxy voice for all black students on campus. UCT had remained ominously silent on the protests, often choosing to speak to the media rather than students directly. It was infuriating. Especially when the university made the foolhardy decision that it would be best to communicate with students by erecting pinboards around the statue for students to express their opinions about the matter. Almost overnight these boards were filled with racial bigotry and slander and they were eventually removed by the institution. The university's position on the removal of the statue at the time was that it first had to engage in a series of consultations with a variety of stakeholders, planned to culminate in a special meeting of Council on 15 April 2015. The process would include a University Assembly, meetings with PASS staff and workers, and a sitting of Senate, a workshop for academic heads of departments, a special meeting of Convocation and a day of no lectures to host workshops with students about the legacy of Rhodes.

The proposal was met with resentment. Increasingly, students felt that Dr Price and his executive lacked both the requisite sense of urgency and the appreciation of what our protest was for. Dr Price and his executive management team, as alluded to before, had explained that they were in favour of the removal of the statue. However, in our eyes, Price's team had, like so many others both within the university and across the country, fallen into the trap of believing that the protest was about the statue and not what it was actually about, namely, the pervasive nature of institutionalised forms of racism on campus. It is an important distinction to make because the misrepresentation of our position often led to the statement: 'It's just a statue.'

We found the university's approach to the removal of the statue flawed for three reasons. The first was that placing the removal of the statue at the forefront of the consultations, rather than institutionalised racism, was putting the horse in front of the cart. For us, the removal of the statue would not impact on the notion of institutional racism; acknowledgement by the university of institutionalised racism on campus would naturally necessitate the removal of the statue. The statue represented a symptom of the problem of the university's score. What we wanted was to cut out the cause. You cannot do this, however, if you don't first acknowledge that the cause exists.

The second reason was based on the experience that within our society no one will ever self-proclaim to be racist, but everyone accepts that racism exists. It is an odd thought process that, once you begin, naturally leads you to illogical conclusions. For instance, one conclusion would be that after the end of apartheid all racist wypipo suddenly became ... not racist. Or that by not saying or proclaiming that you are racist, this means that you are somehow immune from being or acting racist. So many are so consumed by the act of not articulating their racist views that they often forget to not act out these same views.

UCT fell victim to this flawed form of reasoning as it publicly proclaimed that it was not institutionally racist but in the same breath would acknowledge that racial discrimination did occur on campus. As an institution, UCT felt that if it could distance itself from those who were racist, it would not have to confront itself, as an institution, about the experiences of black students on campus. As a result, the removal of the statue was less about the acknowledgement of one's racist acts and more about silencing racist voices. A seemingly righteous act, but one that belied and hid the truth of the matter.

Our third reason for not accepting the flawed nature of UCT's process to remove the statue was that by opening the discussion to all stakeholders, we opened the dialogue to Step 2 of why race discussions in South Africa often collapse. You could immediately see this taking place with the suggestion from 1652s that we find some reconciliatory arrangement that would not see the statue removed. Some suggested we create a historical context for the statue by placing a plaque on its plinth that gave an honest and balanced account of Rhodes's contributions to the country. Others took on what I can best describe as the Mandela Rhodes Foundation approach to the statue, by juxtaposing Rhodes with Mandela by both physically and metaphorically erecting a statue of Madiba next to Rhodes. As a Mandela Rhodes scholar, I found the notion of a statue of Mandela resting his arm on Rhodes's shoulder romantic in its elucidation of the complexities of our society. However, both my view and the many others that resisted the completed removal of the statue from campus suggested a level of acqui-escence towards rainbowism as a means of compromise within a heated racial debate. For #RhodesMustFall, setting a firm date for the complete removal of the statue from campus would circumvent the appeasement of whiteness and avoid a rainbow nation-informed compromise.

Once it became clear that the university would persist with its process regardless of the thoughts and views of #RMF, it was decided that we would march on Bremner Building – the administrative heart of the university – on Friday, 20 March 2015, and demand a date from the university for the removal of the statue. Whether it was during or after apartheid, the Bremner Building was no stranger to protest action or marches, with the most iconic protest involving a nine-day sit-in of the building in 1968 protesting the removal of Dr Archie Mafeje – about whom I will talk more later.

The march comprised two hundred or so people and included workers, students and academics. It made three clear demands: (1) a date for the removal of the statue, (2) ceasing the investigation into Chumani's actions and the students who had joined him on 9 March, and (3) a plan of action to redress the institution's failing transformation efforts.

The mood was tense from the onset and when we arrived at the gates of Bremner, the tension rose. The event began with a speech by Ramabina Mahapa from Aluta (then SRC president), followed by members of SASCO, the ANC, NGOs (for example, Ses'khona People's Rights Movement) and a scattering of other students. Interestingly, Wanelisa Xaba, a relatively unknown student (to me at the time), who represented the South African Young Feminist Activists, used the platform to criticise the ANC, which move was resoundingly booed by those in attendance. The moment was significant, because it showcased the political leanings of the movement at that stage. These leanings would change as the weeks went on.

Vice-Chancellor Max Price began his response to the protesters by exclaiming that the group in front of him were the already 'converted' and that the consultation process was meant to open the discussion to the majority of the 26 000 students on campus. This remark did not go down well with the crowd and there was no patience for Price, who was immediately booed for his comments while chants of 'We want a date!' rang out. Students began to sense Step 2 when Price maintained that more voices needed to be brought into the debate to ensure that the Council meeting would vote to remove the statue. His argument focused on the role of due process and maintaining academic liberalism within the institution. His strategy was to garner enough support to win a vote to remove the statue at Council within the ambits of the score of the university.

Upon reflecting on this argument, I find it bizarre that the executive management team could believe that we would simply trust Council with this decision. The same Council which on numerous occasions had voted to maintain the score of the university by continuing outsourcing at UCT and voted to change the university's race-based admissions policy. A Council that had failed at ensuring any form of academic transformation. That this same Council would suddenly take on a pro-black position was not going to happen.

Once the belief settled in amongst those in front of Bremner that afternoon that we would not receive a date for the removal of the statue, controlled mania took over our group as we stormed past the vice-chancellor standing on the steps of Bremner and into its foyer. Our act of defiance was not a result of uncontrolled hooliganism, but the realisation that if we wanted to change the score of the university, we would have to do it ourselves.

The first days of the occupation of Bremner (Azania House) were euphoric. There was a sense throughout the building that we were on the verge of something bigger than ourselves. The occupation which had originally been intended to last a day managed to extend itself through the weekend and into the following work week. There was an uneasy tension between students and staff in the building. The Monday morning began interestingly, with Athabile Nonxuba taking an unexpected ride on the hood of the vehicle that had brought Deputy Vice-Chancellor Dr Sandra Klopper to Bremner. The incident was due to the insistence by some students that no executive member of the university would be allowed to set foot in the building until a date for the removal of the statue had been determined.

I found myself spending most of my nights in the office of Enrico Uliana, the then Executive Director of Finance, hoping that no one would disturb my small moment of tranquillity outside of the intense nature of Azania House's central watering hole, the Mafeje Room. The Mafeje Room became our ideological incubator. It was where many of us either unearthed or polished the raw arguments we had about race and identity. Quotations and abstractions from authors such as Frantz Fanon, Steve Biko, Pumla Gqolo, Robert Sobukwe, WEB Du Bois, Albert Memmi, Malcolm X, Achille Mbembe, Marcus Garvey, Maya Angelou and Kendrick Lamar became common currency within the space. Art became our blood, with music sending it pumping through our veins. I don't remember a day of the occupation without song or dance. The space would often feel lost without it. Whether it was listening to it early in the morning while I prepared myself for class or late at night when I reflected on the day's discussions and proceedings, Azania House was always alive. Always bursting with ideas and new opportunities. We had created a space of learning that many felt was providing them with more tools for understanding the world than any degree the University of Cape Town could offer.

Every plenary session held the chance to explore a new form of not only knowing but being. We had become the captains of our ship, with each of us embarking on our own journeys of enlightenment. Enlightenment not in the sense of the modernist perspective of bringing rationality to the world, but becoming enlightened to what Walter Mignolo, a prominent but flawed decolonial author, described as the darker side of modernity: coloniality. How systems of oppression that find their logic and origins within the colonial system continued to play out in our everyday lives in a post-colonial society. We became adept at explaining why we as black students felt the way we did at UCT. I remember speaking to white students for an hour or more about #RhodesMustFall at the beginning of the occupation and how our conversations would only scratch the surface of why we needed such an organisation. After a week, these conversations were whittled down to ten or so minutes. We had become orators of our circumstances and warriors of its change. We were disciples of the message of decolonisation and teachers of its practice. We learned how to love ourselves as black children of South Africa. This is a lesson often misunderstood as the need to love diversity for the sake of peace. #RMF taught us that no peace is worth the betrayal of ourselves as black people.

We drew our anger against UCT not only because of its current institutional culture but because of how historically pervasive this discriminatory culture was. UCT consistently managed to demonstrate how the institution had traditionally treated black students, academics and workers who challenged the score of the university. An example, which I touched on earlier, was when, in 1998, the university embarked on a set of extensive retrenchments and the outsourcing of 'non-core' support services such as catering, maintenance and cleaning.[4] This decision had been made within the context of the rise of managerialism in higher education institutions globally. The end of apartheid required a renewed sense of egalitarianism within institutions with racialised pay differentials. Rather than include support staff workers within this newly formed egalitarian institution, universities opted to reduce pay differentials, but also, they removed the bottom sector of the wage scale by excluding them completely from any comparison with other salaried workers because they were employed by outsourced companies.[5]

Regarding academic staff, the Archie Mafeje affair rings the loudest. Prof Mafeje was appointed a senior lecturer in Social Anthropology in 1968. Although Mafeje did not directly oppose the ideology of the university, his mere physical presence as a black academic drew the ire of the apartheid government and allegedly forced UCT's Council to rescind their offer.[6] It is no coincidence that #RhodesMustFall's 'headquarters' were situated in the Mafeje Room, in the heart of UCT's main admin building. In 2008 the university apologised for their treatment of the professor and for their failure to 'defend adequately the right of the university to appoint academics without political interference, and hence its failure to protect Archie Mafeje's right to work at UCT'.[7] It took the institution 40 years to rectify its mistake and even then Mafeje and his family refused to forgive them.

The 'Mamdani affair' also piqued our interest. This incident spoke to how advocates for a change in our university curriculum had been removed from the university. The affair related to the suspension and eventual resignation of Prof Mahmood Mamdani in 1997 after he christened UCT's Centre for African Studies as 'the new home for Bantu Education'. Prof Mamdani confronted the dominant ideology of UCT when he posed the question of how to teach Africa in a post-apartheid university. As Prof Jonathan Jansen noted in 'But Our Natives Are Different!', Mamdani raised several critical issues about the nature of the undergraduate curriculum on Africa. Vociferous responses came from a host of senior academics, including the vice-chancellor at the time, and Prof Mamdani was suspended. The university, said Jansen, failed to 'provide an intellectually honest response to Mamdani because the issues he raises challenges at its very roots a knowledge/power regime at UCT which is intimately connected to the history and politics of a white institution in the shadow of apartheid'.[8] Prof André du Toit, previously in UCT's Politics department, commented at the time that the suspension of Prof Mamdani from the team which had been set up to redesign the foundation course on Africa was because he raised basic issues of academic freedom and accountability. Mamdani was forced out of UCT because he wanted to expand the academic canon by decolonising the way it was taught. He posed a direct threat to the predominant ideology within UCT and for his efforts he was removed. Mamdani has yet to receive an apology from the university for his resoluteness.

In order to understand the #MustFall movements and the creation of #RhodesMustFall, you need to see the organisation outside the context of the events that took place after its beginning, but as the result of a series of punctuated equilibria that have helped in the evolution of our conception of race, class and gender. We learned to identify the moments of punctuation in the past and from each, we gained a deeper understanding of what is required to undo the way our society has been woven together. We learned to understand and view the university not only as a microcosm of society but a reflection of society's morality. We learned so much within the space at the beginning. But things changed.

#RhodesMustFall only truly began during the second week of the occupation. The first week was dominated by plenary sessions and work-shops purposed towards understanding ourselves and the ideology of the movement and stamping our authority on the university landscape. During the second week, the university hosted a University Assembly in Jameson Hall. This was intended to be an open platform where all students would have a chance to speak about the experiences of transformation at UCT and discuss a way forward.

We hijacked the proceedings, removed Barney Pityana as the chair of the session and began to ensure that our message was heard by not only the university community but the country at large. From speaker to speaker, each was carefully selected to speak truth to the proverbial white power in Jameson Hall that evening. One speaker, Danai Musandu, a Zimbabwean national, encapsulated the mood in the room when she stated:

> Let me tell you one thing. If you are a white South African and you think that you can isolate yourself from being African and that statue outside doesn't bother you, you need to think twice, because the future is moving a lot faster than your consciousness.[9]

Workers, black academics and students alike spoke about their experiences of racism on campus. The Assembly was a sounding board for us. A means for our expression. The stage was too important to allow the inevitable Step 2 discussion to follow or to take any form of prominence. We marched out of the hall, celebrating what had become the most meaningful discussion about racism on campus the university had ever experienced. We were on a high, taking advantage of our national prominence, but we had not begun to scratch the surface of what was to come. We had no idea that we were starting to give ideological legs to an idea which in the past had been nothing but empty rhetoric. We began to imagine a world that was different from our own, but to do so, we had to relearn how to dream.

This moment came during a panel discussion after a screening of *Miners Shot Down* – a documentary depicting the events of the Marikana Massacre in which 35 protesting miners were shot and killed by the South African Police Service in 2012. Before that point, #RMF had merely been a vehicle for the expression of students' grievances against the institutional culture of the university. It was a movement with purpose, but without identity or ideology. As the chairperson began the question-and-answer session after the screening, Masixole Mlandu, who at the time was unknown to me but would soon become an unforgettable individual, rose to his feet. Coldly, and with his eyes fixed on the panellists, he bluntly professed that it would not be possible to discuss the killing of black bodies at the hands of the state in the presence of white people, especially those on the panel. He believed that it would not be possible to have an honest and earnest conversation about the traumatic effect that Marikana had had on our society while in the presence of white people.

Masixole was engaging in a form of discourse that, while not new to South Africa by any means, had not emerged in universities in a post-1994 context. It has since become a trope in the student movement. In a moment, Masixole, almost single-handedly, altered the discourse on race at UCT. An alteration that I don't believe can be undone. Whether you agree with him or not, at the heart of Masixole's argument was not that there was a dearth of discussion at UCT about racial discrimination, justice and/or prejudice. Throughout my time at the university, there were countless spaces in which discussions about social issues occurred. Whether this was at an organised workshop, in the dining halls of student residences or on the picturesque steps in front of Jameson Hall, discussions about these issues did happen. What Masixole was pointing to was not that we were not discussing these issues, but the power relations that defined them. As is the case in any organisational structure, the power relations and culture within the structure will guide the behaviour of agents who function for its benefit.

At UCT, it is primarily white students, academics and administrators who have perennially been privileged over their black counterparts, who enjoy both the intended and unintended benefits of this power arrangement. They enjoy a form of privilege that is both circumstantial and a result of the culture of the institution. Whether one seeks to look at it through student enrolment numbers, throughput rates, employment structure, academic hiring practices, or administrative services, there is no denying that there are groups who have found it easier to navigate their identity within the rhythm of the university than others.

By asking that all white people in the Mafeje Room leave, Masixole was trying to signify that a discussion about race would not be able to be had in earnest with the direct beneficiaries of racial discrimination present. There had been murmurs of taking such a stance in the days prior to this moment, but nothing had come of it. Masixole, always brazen in stead-fastness, began speaking in a similar spirit to that of Steve Biko, whose approach to racial discourse was almost diametrically opposed to the notion of nation-building and the rainbow nation. It is an approach that is frequently dismissed in a variety of ways. Some believe that it is indicative of how young students are unable to engage in critical debate. Others suggest that it is part of broader issues of millennials and the notion of not being able to handle emotionally sensitive discussions. In my mind, at least at that moment in time, I experienced what it meant to be racist to someone – and I enjoyed it.

Racism is not the discrimination of someone based on their race. I could deny a white person my pen because of the colour of their skin, but that act wouldn't be racist; it would be prejudice. The white person in question would feel aggrieved about my discretion but would not feel inferior to me because of it. Neither would they feel as if they existed in a society that viewed them as less than. The act of denying a white person a pen is not meant to remind the person about their place in the hierarchy of society for arbitrary reasons. It is an expression of prejudice. To discriminate against a white person because of their skin colour does not make me racist, just prejudiced. Racism is not a universally experienced phenomenon because it was neither created nor maintained to be used as a universal tool of sub-jugation available to all who wish to wield it.

Racism is about the use of or exacerbation of racially motivated power relations meant to discriminate and/or oppress people of colour. It is about the erasure of the existence of a racial group. Institutionalised forms of discrimination that systemically ensure the inferiority of people. Racism is the culmination of all the above in a web that entraps people of colour and never allows them to escape. My experience of racism is not linked to

114

feeling unfairly or unjustly treated. It is linked to my experience of being made to feel inferior, not simply discriminated against. The inferiority is linked to the use of authority by someone who has been given an arbitrary superiority over me. In the moment of Masixole removing all white people from the hall, I realised that within those four walls I was truly superior to all white people there and through the act of their removal made them inferior.

That evening was the first step towards the creation of Fallism as an ideology. The focus in Jameson Hall was primarily on race and institutional racism, which naturally led to the promotion of black consciousness. The emergence of black consciousness, within the Biko-ist understanding of it, led to the emergence of several other themes, such as the role of white liberals, black assimilation and co-existence. However, the expansion of our cause to other forms of oppression only took root when the black women in the movement noticed, rightfully so, that they had been excluded from the space and marginalised to its fringes.

In response to the desire to not be written out of the history of #RhodesMustFall, the prominence of Black Radical Feminism took root. Concerted efforts were made to educate men within the space about how they perpetuated a form of oppressive patriarchy. For the womxn in the movement, a civil war was waged against the men. War was declared during the second weekend of the occupation when the instruction came that all men must attend a plenary session if they wished to be part of #RhodesMustFall. The meeting was intended to bring issues of sexism, chauvinism, patriarchy and the dominant rape culture within #RMF to the surface and away from the whispers in the corridors. We had been living together for over a week and too many lines were crossed by the men in the room, who often silenced womxn through both physical and emotional intimidation. For many, they felt they faced a level of violence from men on two fronts: not only from a society filled with a variety of ills but also from those alongside whom they were fighting to heal that society.[10]

Drawing their inspiration from Flavia Dzodan, the womxn of the movement eventually decided to stand their ground. They declared that either the revolution would be intersectional, or it would be bullshit. Self-described

as 'radical, intersectional, African feminists', their presence in the movement was hard fought and immense. They demanded respect because they,
by and large, commanded a level of intellectual aptitude not match by
most of their male counterparts. You would find them in every meeting,
every plenary, and every discussion. They took their role and responsibility for guiding the movement seriously. Male leaders would come and go,
but the womxn of the movement remained. Not only were they the pillars of strength for the movement, they were also often its moral compass.
Black Radical Feminism wasn't let into the space; it brought a crowbar and
forced its way through the movement's male gatekeepers.

The emergence of Pan-Africanism in #RhodesMustFall came about
because of growing unease with SASCO during the occupation and
PASMA's growing influence. Slow and calculated, PASMA began to chip
away at the support SASCO enjoyed in the space. Racialisation of the space
was at odds with SASCO's stance of non-racialism. At the beginning of the
occupation, it was common currency to allow SASCO a platform to speak,
but by the third week, these opportunities came few and far between. What
hamstrung SASCO was its focus on creating a delineation between race
and class in the movement. The removal of white students from certain
plenary sessions created an ideological schism for SASCO as it argued that
even though black people should be allowed freely to express themselves in
a black-only space, we should not treat all black people the same.

My own introduction to SASCO involved me being brought to meet
Luntu Sokutu, a tried-and-tested political orator of the ANC's National
Democratic Revolution, who immediately lambasted my friend for bringing a 'bourgeois' into his room. The clear working-class bias of SASCO
necessitated asking a question of #RhodesMustFall that had been routinely
ignored. What about class? It was a question that many coconuts in the
movement opted to ignore because of the consequences it might have had
on its structure at the time. Because of the threat of facing a similar consequence to their white colleagues, coconuts had to ensure that class was
never brought into any meaningful discussion during plenaries.

Within this aversion to class discussions, as well as the explicit abdica-
tion of non-racialism in Azania House, the influence of PASMA grew and,

with it, Pan-Africanism. The phrase 'Izwe Lethu' and the accompanying palm-up salute were invisible at the beginning of the occupation; after a week they became ubiquitous. It should be noted that #RhodesMustFall was not an African space. For a variety of reasons, African foreign students never felt comfortable there. Some would attribute this to a level of xenophobia in the room, while others linked their reluctance to engage in protest action with the fear of jeopardising their visa status. Regardless, Azania House, ironically enough, was not necessarily open to all African students and its Pan-African leanings should not be misinterpreted as a pro-African approach to issues. For #RMF, it was South Africans first, African-Americans second and Africans at large third. PASMA continued to bring its Pan-African ideology into the space. Day by day, songs traditionally associated with the ANC were replaced by PAC anthems.

Without going into a deep ideological dive, I want to debunk the notion that Fallism as an ideological framework was conceived overnight or through a process of deep meditation. It would be egregious for anyone to proclaim that we perfectly understood all these concepts, let alone felt that we could express expert opinions on them. The formulation of Fallism was the result of a variety of political contestations. Fallism was forged in a variety of different ways, depending on the institution it emerged from. Where a university such as Stellenbosch was never able to incubate its own conception of Fallism, students from the University Currently Known as Rhodes found themselves further along in their development of Fallism than any other university. Fallism, which is best considered as a subset of #MustFall politics and often its ideological driver, is the ideological nexus of black consciousness, radical black feminism and Pan-Africanism working in conjunction with a protest culture informed by radical civil disobedience.

Fallism was able to infiltrate previously white institutions and capture the hearts and minds of coconuts because it gave the necessary language to understand not only your own experience of the 'oppressive' nature of the university but the experience of others as well. This is not to say that Fallism did not resonate in traditionally black institutions or among students who would not identify as coconuts. Like the broader MustFall

117

narrative, Fallism takes lightning-rod issues as a means of bringing attention to broader complex issues that have taken root in South Africa. #RhodesMustFall was a prominent example.

Fallism creates for itself a platform that leverages discussions about the nature of the South African society to allow for an expression of black pain without any countering force. It creates a veil of secrecy over a black person's class difference to place focus on the broader struggle of black people. This is a stance not taken by happenstance. If the ideology of Fallism was formed from political contestation, it stands to reason that those with political strength would benefit from creating an ideology that benefits them. It is often claimed, by black students in the main, that white people have a heightened level of ignorance of the plight of black students at previously disadvantaged universities because little media attention is given to these institutions. However, I would argue that in addition to white students, coconuts within the 'revolution' further exacerbate this issue. It is not necessarily that they lack empathy for students experiencing, among many other impediments to black success in higher education, heightened levels of academic and financial exclusion. Exacerbation is due to the role a white institution plays and the exertion it uses in coconuts' assimilation to the score of the university. The need to assimilate within these institutions plays to the benefits that are accrued to coconuts if they do – upward social mobility, white acceptance, class privileges. Thus, to bring the class question into the discussion requires removing the benefits white institutions imbue upon coconuts who choose to accede to the score of the institution. Fallism became, for coconuts, the first ideology that privileged the notion of black consciousness on campus without having to ask itself the class question.

Fallism is everywhere and nowhere at the same time. Its existence is predicated on whether it continues to play fiddle to the desires of coconuts. That class is the Achilles' heel of Fallism can be seen by the collapse of #RhodesMustFall, #FeesMustFall and other similar movements. Fractures in these movements were driven by two factors, both linked to class. The first was because of the inability of political organisations linked to the Freedom Charter – the EFFSC and SASCO, for example – to include the ideas of Fallism with their own and their rejection of the idea that class should be relegated in favour of race. PASMA's proximity to Fallism is because of the lack of attention the organisation gives to class differences. However, its schisms with Fallism were a result of its lack of awareness to the violent forms of patriarchy that exist within its ideology. The second factor, and probably the most important, is when a movement realises its own class differences and can no longer rationalise them.

Chapter 9

The Silent Revolution

The desire to enter university was palpable when I found myself standing with my cousin outside the University of Johannesburg at 3 am back in 2011. The evening before, my cousin had asked me if I would be willing to help him and his girlfriend register at UJ and I had agreed, not actually realising what this would entail. His girlfriend wanted to study tourism while he wanted to get into marketing. Both had been in a similar predicament by not applying to any university the year before, believing that their matric results were not good enough. They were placing their hopes on UJ's walk-in system. Walk-in systems were commonplace at the time. The intention was to ensure that universities would be filled if they found certain programmes were undersubscribed and it also gave an avenue for prospective students who had missed the previous year's application deadline another chance at a university education. The system, for most who used it, became a backdoor into the university. I remember trying to take advantage of this system myself in 2010 after I'd been rejected by all the universities I'd applied to.

The morning was long, to say the least. My cousin and I stood together in a line of a couple of hundred people, everyone waiting for the gates to open at 8 am. Armed with their official matric results, most had arrived at the university at 1 am. By the time we arrived the line was almost a kilometre long; it was twice that length a couple of hours later when the gates opened. Some people had brought camp chairs and blankets to keep themselves warm, others had barely anything on them, having travelled from various provinces across the country with nothing besides the dream of gaining acceptance into the university.

When the gates eventually opened there was a general sense of excitement, a belief that the wait had been worthwhile. However, it took another three hours before we even got into the university. At this point, I remember sensing a level of agitation from my cousin and his girlfriend. The flaw of the walk-in system was that it gave the impression of a first-come, first-served process. Though this wasn't the case, the wait gave the impression that the longer you spent in the line, the less your chances of acceptance became. With each passing hour, I could see the hope drain from most of the people standing around us. Most of us had been in line for over six hours, with no sign that we would get entry into the university any time soon. By this point we had been joined by my cousin's girlfriend's family and a decision was made that we should change our tactic. I would go with my cousin and explore other opportunities at private colleges such as Boston City Campus, Varsity College and City Varsity in Johannesburg while she stayed in line updating us on her progress. As my cousin and I drove around Johannesburg looking for any private college that would take him, desperation began to seep into the situation.

At the end of the day, neither my cousin nor his girlfriend got into UJ, with my cousin barely scraping into Varsity College and his girlfriend being accepted into Boston City Campus a couple of weeks later. It was a win, but at the same time, it felt like a loss. Failure to get university acceptance, in the eyes of most, meant that your prospects were severely hampered. We were lucky in 2011. Most people who went through this process that year were unsuccessful. The dream of attending university would have to be deferred for another year. In its place came the need to enrol in a technical vocational education and training college, improve their matric results or find a job.

I often use this moment with my cousin as a frank reminder of the lengths some will go to enter university. A desperation so profound that some would even risk their lives for the opportunity. Something that would happen the following year, 2012, as a mother standing in the exact same line, facing the exact same situation, lost her life as desperation turned into panic. On that fateful day, the patience exhibited the year before dissipated as students forced their way into the university, causing a stampede that injured several people and claimed the life of one. The mother of two was trampled to death. Her name was Gloria Sekwena. She was a victim of a broken system, the first casualty of a war that had already been taking place at the university. It was not the last stampede UJ would experience and not the last that would take place within the higher education system.

There is a persistent misconception that #FeesMustFall began in October 2015. This misconception is compounded by the belief that it was the University of the Witwatersrand that sparked the tinder for the flames that engulfed the higher education system in South Africa over the next two years. This was not the case at all. The death of Gloria Sekwena was just one example of an ongoing war of attrition taking place in the higher education sector. The narrative that #FMF began at Wits is especially peculiar because it shows a complete misreading of the state of the sector before that fateful protest on 14 October. But then again, I have never been too surprised by it. A similar misreading of our society is always present. The higher education system in South Africa had already been failing for a few years leading up to #FeesMustFall. The actions of the Wits SRC were only endemic of this.

I found the infatuation with the protest by 'seasoned' political commentators both nauseating and revealing. They were the source of much of the ire I felt. It seemed to me that they were nothing more than political witch doctors, looking into their proverbial tea leaves as a means of understanding the politics of the country. Political witch doctors, having mastered the art of using crumbs of information to build grand narratives, became the biggest providers of misinformation during the protests. They would gather information at coffee-table discussions during workshops or conferences to weasel their way onto talk radio, where they held forth about things they knew little about. Listening to them, one would think #FeesMustFall was a flash-bomb that took the sector by surprise and disorientated it. The coverage of the protest across various media platforms completely missed the mark about the drivers of the movement.

Public commentary during the first week of #FeesMustFall centred on a level of surprise about the students' actions. In week two the narrative changed twice. At the beginning of the week, it focused on labelling the students as naive hooligans who didn't understand how lucky they were; the latter half focused on equating our actions to those of young people in 1976. We had become modern-day revolutionaries in the eyes of the media. Even publications that were more in tune with the heartbeat of the protest, such as *The Daily Vox*, often placed an unreasonable amount of significance on the demonstrations of 14 October as the beginning of the revolution. Most hadn't realised or chose not to explain how this 'revolutionary war' had already begun long before that fateful October.

The fight against fees had been an ongoing battle within the higher education sector for a time longer than I can remember. Scheduled negotiations between SRCs and vice-chancellors had always been an adversarial rather than co-operative effort and the negotiations that took place at Wits that year were no different. Fee negotiations were the hallmark of any SRC term. It was usually the way your time in office would be judged. The higher the increase in tuition, the worse your performance as an SRC. Regardless of all their other efforts, students used the financial impact of fees as their measuring stick for their SRC's performance. Among universities at Historically Black Institutions (HBIs), the fight was not only with university management but with the National Student Financial Aid Scheme (NSFAS) as well. It would be unusual for there not to have been a protest at an HBI at the beginning of a given academic year due to a lack of funds distributed to these institutions from NSFAS. However, protests at HBIs generally failed to garner any national attention compared to their colleagues in HWIs.

There had been a level of animosity flowing back and forth between Vice-Chancellor Adam Habib and the Wits SRC throughout 2015, beginning with the '1 Million, 1 Month' campaign which sought to find the requisite funds for the registration fees for just under 3 000 students who had been left stranded by NSFAS due to insufficient funds.[1] Led by Mcebo Dlamini (SRC president and a rising star within the ANCYL, but not an uncontroversial figure), the campaign was a damning indictment of the inefficiencies of NSFAS and the inability of the university to account for the premature financial exclusion of almost a tenth of the university. The campaign was a success, raising over R2 million, with contributions from luminaries such as George Bizos and former Deputy Chief Justice Dikgang Moseneke, as well as Vice-Chancellor Adam Habib himself.[2] The campaign, however, became indicative of the problems that existed not only at Wits but in the higher education system as a whole.

As Wits celebrated the success of its campaign, the Tshwane University of Technology, only an hour's drive up the N1 from Wits, experienced a series of shutdown protests. These had been happening since September the previous year and they rolled over into the beginning of 2015. They would delay the opening of the university. A full year before the protests at Wits, TUT had embarked on its own version of #FeesMustFall and it was not alone. Half a dozen other institutions had also embarked on their own #FMF programmes. For many of these universities, the protest scenes that grabbed the attention of South Africa towards the end of 2015 had become commonplace on their own campuses.

The misconception that #FeesMustFall began in 2015 was primarily driven by the general assumption that the higher education system in South Africa circa 2015 was a well-oiled machine. Compared to the basic education sector, I guess most just assumed it couldn't be as bad. On the surface, the sector evoked an allure of economic emancipation among the financially impoverished matriculants of South Africa and their parents. The majority of students who sought entry into the higher education system believed that higher education would increase both their skills and their income potential.[3] A university degree, against the backdrop of the failures of the basic education system and rampant economic inequality, became the most reliable signal of a student's cognitive ability – thus a strong signal of employability in South Africa's job market.[4] The allure of the economic freedom a university degree promised was not unfounded: South Africa has the highest rate of individual private returns to higher education in the world.[5]

This allure also entices the rich of the country. For the parents and students who are able to attend the more prestigious schools – St John's, Hilton College, Michaelhouse, Herschel Girls' School, and so on – South African universities gave credence to the notion that their investment in their children's private education (a means of avoiding the dysfunctional basic education system) would reap its greatest returns within a university context in South Africa. For many of these parents, sending their children to a foreign university was not an economically viable decision. The Harvards and Oxfords of the world were beyond their reach, but the University of Cape Town and Wits were not. They were viable alternatives. The need to not only educate one's children but to ensure they are employable ensured that most parents were unable to look beyond the sector's façade and the many ills it masked.

South Africa's higher education sector is intricately interwoven with the society in which it is embedded and is as much a creature of South Africa's past as it is a creature of the sustained efforts to redirect and transform the country. The sector was both small and fragmented after 1994, with a severe level of under-representation of African, coloured and Indian students, who mostly found themselves confined to HBIs.[6] A restructuring of the sector in the early 2000s was meant to rectify this problem by merging HBIs and HWIs and forming universities of technology in the place of technikons. Thirty-six public institutions soon became 20, with the sector attending to its mandate to create equity in access as dictated by the 1997 White Paper on Higher Education.[7]

The state after the end of apartheid placed its focus on increasing enrolment and improving access to higher education. As a result, the Post-School Education and Training (PSET) system in South Africa currently comprises 26 public Higher Education institutions (HEIs) (12 traditional academic universities, 6 comprehensive universities and 8 universities of technology), 50 Technical and Vocational Education and Training (TVET) colleges, and 9 Community Education and Training (CET) colleges. In addition, the private PSET system is made up of 124 private HEIs and 252 private colleges.[8] Currently, there are 1.1 million students enrolled at public and private PSET institutions.

In 2015, public HEIs comprised 985 212 (87%) of those enrolled in the PSET system.[9] Enrolment since 1994 had grown by 80%, with most of the growth as a result of the strong demand by black students. In addition to the racial diversification, enrolment by gender underwent its own changes, with women making up over 50% of undergraduate students.[10]

For all its successes, in a 20-year review of the sector undertaken by the Council on Higher Education (CHE), it was found that the restructuring of the sector's institutional landscape and systemic intervention had had no real overall effect on the quality of its educational process. It highlighted that the output of the sector was not meeting the country's needs, was characterised by low internal efficiency (optimisation of human and material resources), and that the scale of the failure and dropout rates indicated that there were substantial systemic problems within the system. Graduate rates within the sector had been generally awful, with throughput rates generally low and dropout rates absurdly high, especially among black students.[11] Both rates were exacerbated by students' financial woes, which would often dovetail with academic performance.

Many of the ills that affected the university system were due to decreasing state subsidies, which inevitably led to the increase in student fees. University funding in South Africa is derived from three streams: government subsidies, student tuition and third-stream income (that is, research income, investments, donations, ring-fenced contributions, etc.). The current crisis in the higher education sector was precipitated by the decrease in government subsidies as a component of total university income over the past decade and an increase in student tuition. In 2000 the government accounted for 49% of university funding; by 2014 this had been reduced to 40%. In response, universities began to increase fees to compensate for the reduced government income (during the same time 21% to 31%).[12]

Although there was more government-sanctioned financial aid available for students, from the university's side the increased burden for the funding of higher education was transferred to the shoulders of students. Shifting the costs of higher education onto students became a strategy that masked the inability of universities to find new methods of generating third-stream incomes.

Universities found themselves in a peculiar situation. For some time, they had been warning the government about the impending chaos that would run rampant through the sector if nothing was changed. Vice-chancellors had been appealing to the state to increase government spending to higher education. The state spent between 0.68% (2004/15) to 0.72% (2015/16) of GDP on higher education. The figure compared well with other African countries but it was still a far cry from the sector's competitors from the Organisation for Economic Co-operation and Development (OECD), which routinely spent over 1% of GDP.[13] The thought process of shifting costs onto students relied on the belief that the state, realising that increasing outstanding debt would threaten the existence of certain higher education institutions, would need to create some form of financial aid for students from previously disadvantaged backgrounds.[14]

The National Student Financial Aid Scheme (NSFAS) had been in place since 1995. Its sole purpose was to ensure that those without the financial means would still be able to access higher education. The scheme functions as an income contingent loan and bursary which allocates state funds to universities – determined by the number of eligible means-tested students. Universities facilitate a transaction between the student and NSFAS. Students receive their funding in the form of a loan and must start their repayments only once they are employed and are earning above the threshold level of income of R30 000.[15] The loan is calculated by determining the full cost of study at an institution less loans or bursaries received by the student and less an expected family contribution to the fee amount. A portion of the loan is then converted to a bursary dependent on the academic success of the student. Those students who score a 50% pass rate will have their loan automatically renewed the following year.[16]

In a study from the Human Sciences Research Council (HSRC) regarding NSFAS, the council found that between 2000 and 2012, on average, 91% of NSFAS recipients were black, 4% coloured, 3% white and 1.5% Indian. In addition to this, of every 43 NSFAS recipients '1 student was from a historically advantaged background, while the remaining 42 students were from a historically disadvantaged background'.[17] Even within HWIs – 70% of the student population at HWIs were black students – the majority of NSFAS recipients were black (91%) in 2012.[18] Although it was overwhelmed by the demand for its services, when it was first legislated in 1999 NSFAS became the envy of student loan schemes across the world. As demand grew, a variety of administrative issues and inefficiencies began to affect its ability to allocate funds to institutions and collect on its debt. These problems would lead to the creation of peculiar distortions in its distribution of funds. It would be these distortions that would eventually galvanise the 'missing-middle' and coconuts across the country.

The intention was that over time the scheme would fund itself and become self-sustaining. As more students joined the scheme, there would eventually be an increase in income from debt collection, thus allowing for the financing of new loans. However, this turned out not to be the case. In less than a decade the scheme became riddled with administrative inefficiencies. By 2006 NSFAS was nearing a level of sustainability as debt collection reached a high of 28.9% of disbursements.[19] Despite the five-fold increase in funding of NSFAS between 1999 and 2009, the rapid growth in the demand for its funds outstripped its ability to cover the full cost of study for students, creating a massive shortfall.[20] By 2008 NSFAS allocations to HWIs could only cover 51% of the full cost of study, while allocations at HBIs could only cover 36%. The disparity between the HWIs and HBIs was largely due to how high the full cost of study was at HWIs, and the way the formula that determines an institution's NSFAS allocation was determined.[21]

Although HBIs had a higher annual growth rate in their NSFAS allocations when compared to HWIs, they were still unable to fully fund students who were both eligible for NSFAS funding and had been accepted into their universities. The situation created a perverse system of funding within these institutions often described as top-slicing. Top-slicing meant that rather than using the means test to determine the allocation of financial support to an individual student, the NSFAS allocation to the institution was diluted among all students. As a result, NSFAS recipients would have to share these funds as a collective rather than according to each student's individual needs.[22] It became a distributive mechanism that allocated funds to all qualifying students that were less than the recommended amount by NSFAS.[23] The process incentivised universities to accept more NSFAS-eligible students than NSFAS could feasibly afford to cover according to their own means test.

Although it was state policy to increase student enrolment across the sector, what HBIs were embarking on was a get-rich-quick scheme. With every NSFAS-eligible student who was accepted into an institution practising top-slicing, the NSFAS payment to each student decreased, while the amount owed to the university increased. As a result, HBIs entrenched a system that meant that rather than the NSFAS allocation covering 80% of a student's full cost of study, with the remaining 20% being the student's expected family contribution, the NSFAS allocation would only cover 20% of the full cost of study, with the student's family contribution amounting to 80%. It created a situation where institutions would enrol 5 000 NSFAS-eligible students instead of 3 000 students who would have received 100% of their full cost of study covered.[24]

HBIs were, for all intents and purposes, shorting the market for enrolment. They were betting on students eventually passing and paying off their university debt, thus profiting as students paid more of their debt to the institution rather than to NSFAS. However, if the students failed to pass, whether through financial or academic exclusion, both NSFAS and the institution would accrue the debt, with the university bearing the brunt of it. This risky practice saw many HBIs fall into debt and/or bankruptcy while simultaneously placing a greater burden on NSFAS's debt collection capabilities.

The Department of Higher Education and Training believed that the discrepancy between funding allocation between HWIs and HBIs was unjust because it meant that the 'affluent' black students at HWIs – 'affluent black students' was how the department described coconuts – benefited from a NSFAS allocation that gave less to those in need and more to those who were not in need. In a similar approach to UCT's admissions policy, the department increasingly felt there was a need to determine NSFAS allocations according to the socio-economic background of students rather than race.[25] It would be a decision that, in a similar manner to how things played out at UCT, planted the seeds for a lash-back from coconuts.

Debt collection began dramatically to increase in the face of all the pressures facing NSFAS. The increase in enrolment numbers and stable but low throughput rates ensured that loans were increasingly converted into bursaries. In addition to this, due to the National Credit Act of 2005, under the terms of which NSFAS had to remove all their blacklisted loan recipients from certain credit bureaus in 2007, and again in 2011 when the minister of Higher Education, Blade Nzimande, sought to find a new way to encourage blacklisted loan recipients to begin the process of repayment.[26] The disbanding of the NSFAS board and a range of changing processes to debt collection saw debt collection drop from a high of R638 million in 2010/2011 to R248 million in 2014/2015.[27] By 2014 only 3.6% of loan disbursements were being recovered by NSFAS. As it continued to toil to find new ways of recovering its debts, to all intents and purposes NSFAS had in effect become a grant-making scheme.

Top-slicing, the uneven distribution of NSFAS funding across institutions, the increasing demand for NSFAS funding, decreasing government subsidies, increasing tuition fees, low amounts of third-stream income, low throughput rates in conjunction with high dropout rates, administrative inefficiencies in both NSFAS and universities where funding allocations were not made to students at the beginning of the academic year, and the belief that higher education held the key to economic freedom – all these factors created the perfect storm for a break in the system.

Though international prestige was bestowed upon some of South Africa's higher education institutions, most faced severe liquidity issues, bankruptcy or even a complete shutdown. For all the good of employability the sector promised, it also perpetuated a different form of inequality in South Africa. The poor in the main attended HBIs, while the rich and coconuts attended HWIs. Those who were not rich or a coconut, who through sheer will managed entrance into a HWI, often found themselves facing the exit door due to financial constraints. Inequality between universities in the sector mirrored inequality in society. What was worse was that if a student found themselves financially excluded and was dependent on NSFAS funding, they would be forced out the door of the university drowning in debt. It was like stepping into a revolving door: being brought into the higher education sector, given a glimpse into a better tomorrow and then being shot back out into poverty when they failed. The financing within the higher education sector became barbaric to those who faced financial exclusion. It left them worse off than when they had entered the system.

In my experience, it was those who were beholden to the notion that universities were the home of the academic elite, who were somehow shielded from the perverse nature of our economic system, who were the most shocked about the emergence of #FeesMustFall. In a similar vein to society's urban elite, who generally ignored the day-to-day protests that gripped hundreds of communities across the country, the protests that ripped through the higher education system over the years were also ignored. If the logic of #FeesMustFall was the intention to shut down a university due to a fee- or financing-related issue, then HBIs across the country had fully embraced the idea of #FMF since the mid-2000s. The urgency from 2007 onwards as NSFAS began to fall apart was evident everywhere if you only took the time to look.

Although many protests of this nature took place much earlier than 2015, I want to show that even as the restructuring of the sector was intended to create greater equity, it was engulfed in a war of attrition between students and university management.

On 4 February 2008, at the Steve Biko campus of the Durban University of Technology, there was a showdown between students and police. Tensions had been high on campus the week before as the SRC and university management were unable to come to an agreement on how to handle growing student debt. Students gathered in front of the vice-chancellor's office, clamouring for management to respond to their demands and threatening to halt the registration process for the beginning of the academic year. The SRC accused management of failing to appropriately apply the NSFAS means test and demanded that the university roll over the current outstanding student debt to the following year. In response, the vice-chancellor, Prof Roy du Pre, claimed the university could not afford to do so, stating that student debt already stood at R175 million, with R72 million being accrued in the previous year.[28] It is not certain who attacked first, but the Steve Biko campus of DUT quickly became a war zone. Students hurled bricks, stones and bottles at police officers, with SAPS retaliating with rubber bullets and stun grenades. By the end of the day, one police officer was injured, five students had been arrested, and the university was closed for the rest of the week.[29]

It was a situation not unique to DUT. Demonstrations had also taken place at the University of Limpopo and Tshwane University of Technology (TUT). The University of Limpopo's Medunsa campus found itself embroiled in clashes between students protesting increasing student fees and financial exclusion and police officers armed with rubber bullets.[30] TUT's Soshanguve campus had been embroiled in protest action throughout January, their focus on disrupting the registration process. A 9% increase in tuition, the increase of bus fees from R1 to R2 and concerns that the percentage of NSFAS funding covering the full cost of study was far too small led to this student protest situation.[31] On Wednesday, 20 February 2008, ten students were arrested at TUT following violent protests and clashes with SAPS, which brought the campus to a standstill.

The protests described above became a regular occurrence at the beginning of each academic year. Though primarily affecting HBIs, even Wits had faced its own fees-related protests, which had shut down the university in 2007. Most protests across the country during the years before #FeesMustFall were led by an affiliate from the Progressive Youth Alliance (PYA) – an alliance of ANC-aligned youth structures on university campuses – who used their position on the SRCs as a means of galvanising student support against management. During these heightened times of tension on campuses across the country I often wondered why, if SASCO's national offices were located in the ANC's headquarters in Luthuli House, they didn't simply take the elevator up and demand the party place pressure on the state for free education. It was not as if the organisation had not done so in the past. In 2007 it had lent its support to President Zuma as it sought to gain enough favour in the party to establish free education as a formal ANC policy.

Alternatively, PASMA would be the organisation leading the charge, often working outside the SRC framework to achieve a shutdown. Independent protest action outside of these two groups was extremely rare.

The protests all followed a similar formula, focusing on student registration at the start of the academic year as a means of gaining the university's attention. Students would then deliver a memorandum to management, with management responding that most details of the memorandum had already been discussed with the SRC. The stand-off between these two structures would eventually boil over, with protests taking place on campus and police called onto campus to quell the unrest. Police presence on campus became the norm for the majority of HBIs as protests rocked these institutions from 2009 to 2015. The Durban University of Technology, the University of KwaZulu-Natal, the University of Limpopo and the Cape Peninsula University of Technology all faced shutdown protests in 2009 linked to inadequate student accommodation, a lack of NSFAS funding, inadequate funding of academic staff and a variety of other finance-related issues. Often described as 'violent', these protests either took place at the beginning of the academic year with the purpose of disrupting university activities or towards the middle of the year before the conclusion of fee negotiations.

DUT's protest in 2009, related to wage negotiations with workers, highlighted the nature of how the fight against the financial system backing higher education did not exclusively affect students, but workers and academics too. In a tactic that would later be adopted by #FeesMustFall, the students at UKZN refused to hand over their memorandum to management or meet with them until the student leaders who had been arrested at the time were released by the police.[32] The arrest of students and targeting of student leaders during these protests became standard practice. SAPS would charge students with either trespassing, public violence or illegal public gathering as a reason to put them behind bars, a tactic that shared large similarities with SAPS's apartheid past.

In 2011, fee-related protests took place at UKZN, DUT, CPUT and Mangosuthu University of Technology (MUT), culminating with TUT being put under administration by the Ministry of Higher Education.[33] In 2012, protests rocked TUT again and UKZN saw protest action related to a lack of accommodation provided to students as well as the quality of said accommodation.[34] The protests at UKZN would foreshadow the protests that took place on campus in 2015 in the lead-up to #FeesMustFall, which led to the burning down of a university residence there.

In 2013, DUT was shut down by protesting staff and Walter Sisulu University of Technology (WSU) stopped functioning, for all intents and purposes, as a university when students, academic faculty and workers all proceeded to embark on strike action one after the other.[35] In 2014, which was an extremely volatile year, the Vaal University of Technology (VUT), UWC, VUT, TUT, DUT, and UJ all embarked on protest action, resulting in the suspension of classes.[36]

Against this backdrop of years of student protests, it is bizarre to claim that #FeesMustFall took the country by surprise. What should be said instead is that the country had been placed under a veil of ignorance about the plight of students on many of these campuses across the country. What set the 2015 protests apart from ones that had taken place in the years gone past was that they happened on the country's more 'prestigious' campuses, the universities most white students attended. The emergence of #FMF not only at Wits but the white establishment's pride and joy, the University of Cape Town, brought a war that was already well under way, in from what the parents of children who attended IEB schools believed to be the far-flung areas of the country and onto their doorsteps. The protest also became what it was because black students at HWIs, and coconuts, in particular, were beginning to be affected by what was a failing sector of our economy.

Through the narrative of the missing-middle, black students were able to place their plight under one banner regardless of their economic standing in society. In doing so, they created for a grouping of black students from across the country a clearly defined identity. As a group, they saw it as their collective responsibility to restructure all institutions. More importantly, as a group, they believed they could achieve this.

In the months leading up to October 2015, UKZN students torched residence buildings, citing that residences were insufficiently financed and that the system was completely under-capacitated. Walter Sisulu University was still no longer functioning as a normal university, while the University of South Africa (UNISA) also saw protest action on its Durban campus.

Alongside the plethora of #MustFall movements formed after the emergence of #RhodesMustFall, the ground was fertile for a national explosion.

The narrative that South African universities house society's elite – an elite that is somehow shielded from the inequality, poverty and unemployment that runs rampant in our country – is one that deserves to be debunked. During #FeesMustFall there seemed to be a concerted effort to create an image of students who were not grateful for the opportunity given to them to study and that said students should be grateful that they had survived the basic education system of the country. These were false illusions, and black students were not fooled for a second.

Chapter 10

Identities of #FMF

My time in student politics taught me one valuable lesson: party politics is far easier to understand than the politics of people. Party politics generally functions within a demarcated area of understanding. One can predict the responses of political parties and act accordingly. It is rare for a political party, especially those with a functioning mother body, to suddenly change tack. One could easily predict the reaction to the student protests of DASO, the student wing of the Democratic Alliance, the official opposition party. They distanced themselves from the tactics employed by protesters and placed themselves as the political home for the silent majority. The decision by DASO was not without merit and, as one DASO member told me in an interview, was the result of 'political pressure from the party'.

DASO choosing to distance themselves from the protest was most likely due to how #FeesMustFall not only rejected both Mmusi Maimane (the national leader of the party) and Helen Zille (the provincial leader of the party in the Western Cape) but sought publicly to humiliate them. This was a tactic often employed by protest leaders. But regardless of the reasons for their self-removal, DASO's distancing from #FeesMustFall was predictable.

People politics, on the other hand, is notoriously hard to understand and predict. One could not predict, whenever a disagreement between two people within the protest movement arose, whether this was because of ideological differences or personal antagonism. This is not to say that one should delineate one's personal differences with one's ideological ones, but rather to point to how using an ideological difference to mask the personal differences you may have with someone had a profound effect on the movement. This became even more complicated when you understood that #FMF at its core focused on the politics of identity.

#FMF was much more than a national movement for the organisations involved. It became a potential political vehicle to redefine youth politics in South Africa. As a result, the contestation for the driver's seat of the movement was fierce. Bribery, assault, theft, blackmail, vandalism, bullying – you name it. All these things became everyday occurrences within the movement. To gain prominence within the movement, you had to be willing to denigrate the character of others and embolden others to question not only someone's commitment to the struggle but their commitment to being a black person. Even I fell victim to this growing culture when I was once accused of stealing money from the movement, when in fact I was trying to ensure that certain students would not gain prominence within the movement.

#FMF had a few key stakeholders. From protest to protest, university to university and region to region, one or two of these parties would hold the baton of responsibility for the movement. Those who claim that #FMF was one nationally co-ordinated protest should be branded as liars. #FMF was a coalition of various city-state-like alliances with the purpose of getting rid of Rome. Different universities functioned differently. Some formed regional alliances while others shunned their neighbours over political differences. However, incidents at key universities would often have more considerable repercussions, which extended across all universities. Because of this, I think it's vital for us briefly to undertake an analysis of the various political players within the game that became #FeesMustFall.

The Progressive Youth Alliance (PYA) and the South African Student Congress (SASCO)

The first significant stakeholder in #FMF was the Progressive Youth Alliance (PYA). As I've already mentioned, PYA was a coalition of ANC-aligned youth organisations such as SASCO, ANCYL, Young Communist League (YCL), the Muslim Students' Association (MSA) and the Congress of South African Students (COSAS). Contestations within the PYA were not unusual, however, with the ANCYL often competing against SASCO at a variety of institutions, often leading to the shutdown of these universities – TUT being a case example. In general, though, SASCO remained the dominant structure within the alliance.

SASCO was formed in 1992 as a result of a pact between the traditionally white National Union of South African Students (NUSAS), which was established in 1924, and the South African National Student Congress (SANSCO) – a descendant of Steve Biko's Black Consciousness South African Student Organisation (SASO), which was formed in 1984 and quickly became the most influential student organisation in the country.[1] NUSAS and SANSCO, both aligned to the ANC and the Freedom Charter, often found common purpose, with SANSCO, in particular, seeking an ally within English HBIs to establish black-centric structures – Black Student Societies (BSS) – in these universities.[2]

The formation of SASCO in 1992 set in motion a variety of ripple effects for student governance within the broader higher education sector in South Africa. Though linkages between the two organisations focused on ideas such as non-racialism and non-sexism and were able to bring together black and white students (becoming a precursor model of the rainbow nation project within universities), after the merger SASCO drew most of its membership from the black student population. As a result, white students opted out of SASCO over the following years, choosing instead to create piecemeal independent coalitions of white students. The concern was that SASCO was too subordinate to the ANC and there was a general unease around their dominance of SRC elections.[3] Unlike the other structures within the PYA, SASCO remained omnipresent within the higher education sector, often contesting SRC elections.

SASCO has traditionally been affiliated with the African National Congress throughout the years but has been known to disagree with its stepmother-body from time to time. The organisation follows a Charterist approach in ideology, with a Marxist-Leninist leaning in its understanding of society. Its role in student politics has primarily been to ensure that the ANC's National Democratic Revolution finds resonance within universities across the country and to provide a voice for ANC ideals on campus, without the need explicitly to pay homage to the party. As a subset of the PYA, SASCO's influence within #FMF should not be downplayed. Due to its omnipresence on campuses, SASCO naturally became the leader at the majority of SRCs, a role they would continually exploit to their advantage. It should be said that SASCO's advantage over the other stakeholders in the country allows them to control the South African Union of Students (SAUS), which is one of the only nationally recognised structures with a direct line to the Minister of Higher Education and a seat on the board of the National Student Financial Aid Scheme.

Economic Freedom Fighters Student Command (EFFSC)

The EFFSC is a fascinating organisation, primarily due to the way it rapidly grew across the country, providing the first truly legitimate threat to the dominance of SASCO on a national level. Formed alongside its mother body, the EFF, in 2013, the EFFSC would only need a year before it began to make inroads on campuses traditionally dominated by PYA and SASCO. Identifying themselves as the vanguard of the revolution against the class enemy, the EFFSC swept the SRC elections at the University of Limpopo's Turfloop campus in 2014, winning 10 of the available 17 seats.[4] Until then the University of Limpopo had always been a stronghold of the PYA (who only won 5 seats that year). As the EFF had done in the national elections a few months earlier, the EFFSC announced themselves on campus in grand fashion. The following year they would go on to win elections in the University of Venda and the Vaal University of Technology, further indicating their prominence within previously disadvantaged universities; and they would competitively compete against PYA stronghold institutions such as the Tshwane University of Technology.[5]

However, the EFFSC had some teething problems in the HWIs, some-times managing to win only one seat at universities such as Nelson Mandela Metropolitan University, the University of KwaZulu-Natal and the University of Pretoria. Both their inability to win any seats at Wits between 2014 and 2015 and failure to even appear on the ballot before 2017 at UCT was indicative of their failure to resonate in HWIs at the time. Yet, with the growth of #MustFall politics in the nation at large and universities, the EFFSC strongly gained traction at HWIs and by 2017, they won the SRC elections at Wits and scrambled their way into a presidential position at UCT.

In typical #MustFall fashion, the EFFSC's constitution states that it seeks to overthrow the neo-liberal anti-black education system, the bourgeoisie within the system and all other exploiting classes. It seeks to establish a dictatorship of the working class 'in place of the dictatorship of the bourgeoisie' in order to ensure the triumph of socialism over capitalism.[6] Although they would not explicitly state it, the EFFSC remains Charterist in its ideology but less so than the PYA and SASCO, positioning itself as a viable alternative to the PYA at HWIs and HBIs while maintaining the more militant characteristics of PASMA and Fallists. The continued growth of the EFF at a national political level, unlike SASCO or DASO, has not detracted from students voting for the party's student command. On the contrary, it seems to be attracting students. The EFFSC would leverage this realisation in their pursuit of controlling #FeesMustFall.

Pan-African Student Movement of Azania (PASMA)

PASMA was formed on 19 June 1997 at the University of the Western Cape after a decision to split the responsibilities of the Pan-Africanist Congress's student wing, the Pan-African Student Organisation (PASO), between higher education and secondary education.[7] PASMA is an especially interesting organisation. In the years before the emergence of the EFFSC, traditionally it was SASCO's primary opponent at HBIs, but at HWIs it lacked a certain level of gravitas. While it competed in elections at, for example, the UFH, NMMU, WSU, UL and TUT, a single electoral seat was usually the most it secured. It found most of its success at UWC, often interchanging electoral wins at that institution with SASCO from one year to another.

In a similar manner to the EFFSC, the rise of #MustFall politics allowed for PASMA to gain increased prominence within the student movements and SRCs across the country. PASMA's influence on student politics has evolved over the last few years. Sometimes seen as the perennial opposition party at most institutions, with fleeting victories dotted across the country, its role in student politics took an upward turn after 2015. Though it would remain an opposition party at most institutions, except for UWC and WSU in 2016, the ideology of PASMA began to percolate through the university landscape. Leveraging the growing influence of Fallism, the organisation would often position itself as the ideology's political home, offering its party infrastructure to Fallists as a place to mobilise. The strategy created an uneasy alliance between PASMA and Fallists, with PASMA seeking control of Fallism without neglecting its own political ideology, and Fallists found themselves at odds with PASMA's patriarchal nature.

Fallists

Fallists are probably the most fascinating stakeholder in the #MustFall movement. Without a political home, they have managed to maintain, at least in their eyes, the position of torchbearers of the ideology of Fallism. I would describe them as a disparate group of politically independent students, one that includes coconuts and non-coconuts, connected only by the notion of envisioning 'a more just and appropriate system of education which provides them not only with useful skills and chances to further their own career, but to help their families and communities, and to position (South) Africa in its rightful intellectual place'.[8] Limiting the role of Fallism to just the educational system seems unfair, but I have yet to see 'true' Fallism gain prominence outside of the university or educational space.

This is primarily due to the broad spectrum of Fallist movements across the country and the lack of a unifying definition of what a 'real/true' Fallist is. In a similar way that some people identify as Christian but do not necessarily practise Christianity, those who identify as Fallists do not necessarily fully subscribe to the ideology of Fallism. The discrepancy between the nature and composition of what is a Fallist is because, unlike the political stakeholders that comprise the student #MustFall movement, Fallists do not have their own membership card. What sets them apart from 'pseudo-Fallists' is their commitment to all the pillars of Fallism without fear or favour, and their role as gatekeepers for Fallism.

Within #RhodesMustFall at UCT there was a dire need to separate the proverbial 'Day Ones' from those students who joined the movement after its inception and differentiate between the more knowledgeable students from those who were just beginning their journey to (ironically enough) enlightenment. Though many will claim that #MustFall movements had a horizontal structure, there also existed an intellectual ladder that one was expected to climb to gain clout within their ranks. It was this intellectual ladder that disaggregated students within the movement and thereby created an artificial hierarchy of unelected leaders. It was this band of students who often became the leaders of the protests and more often than not, if not politically affiliated, would take on the identity of a Fallist.

As a result, identifying a Fallist in their purest sense is a difficult task. 'True' Fallists are a reclusive group, often reserving admission to their inner circle in arbitrary ways. Some Fallist groups might insist that you show a proficiency in the language of decolonisation through the lens of Biko and Fanon, while others required that you demonstrated a firm commitment to the notion of black radical feminist or showed an appetite for a militant attitude deemed useful for politics. In some cases, one merely needed to have access to resources unavailable to other Fallists. To climb the ladder to the status of Fallist requires a level of self-discipline and the courage/cowardice to disregard old friendships in the search for new and militant comrades in arms.

In my experience, Fallists and coconuts seem to find themselves in the same WhatsApp group. Why this happens is difficult to determine, but it is a bizarre coincidence (if one wants to call it that) that the majority of prominent Fallist leaders across the country are also coconuts. It could be the ability of coconuts to speak 'the Queen's English' and the trust that this bestows upon them. It could be a coconut's access to resources that allows them to progress up the ladder of Fallism faster than most others. It may be that students feel that coconuts would be trusted by university management more than non-coconuts. Maybe coconuts are just more adept than others at navigating these various spaces that you find in South Africa. Whatever the truth, what I can say is that Fallists' inability to challenge the notion of class differences as one of the drivers of inequality in South Africa was what allowed coconuts freely to navigate the world of Fallism without fear or favour. The level of scrutiny enacted against white people, black cishet men, homophobic men, or transphobic men was never exhibited against black students with a clear class difference from the majority of students in the movement.

This lack of class introspection would become, either directly or indirectly, the primary driver of the internal conflict that would play out in #FeesMustFall. However, before this contestation took root, there was general agreement within #MustFall politics that it was SRCs that stood in their way. There was a need to delegitimise these structures because of their inherent nature, that is, to be representative of all students. This need ran contrary to Fallist ideology.

Increasingly, the notion of Black Pain began to be employed as means of not only having the authority to speak on behalf of black students but in place of democratically elected SRCs.

Chapter 11

The Beginning of #FeesMustFall

During the process of writing this book, I often found myself feeling angry at my parents. Being angry at my parents' friends and my friends' parents and so on. I found myself feeling angry at all the generations who came before me. I grew angry because to me they seemed to have failed. Harsh as it may sound, the mistakes made by generations past are so glaring at times they are hard to ignore. But it is a different type of anger. It is not informed by dislike or hatred or by some other emotion that brings the blood to boil. Rather, it is the anger that is reminiscent of the feeling experienced during a failed handover during a 4 x 100 metre relay race.

No one ever drops the baton during a relay race on purpose, but the anger at the individual who does drop it is no different than if the intention had been there. Though you are rightfully expected to carry the baton after the handover, you are completely reliant on your teammate, or in this case the previous generation, to hand it over to you. We expect our teammates to run the race to their fullest capabilities and ensure that when we begin our jog as they approach, they place the baton in our hand in one fluid motion. When I think about my parents, their friends and the older generation in general, I feel that they ran the race as hard as they could and fought to end apartheid to its bitter end. Yet when it came to handing over the baton, they dropped it, and we missed more than 20 years of development trying to pick it up.

Over a period of a week and a half, #FeesMustFall did what others took decades to complete. We picked up the baton. We began a movement with one aim, and in a week achieved it. High off this victory, we rode the momentum of the moment and proceeded to demand more. Demanding more sometimes led the movement astray and threw its multiple moving elements into disarray, but despite all the hurdles, we did it. Free Education had been little more than a pipe dream when I entered university, but to know that some dreams do come true, I couldn't be prouder of all the sacrifices students from around the country made to achieve this goal. Though we were able to pick up the baton dropped by past generations, we needed to be careful not to drop the baton ourselves. #FeesMustFall teetered on the edge of dropping the baton for two years.

The story of #FeesMustFall is complex and can't honestly be told by one person in one book. Too many stories would go untold and too many heroines and heroes would be forgotten. What I can do here, though, is show how important moments in the movement helped shape and form the movement into what it became.

For two years the higher education system engaged in open warfare between students, academics, workers, university management and the state through the police force. In most universities, alliances were formed between students, workers and academics, so long as these alliances supported the vested interests of each. For students in the early days it was fees, for workers it was insourcing and for academic staff it was, in the main, increasing diversity in academia. These alliances, however, were not set in stone. #FeesMustFall at UCT on the odd occasion found itself at war with the National Education Health and Allied Workers Union (NEHAWU) on campus in a disagreement between shop stewards, workers and an agreement with management that would see workers return to work in the middle of the protest. At the beginning of 2016, residual anger from workers towards the Wits SRC from the 2015 protests still lingered. Academics became split between those who were proponents of the continued protests on campus and those who were supportive in spirit but thought it was time to return to class. Long snarky email chains and competing WhatsApp groups became common among the staff in various departments.

The protests across the country had hundreds of constantly moving parts, making #FMF an extremely difficult movement to track with accuracy. Sites of occupation such as Azania House or Solomon Mahlangu House became the headquarters for protesters at UCT and Wits respectively, with other sites such as the Rooiplein in Stellenbosch, The Great Hall at Wits, Main Road in Cape Town, the Union Buildings in Pretoria, Luthuli House in downtown Johannesburg, the University of Free State's Shimla Park, Kingsway Avenue in front of the University of Johannesburg, and residences across the University of KwaZulu-Natal all becoming locations of confrontation at one time or another. Some became sites of aggression or battlegrounds, all in the broader war for free education, while others were proxy wars for power within institutions. Even espionage became commonplace as spying among students became inevitable. The media, usually barred from student plenaries, became increasingly creative in the way they gathered information. University management teams planted students within the protest to collect information during plenaries. Political parties worked day and night to influence student views and though it has never been publicly proven, it is an open secret that state security inserted themselves into the protests as well during this time.

As I have already said, the story of #FeesMustFall will probably never be genuinely told in full. Doing so would be impossible. There will always be claims of bias and erasure, depending on where on the political scale you reside. So, I am not attempting in this book to tell the #FMF's rollercoaster story, but rather my understanding of how its politics influenced the movement.

* * *

There was no exit strategy for #FeesMustFall because there was never a predetermined end goal for the movement, a signifier that our job was done and that we could return to class. All there was was a deep hankering to keep pushing the envelope of the country's national consciousness and seeing what would happen. When the first protest at Wits took place on 14 October 2015, I don't believe anyone that morning thought that barely a week later thousands of students would march on Luthuli House or, in Cape Town, engage in open conflict with police outside parliament.

There was no specific plan to bring together the ideology of decolonisation and the economic principle of free education. The notion of free decolonised education for all was not conceived at the beginning of the protest; it came about more as the result of contestations inside the movement. Most of the events that happened during the first week of #FeesMustFall were the result of converging circumstances creating unexpected areas of alliances and coincidences. The first protest at Wits was never intended to turn into a full-blown national movement but happened to take place at a time of generally heightened tensions at that university, growing alliances between several groupings self-described as Fallists across the country, and a scheduled gathering of SRC presidents in Durban serving to showcase the level of ambivalence vice-chancellors and the Department of Higher Education and Training had towards student leaders.

At Wits, tensions had been building between students, workers and management. The SRC had been embroiled in fee negotiations with the university management team. Though #FeesMustFall had been in full swing before 2015, its explosion on 14 October 2015 was a reaction to the increasing arrogance and ignorance both within the state and university administrative systems. On 2 October Shaeera Kalla, the Wits SRC president at the time, and Nompendulo Mkhatshwa, the incumbent president, found themselves in a position all too familiar to thousands of former and current student leaders across the country – walking out of a university Council meeting with the feeling that you are invisible. That you are there to make up the numbers, to be seen but never truly heard. This is something not unique to universities as institutions. It is the general attitude to youth issues across the country.

While process and procedure differ at different universities, one constant is that there is minimal scope for students to participate in setting the agenda for a Council meeting. The Wits Council, usually consisting of 30 people and with only two student representatives (the SRC president and one other postgraduate student), is the highest decision-making body in the university. It is the final arbiter on all issues, including fees. Though most stakeholders across the university would regularly cite having the same problem, to remove students, the largest stakeholder in the university, from the agenda-setting process just seemed like a foolish habit to fall into. (Though it should be said that in a similar sense the removal of young people – one of the country's largest demographics – from the agenda-setting process of the country is also a foolish exercise, but that is a story for another day, I guess.)

Council, by and large, functions on the need to achieve consensus on the actions the university will take forward. This principle generally holds true, but not when it comes to fees debates. The Council meeting on 2 October was a resounding failure for the SRC, who lost the fees debate, with all of Council (except for Shaeera, Prof Dickerson and the postgraduate representative) voting in favour of a 10.5% fee increment, a residence fee increase of 9.4% and an increase in international student fees of 10.7%.

It should be said at this point that fee negotiations between students and management is a monumentally flawed process. It disproportionately favours management over students and actively works to handicap students. The negotiations often resemble internal monologues between university administrators, with student leaders making cameo appearances. Through a combination of SRC annual turnovers, a dearth of negotiating skills among students compared to university administrators, the university holding a monopoly on the financial information disseminated to student negotiators, and the general commitments SRC members have outside of the negotiations, a situation is created that can be best described as a toxic Molotov cocktail of frustration. Student ambitions to win these debates under these circumstances are never going to be realised. The situation is so dire that a market for fees-debate consultants has grown as SRCs identify a need to accept external support in the negotiations. The lack of institutional memory at the disposal of SRCs ensures that while management engages in fee negotiations with over 20 years of experience in the space, most SRCs enter it with a basic understanding of the university's finances that have been gathered over a couple of months.

The argument by management for a 10.5% increment was informed by a worsening rand-dollar exchange rate, an increase in the prices of library books, journals, electronic resources and research equipment, a necessary salary increase of 7% for academics, and inflation-related increases. Inflation-related increases often focus less on the country's inflation rate and more on the university's own internally determined inflation rate, which is, on average, above inflation. The warning from the Wits management team was that without the increase, the university's entire academic project would be in jeopardy.[1]

Elsewhere on campus, students and workers had been preparing for the National Day of Action Against Outsourcing planned for 6 October 2015. Commonly known as the 'Oct6 Protest' across the country, the protests that took place at Wits, UCT and UJ would be a sort of test run for #FeesMustFall, but even then, no one could imagine what would happen just over a week later. The Oct6 Protest was meant to highlight the dehumanisation of workers on university campuses due to outsourcing.[2] At Wits, it was attended by 2 000 people, primarily students but also including outsourced workers, academics and administrative staff.[3] At UCT a group of 300–400 students marched from Lower Campus to Upper Campus before eventually occupying Jameson Hall. Most protesters there were students associated with #RhodesMustFall, members of UCT's Left Student Forum and workers from NEHAWU.

The practice of outsourcing, spearheaded by UCT in the late '90s, was widespread in institutions of higher education, creating an exploitative relationship between workers on campus – who had been removed from the university community and placed in the hands of labour brokers – and the university in general. The Oct6 Protest at Wits had its roots in a variety of outsourcing-related protests that had taken place there over the previous years. In 2012 a hunger strike was held in several residences at Wits as students turned a spotlight on how the university had turned a blind eye to the treatment of 17 chefs who were dismissed by an outsourced catering company contracted to the university.[4] In June 2013, panic engulfed workers at Wits as hundreds of workers were summoned to a meeting and told that owing to the expiration of the contract between the university and their employers at the end of that month, all were required to interview for the same jobs they held with their previous employer.[5] Wits WSC, led at the time by Mbuyiseni Ndlozi – the People's Bae and charismatic intellectual of the EFF – noted that several workers had also been given termination notices by their respective companies.[6]

The general attitude towards outsourced workers on campus by management was probably best encapsulated by Vice-Chancellor Habib in a blog about accelerating transformation on campus. Habib admitted that even though it was hard to ignore the super-exploitative nature of outsourcing, the university did not have the 'resources required to insource these services and put the workers directly onto our payroll without throwing the institution into financial crisis'.[7] Hardly a week after the blog post, the EFFSC and Wits WSC occupied the office of Habib in response to a long-standing dispute between workers in an outsourced company and their employers regarding the non-payment of outsourced staff due to the termination of the contract between the university and the outsourcing company that hired the workers. For Wits (though Wits is just one example of the general attitude universities have towards outsourcing on campus) outsourced workers became a means to an end: ensuring the essential services of the university were maintained but maximising the bottom line.

The Oct6 Protest at Wits, therefore, wasn't about a new problem on campus, but an existing issue that had taken firm root. What marked this protest as different from others was that for Fallists it became the trial run for #FeesMustFall. Since the advent of #RhodesMustFall, Fallists from across the country had begun to communicate and co-ordinate their actions. Leigh-Ann Naidoo, one of the most prominent Fallists and a formidable academic, often found herself crisscrossing the country trying to find areas of convergence among the many disparate Fallist groupings. Though Wits SRC had thrown their support to the Oct6 Protest, unintentionally they were helping facilitate the first attempt by Fallists at a nationally co-ordinated protest.

At UCT the Oct6 Protest was led by #RhodesMustFall, who in a similar vein to Wits WSC, demanded the end of outsourcing on campus as it was a 'deliberate policy to exploit workers in order to cut costs of institutions at the expense of these workers'.[8] Since the fall of the statue, #RhodesMustFall had found itself in a peculiar position, a limbo of sorts. With curriculum reforms intended to decolonise the curriculum under way and the fees debate completed by the SRC, the only lightning-rod issue available to them was outsourcing. In the week before the Oct6 Protest #RMF caused its first public furore in months when it disrupted a lecture hosted by the Nelson Mandela Foundation. The lecture was to be given by Thomas Piketty, French economist and author of the bestselling book *Capital in the 21st Century*. Due to a series of comic mishaps, Piketty was unable to give his lecture and a panel discussion, which included former Minister of Finance Trevor Manuel, was set up instead. The topic of the discussion was Inequality in South Africa. Just as the discussion was about to begin #RMF walked into the auditorium carrying placards reading 'Remember Marikana'. Silent at first, the group of protesters waited for the introductory remarks to be made before disrupting proceedings.

For #RMF, the entire event was a testament to the hypocrisy that defined UCT. How does an institution that claims it wants to find new ways of tackling inequality in society actively support the practice of outsourcing? The group highlighted that while the elite of the university sat and listened to the panel, those most affected by inequality, workers on campus, had been kept outside. In the eyes of #RMF, decolonising the university did not mean only meting out benefits to students, but to support workers as well, who experienced the greatest levels of oppression through racism, exploitation and dehumanisation.[9]

Riding on the Piketty protest, #RhodesMustFall went into the Oct6 Protest on a wave of optimism and enthusiastic supporters. It was more than just a gathering for #RMF. It was a clarion call. It was an announcement that it had returned from its hiatus and had brought friends with it. Firmly established partnerships with UCT Left Students Forum, UCT Workers Solidarity Committee and UCT's NEHAWU Joint Shop Steward Council firmed up its support among workers, and #RMF replaced SASCO as the political voice of students regarding workers' rights. At the same time PASMA, growing in prominence because of the politics that #RMF brought onto campus, managed to establish itself strongly within the movement, giving it a political structure it could work through. It had also renewed ties with the Black Student Movement at the University Currently Known as Rhodes, Decolonise Wits and elements of #OpenStellenbosch, creating for PASMA key allies at previously advantaged universities. Fallists wanted the success of the Oct6 Protest to become a showcase for the movement, to build confidence in their ranks. #RhodesMustFall and Fallists had been placing the pieces together for a national movement to take root in the country. Just a week after the organising of Oct6, however, they were beaten to the punch.

After their failed attempt at convincing Council on their fee proposal, the Wits SRC began plans to tackle the fee debate through other means. It had become apparent to the SRC that normal diplomatic channels would not be useful if they wanted to overturn Council's decision. It was decided that a demonstration should take place on campus to highlight students' displeasure at the proposed fee hike. On the morning of Wednesday, 14 October, a group of PYA-aligned students began to form human barricades across the university's various entrances. Utilising the moniker of #WitsFeesMustFall, the protesters hoped to evoke a similar resonance with its cause as #RhodesMustFall had done only a couple of months earlier.

Forgoing an invite to attend the Higher Education Summit taking place in Durban at that same time, Shaeera and her SRC remained at Wits in the hope that they would be able to take advantage of the university being without its vice-chancellor, Adam Habib, who had decided to head to the summit instead. The VC's decision to travel to Durban was ironic when only a month earlier he had written that South Africans should begin to question the conventional wisdom that guides our society to fashion solutions that would allow us collectively to transcend many of its challenges. He described it as our 'Moment of Reckoning' as a nation.[10] Yet there he was flying to Durban while South Africa's moment of reckoning was taking place right under his nose.

The SRC notified the university management team that the protest would take place at 12 pm on Wednesday, but the day would not unfold in the manner management expected it to. As the protest – which began at 6 am and with only a handful of students – unfolded throughout the morning, there was a fair amount of confusion on campus. Although the protest had been sanctioned by the SRC, during the early hours no clear leader was leading the charge, just a few puppeteers pulling strings in the background. This would be normal within #FeesMustFall going forward, but on this occasion, it was unique. As the morning progressed, more students joined the fold as news spread over social media that students were staging sit-ins across the university. Videos of students being forcibly removed by motorists trying to gain entrance to the university spread like wildfire. One video showed a man on a motorcycle trying to ride over students to enter while another showed a driver driving at full speed towards a group of students in what appeared to be an elaborate game of chicken (the motorist lost). The sight of students facing a barrage of insults galvanised other students to join the cause as students began to roll into the various sit-ins. Soon the protest numbered in the couple of hundreds.

By 9 am the protest looked like an exclusively PYA-driven programme, with support from independent students helping to bulk up their numbers. At this point, there had been no consideration to open the protest to other political stakeholders. However, as the day progressed a decision was made to invite the EFFSC to join as well as other political organisations. Initially, the EFFSC rejected the invitation. (They would only join the next day after a failed attempt to discredit the Wits SRC by claiming that their failure at Council was a result of them being stooges of management.) The opening of the protest to all stakeholders lent stronger credence to the SRC's efforts. By midday, the protest numbers had increased to thousands and the university announced that all classes were cancelled. Staff and outsourced workers also joined. The protest culminated with a mass meeting in Solomon Mahlangu House (Senate House at the time) where it was decided that students would only leave once the university had changed its position on the fee increase.

Police were deployed onto campus late in the evening and early the following day, ostensibly to maintain control of the protesters. Clashes between students and police had mainly been in the form of officers trying forcefully to remove protesting students, a rather foolish errand at the time as with each student removed, three would take their place. Furthermore, SAPS's task was made extremely difficult because even though the protest had been illegal, the disruption remained mostly peaceful. The police were asked to control the perimeter to ensure the free flow of people in and out of the university. It would be to no avail as by the morning of the 15th the university had been successfully shut down again.

It was at this point that Nompendulo's prominence grew. As the incumbent SRC president and with PYA taking charge of affairs, she worked tirelessly to cement her base as a leader of the movement. Already a renowned leader on campus, her signature ANC doek made it clear where her allegiance lay. Day two was owned by the PYA and Nompendulo. In one of the speeches she gave that day she proclaimed that they would not leave or stop the protest until Adam Habib returned from Durban and faced his own day of reckoning.[11]

A dominant critique of the protesters at this point was why 32 000 students and academics should be denied entry into the university by only a couple of hundred protesters. It would be a critique that would fall flat among many protesters and even those who were just bystanders. They all faced the same threat: financial exclusion. The critique presupposed that the student protesters did not represent the majority, a premise that came from the belief that it would be impossible for any small group of students to truly comprehend the various demands and interests of thousands of students. At Wits, this argument was largely displaced because the protest was led by the SRC, the official representative of the student body. The SRC was the legitimate voice of students. One could talk about how the SRC should work through official channels, but if the SRC (who represents over 30 000 students) is continuously marginalised within these channels, it stands to reason that it will, as any public representative would, find another way to make sure its constituency is heard. Meetings with student leaders and the Department of Higher Education and Training had always been repetitive talk shops. The only substantial policy change that had taken place in the sector had been through the release of the White Paper on Post-School Education and Training in 2014, which allowed the minister to dissolve university councils if they failed to transform. Other than that, students barely ever set the agenda of the sector's policy cycle, even though they bore the brunt of its consequences.

DHET-organised gatherings, therefore, seemed always to function as little more than social events. This year, however, things were different. The DHET Transformation Summit in Durban, scheduled to run from 15 to 17 October, began under a cloud of mutual uncertainty amongst those stakeholders present due to the events simultaneously taking place at Wits. Included at the summit were SRC presidents, student political organisations, government officials and vice-chancellors. It was being hosted against the backdrop of the Parliamentary Portfolio Committee on Higher Education and Training's decision to greenlight the establishment of a task team to investigate the funding issues plaguing the sector.[12] Though these meetings are usually exclusively attended by SRC representatives, this year DHET also opened the meeting to organisations such as #RhodesMustFall.

The first day of the crisis was acrimonious. As unrest in the sector had grown, students' anger, for the most part, was usually directed at university management. In a paper he had prepared for the summit, David Maimela, a former national president of SASCO and a researcher at the Mapungubwe Institute, suggested that there was a need to democratise universities and give students a greater voice on university issues. As seen by the events at Wits, the core driver of the desire to cause disruption, he said, was not to cause disruption for disruption's sake, but was the feeling of marginalisation the current fee negotiations had evoked among student leaders. Maimela even went as far as to recommend the disbandment of university councils and institutional forums in favour of university general assemblies.[13] Anger at the summit finally bubbled over, with students questioning the presence of VC Adam Habib in proceedings when students at his university were demanding that he return to answer their questions.

In a letter sent to the conference, the Wits SRC called on other SRCs to join them in the trenches. The letter read:

> *We are deeply humbled and amazed at the levels the voices of students are reaching. As I type this to you we are standing in the sun with students*

who are united behind the call for access to higher education for all. We are here singing 'Senzeni Na' the most apt question we ask! What have we done to be born poor, what have we done to fail our parents, brothers and sisters, fail them not because we are incapable of succeeding, but because we are too poor to succeed.

We are still unapologetic in our systematic and strategic shutting down of all the entrances to Wits University. I must commend students at our University in spite of being called kaffirs, animals, told to go back to the zoo, threatened to break our jaws and numerous other hurtful insults and threats we have remained resolute, determined and have abstained from violence.

Wits University has taken a deliberate and anti-progressive decision to once more entrench the financial exclusion of poor students by exorbitantly increasing the upfront fee payment in particular and fees in general. There is currently an upward trend in fees at all universities around the country and NSFAS is not increasing at the same rate as Wits fees. Wits proposed fee increases are simply unjust and unjustifiable. One must then ask, how much longer is this going to go on for? How long is Wits University going to continue to exclude poor students? How much longer is the gates of higher education continuously going to be shut in the faces of the poor students. We implore students from all over the country to support us as we demand that the gates of higher education, the gates that allow us to escape from poverty, the gates which allow our people to uplift their families and communities, we demand that these gates be opened absolutely to all!

Through the '1 Million, 1 Month' campaign, we have proven, by the fact that 80% of the students we registered secured funding/bursaries, that upfront payment cannot be used as a measure of which students will pay their fees and which will not.

We call on all students to stand with us in opposing these increases. Wits University is not a business and cannot be run in the interests of the minority. We are tired of the blatant lack of transparency and financial accountability on the part of the management. Enough is enough, the socio-economic reality of students on this campus cannot be continuously ignored and deliberately undermined.

If our calls are not met we thus sincerely implore students all over the country to render this failed higher education system unworkable and untenable.

Join us on the picket lines Comrades![14]

The letter was the first public and formalised rallying call to all institutions of higher education to join the protest instigated by Wits. Ironically, the letter was read out by a delegate from #RhodesMustFall, who had been planning its own clarion call of sorts. In fact, one could surmise that attendance at the DHET summit was part of a larger plan to infiltrate and eventually discredit SRCs across the country as Fallist groupings would go on to do over the next two years.

There were mixed reactions to the letter. It brought up arguments between student leaders about their responsibility to their comrades at Wits. Although the summit was attended by SRCs, many of the students in attendance were PYA members. Old debates about the differences between HBIs and HWIs regarding fee issues came to the surface as student leaders struggled to come to a consensus about whether to give support to the protests or not. It would take a rallying speech from Ramabina Mahapa, SRC president at UCT and a member of Aluta, to galvanise support for the students' efforts at Wits. It set the stage for the events that would take place the following Monday as students used the weekend to create coalitions of support on their own campuses to support the efforts of Wits students.

The week's proceedings at Wits culminated with a mass meeting in Solomon Mahlangu House and a statement to be conveyed to Council that students would not stop the protests until Council declared that there would be no fee increase in 2016. An emergency Council meeting was called, but students demanded that the meeting take place in front of them. Unwilling to be swindled by the Council for the second time in two weeks, the students were uncompromising in this demand. The idea of holding Council accountable using a public spectacle was not new. Earlier that year #RhodesMustFall had stormed a UCT Council meeting gathered to determine whether the statue would remain on campus or not. The Wits demand was different. Rather than storming a meeting of Council, students sought symbolically to bring Council down to the rough-and-tumble level of local student politics. As a compromise, students chose to engage with the Executive Committee of Council (Exco) and the vice-chancellor on the floor of Solomon Mahlangu House in front of all the student protesters. The mob rule of democracy was in full effect. For students, this was a significant symbolic shift and would be a warning shot to the university governance system that negotiations going forward would be done under new terms and conditions.

It was at this point when the EFFSC, led by the charismatic Vuyani Pambo, firmly established itself within the protest. Vuyani brought an interesting element to proceedings, being a natural populist and an immaculate orator. With Shaeera Kalla mainly remaining in the background, working as a puppeteer rather than a leader, and Nompendulo lacking the populist charm (although if you were to hear her speak, you would be hard pressed not to follow her), many students gravitated towards Vuyani. He became the clear face of the protest. This was probably mainly due to the patriarchal nature of the protest, which began to shun female leaders in favour of male leaders.

In reaction to the growing prominence of the EFFSC, it was not surprising that the PYA let loose their trump card: Mcebo Dlamini. A former president of the SRC (before his Hitler-praising comments), Mcebo had been an extremely popular student on campus and among student leaders. Populist to the core, he could rally students to undertake almost any action he asked of them. If he said they should march to the Education Campus, students would march to Education Campus. If he demanded they march to West Campus, students would march to West Campus. Mcebo became the populist answer to Vuyani. With Mcebo and Vuyani on board, joining Shaeera and Nompendulo as the faces of the movement, 'the fantastic four' was born. As men in the movement began increasingly to dominate, the two leading women of the movement were pushed to the sidelines.

Adam Habib made an early return to Wits from the DHET Transformation Summit. As soon as he got there, students demanded that he address them. He waited for hours before he was able to engage with students because protesters had to wait for their colleagues to return to Wits's main campus from their various excursions to its satellite campuses where they had gone to garner support. After being shifted from location to location, when Habib was about to speak, protesters demanded that he not address them until he sat down. Habib made the decision to heed their call and sat on the floor with students in Solomon Mahlangu House until an emergency meeting with Council could be organised.

Speaking to Habib about this moment sometime later, he intimated to me that this was the moment that the 'politics of humiliation' began to run rampant in the movement. It wasn't enough merely to argue your point; you had to humiliate your adversary as well. He used Lenin's notion of infantile disorder to explain how students' positions had been fragmented. The protest, he said, was losing its integrity and coming close to allowing intolerance of others to flourish.[15] In his case, his decision to sit was more tactical than political.

The meeting with the Executive Committee and students started on Friday evening and proceeded throughout the night into the early hours of Saturday morning. The delay in the meeting was because Exco needed to have a quorum, which it lacked. During this time students heckled Exco members, in particular the Chair of Council, Dr Carolissen. Eventually, an agreement was reached between students and management. It read:

> Following an intense and protracted engagement between protesting students and members of the Executive Committee of Council, it was agreed that:
>
> 1. The University will suspend the decision on all fee increments made for 2016. There will be no fee increments until negotiations reach an agreement.
> 2. The negotiations pertaining to fee increments will resume anew.
> 3. In the eventuality of negotiations breaking down, the University will not revert to its initial decision.
> 4. A new framework for negotiations will be jointly agreed upon in which any final decision of Council on this matter will be ratified to a University Assembly.

> 5. *There will be no disciplinary action taken against students or*
> *workers who participated in the protest, and no worker will face*
> *dismissal as a result of their participation in the protest.*
> 6. *The Exco of Council will advance the position of the students for a*
> *no fee increase at Council.*[16]

However, the agreement could only be finalised once a sitting of Council, now set for Sunday, 18 October, approved the agreement. Council committed to reporting back to students at noon on Monday, 19 October. Students waited with bated breath over the weekend. On Monday morning students stormed Solomon Mahlangu House again, leaving Council feeling that they were contravening the spirit of the agreement. Council therefore failed to keep its noon commitment. I always wondered to myself what would have happened if Council had chosen to ignore the occupation of Solomon Mahlangu House and had focused their attention on reclaiming the trust of students. The snubbing of students at Wits set in motion a chain of events that would eventually lead to the largest gathering and march of young people in a post-1994 South Africa – all the way to the halls of the Union Buildings in Pretoria, the offices of the president of the Republic of South Africa.

On Monday, 19 October, students from across the country decided that enough was enough. Protests at Wits the previous week had sparked a series of discussions among students at many higher education institutions countrywide. At UCT a Sunday meeting was called by Busisiwe Mkhumbuzi, which gathered together a variety of political organisations. It was the first meeting since #RhodesMustFall that saw SASCO, PASMA and the Fallist movements all in the same room. The sole agenda item was how these structures would lend support to their comrades at Wits. It was decided that they would shut down the university. Similar discussions were also held at other institutions. After the transformation summit had ended, most SRC presidents returned to their institutions asking themselves the same question, but not everyone would give their support to students.

At this point, the protest was still not a nationally co-ordinated event as much as it was an over-subscribed support group for Wits. A collection of student anger rather than a cohesive movement. On a broad level, the central demand was a 0% fee increment at individual universities protesting. More localised issues would play themselves out at individual universities. At Wits students waited for an announcement from Council about the negotiations over the weekend. At the University Currently Known as Rhodes students and the SRC met not only to discuss fees but also the high value of the minimum initial payment (MIP) needed to register at the institution. At UCT the protests remained focused on the issue of outsourcing.

Although WhatsApp groups had been set up to ensure certain student leaders from across the country could communicate, there is no real evidence that these discussions informed a co-ordinated approach to the protest. The events that would take place over the course of the first day of the national protest would demonstrate just how disparate each institution's efforts were. But more importantly, it would be the consequences of these various actions taken by students across the country that would force them to work together. As events played out throughout Monday and Tuesday, the lack of co-ordination within the movement soon changed into what I came to think of as a chaotic symphony being played by an orchestra without a conductor.

Chapter 12

A Chaotic Symphony

On the morning of Monday, 19 October 2015, protests erupted at UCT and the University Currently Known as Rhodes, while Wits remained quiet. At UCT protesters gathered at university entrances from 4 am, creating blockades and restricting access to students and staff alike. Just after midnight at UCKR, through the co-ordination of the private 'Purple Fees' Facebook group, 500 students began setting up blockades across Grahamstown consisting of burning tyres, rocks and furniture.[1] As the morning ran on, the management teams at Wits and UCKR announced that they would be shutting down their activities for the day. The logic behind the decision at both institutions was so that a time and place to negotiate with students could be arrived at.

At UCT, negotiations were non-existent throughout the day. Management had simply failed to anticipate the protest in the same manner that UCKR had. UCT management was caught on the back foot from the onset and would remain so throughout the day. At UCKR, though, because the protest had begun so early, Vice-Chancellor Dr Sizwe Mabizela was in the trenches at 8.30 am. By 9.30 am he had hosted a meeting with the SRC, diffused tensions between police and protesters on Prince Alfred Street and attended a meeting with the broader student body.[2]

Wits had remained quiet throughout the morning as most students had been instructed to wait for the feedback at 12 pm from the Council meeting held on Sunday. As the students made their way to the Solomon Mahlangu House concourse, a Council spokesperson announced that due to health and safety concerns, the meeting would be held outside the Great Hall instead. Students arrived at 12 pm, but some began to complain about having to stand in the heat. Confusion reigned supreme as conflicting reports about the meeting's location spread over social media and, as tensions rose, students made a move to storm Solomon Mahlangu House and demand that Council meet them there.[3] Solomon Mahlangu House, as Azania House was for UCT students, was not only a strategic point of influence for both students and management because of its locale – where students could co-ordinate and congregate – but it also held symbolic strength as the home of the protests at Wits. As expected, students remained in Solomon Mahlangu House, prompting Council not to address students directly and to email its statement instead.

By midday protesters at UCT had successfully closed the university. Unlike Wits and UCKR, UCT's protest, which at that point was known as #UCTFeesMustFall, was motivated against both the SRC and university management as both parties had agreed upon a 10.3% fee increment. In a line that I feel perfectly encapsulates the anger at UCT, a student was reported as stating: 'It's nice to see white people walking for the first time in their lives.'[4] Before #RhodesMustFall, UCT had developed a reputation within student politics over the years that due to the large number of privileged white students on campus, the only thing students ever protested about was the inadequate parking. For many protesters in 2015, the stream of white students walking up the mountain to attend classes was a rare and unique sight. UCT eventually followed in the steps of the management teams at Wits and UCKR and suspended classes for the day – this after a report emerged that an angry motorist had driven over a student's leg.[5]

At UCKR, the Black Student Movement led by Thenjiwe Mswane – someone I personally considered to be a formidable force within the protest – SASCO and the EFFSC began a march to the neighbouring (and lesser known) TVET institution, Eastcape Midlands College, to support students there who had complained that the college had misappropriated NSFAS funds.[6] Two 'firsts' in #FeesMustFall took place at the Eastcape Midlands College. One was the inclusion of a TVET college in a broader movement, which until then had focused almost exclusively on universities. The second was Public Order Police (POP) officers retaliating against protesting students. Students were met by police who, in response to students attempting to enter the college by scaling its fence, dispersed the protesters by using stun grenades and a water cannon. The water in the water cannon had been treated with chemicals designed to cause severe itching.[7] It would be the first act of aggression against students during #FMF, but it was certainly not the last. Police officers followed students back to campus before the situation was de-escalated through the intervention of VC Mabizela.

Around 4 000 students had occupied Solomon Mahlangu House on the Wits campus before news broke that Council had ordered all students to vacate the building by 3 pm that afternoon. A call that would be heeded by students, not because they agreed with leaving Solomon Mahlangu House but to gain the attention of Council in another way. Thousands of students, arms linked, began a march that streamed onto Empire Road, a major intersection of Johannesburg connecting the CBD with the city's leafy suburbs. The goal was to stage a sit-in on Empire Road with the logic that if the Council would not listen to student demands, maybe they would heed the public outcry from ordinary citizens stuck in traffic. Council refused to speak to students in plenary sessions, fearing for their safety, and chose instead to use SRC members as their conduits. It would be a tactic that would be rejected by both the SRC and students at large. Students wanted to receive the feedback from Council in person.

Around the same time, UCT protesters were engaging with representatives of the university's executive, namely Deputy Vice-Chancellors Anwar Mall, Francis Petersen, Danie Visser and Alumni and Development director Russell Ally.[8] A list of demands was handed over to management. The majority of these related to insourcing, with calls to suspend classes and have a mass meeting on Tuesday to discuss the insourcing of workers and fee-related issues.[9] The men sat and listened to the students' complaints. Then they replied that they could not make any commitments at that time, as many of the students' demands required Council's approval. It was a delaying tactic and students knew it. They declared that the men would not leave until they received an answer. To all intents and purpose, the situation had devolved into a hostage-taking. At one-point DVC Visser, who had a heart ailment, asked to leave the gathering, upon which a debate broke out about whether he should be allowed to leave or not.

In Johannesburg, the protest on Empire Road succeeded in bringing the city to a standstill. Cars were backed up all the way into the CBD as well as on the nearby highway. Tensions rose as motorists, increasingly agitated by the lack of movement, began to taunt students. Until then protests had remained – all things considered – peaceful. Reports of violence were limited to the breaking of windows and instances of unverifiable vandalism, so when a motorist, incensed by the protest, deliberately drove into a group of students in his bakkie, injuring four of them, this came as a shock.[10] In the first public display of overt aggression by students, but also not the last, the vehicle was chased down and flipped over with the driver still inside.

Down at UCT, more students and academic staff had gathered around Azania House, the site of the 'hostage taking'. A kaleidoscope of student groupings was present. #RhodesMustFall, UCT Trans Collective, SASCO, PASMA, #PatriarchyMustFall, UCT Queer Revolution, UCT Left Students Forum, the Muslim Youth Movement, and the UCT Palestine Solidarity Forum all brought their support to the cause.[11] Surrounding the DVCs, students demanded that DVC Petersen hastily organise a Council meeting, if Council was the only body that could make decisions on their demands. Calls by Petersen, however, seemingly fell on deaf ears – 'seemingly' being the operative word, as we would later find out that Petersen had merely been stalling. The events that would take place at UCT over the next 24 hours also set the tone for the manner in which police officers would interact with students in Cape Town the following year.

The first interdict of #FeesMustFall 2015 caught everyone by surprise. Students gathered around Azania House had no intention of occupying the building. At 5.30 pm Ru Slayen, an independent student I had met before the #RhodesMustFall mass meeting and who would soon become #RMF's *de facto* statement writer, took the microphone and announced that the protesters had been served with an interdict from the Western Cape High Court.[12] This was met with widespread anger among students who had resisted the urge to occupy the building, even reprimanding a handful of students who had attempted to break into it earlier that day. All day the protests had been peaceful, a characteristic acknowledged by DVC Petersen, who explained that the issue was the unlawful nature of the protest not how it was being conducted.[13] In the eyes of management, the protest was a threat to the functioning of the university, and thus a court interdict was required to enforce the rights of UCT to be open and accessible to its students. To the students, not unlike the demands of the Wits students the previous Friday, their demand was not unfair: all they wanted was counsel with the Exco of the university, but instead they were being criminalised by the university. One wonders what would have happened if management at UCT had taken a page out of Habib's playbook.

Tensions eventually boiled over, and students stormed into Azania House and occupied the building. Police Casspirs quickly arrived on the scene and a stand-off began. Police donned riot gear and, heavily armed, took their positions in the parking lot. Students positioned themselves within the halls of the building, occupying both floors almost as if they were trying to maintain all possible lines of sight with the police. Outside of Azania House, a line of academic and administrative staff formed a human chain in front of the building. In the eyes of the staff present, the university had abandoned any possibility of negotiation and had resorted to police action to solve what was essentially a political problem. Hours went by with neither party acting. Students sat and sang. Academics watched and waited. Police held the guns primed for action, waiting for orders.

It would be around midnight when police stormed Azania House to remove students. As they approached the building, they were met by a crowd of 30 or 40 students sitting on the ground in front of the main gate. The police demanded that the students leave the premises, but their calls were ignored. Instead, students heckled the police. In response, stun grenades and tear gas canisters were deployed to disperse students in scenes that often made me wonder how anyone could view South Africa as a post-apartheid society. Chaos reigned for the next hour as police marched through the admin building forcefully removing students and staff alike. Students, now caught in a spiral of escalating anger, stood their ground while academics pleaded with police officers to refrain from using force. Their pleas fell on deaf ears. Staff and students were hurled into the back of a Casspir, which began to head down to the Rondebosch police station. In all 23 students and staff members were arrested that night.

Then the Casspir did an odd thing. In what looked like a moment of complete madness, it made a U-turn and drove into a crowd of students. Coming to a sudden stop, police then hurled a second barrage of stun grenades. This unprovoked attack incensed students, who began to spread the word of the night's proceedings over social media. As a result, thousands of students gathered outside Lower Campus, the residential hub of UCT. This was the point when, I believe, #FeesMustFall became antagonistic towards police officers. The ripple effect of the night's chaotic actions would reverberate across the country. The pictures and videos that emerged would see students such as myself, who until then might have been on the fence about the desire to hit the ground, lacing up their boots and readying themselves to risk it all. On that night, #FMF kicked into gear at UCT.

On the Tuesday morning, I found myself among hundreds of students marching through the streets of Cape Town's Southern Suburbs. The march, which traversed the university, its residences and satellite campuses, was meant to gather support from students and workers, and it began on Lower Campus, where hours earlier students had been arrested by police for burning a tyre in public. News had spread among those marching that protests were emerging across the country under the banner of #FeesMustFall or some derivative movement. The scenes at Wits, UCT and UCKR the day before had a resounding effect on students everywhere. It galvanised them into action. One tweet that gained a high level of virality came from Muhammed Aslam, who took a picture of a protest placard that read: 'You can jail a revolutionary, but you can't jail a revolution.'[14] This phrase would become not only synonymous with that week, but with #FMF into the following year. Protests spread to the University of Pretoria, University of the Free State, the University of KwaZulu-Natal, Tshwane University of Technology, Nelson Mandela Metropolitan University,

North West University, Stellenbosch University and the Cape Peninsula University of Technology.

Students at Stellenbosch who had occupied the 'Winnie Mandela' admin building the previous night found themselves firmly in the sights of the police force, who entered the building and forcefully removed them. At NMMU students who were quietly sitting on the ground blocking a road found themselves on the wrong side of gunfire from police officers. Another driver attempted to mow down Wits students outside the Medical School campus. It was also reported that even though protests at Wits were still under the ambit of the PYA, protesters began to turn their ire on Blade Nzimande, the minister of Higher Education and a member of the ANC and its alliance partner, the South African Communist Party. Classes were cancelled at CPUT as students blockaded all entrances of the university, even threatening to not allow management to leave campus.

UFS, one of the few universities under the leadership of DASO, also engaged in protest action, which initiated day-long negotiations with management.[15] UFS attempted to pre-empt the protest by sending out an email detailing what they were doing to mitigate against the increase in tuition. It would be an email that was largely ignored, however, as students gathered to show support to students across the country.[16] Protests emerged at both the Howard and Westville campuses of UKZN, which had both been contending with fee- and residence-related protests all through the year.[17] At NWU, anger had begun the week before when students with outstanding debt had their student cards deactivated; this move culminated in protest action all through Wednesday. Students at the University of Limpopo, meanwhile, proceeded to disrupt exams.[18]

At UCT, students marched on Rondebosch police station, demanding that those who had been arrested the night before and earlier that morning be released. Hundreds of students pushed against the gate of the police station, singing and demanding a time for the release of the students, who at that point had not been charged with any crime. As tensions rose, the police began to mobilise inside the precinct, anticipating that students would burst through the gates and physically free their comrades. Instead, students who saw the police get into formation reacted in a manner that surprised the officers. A call was made for all white students in attendance to form a line between the police and protesters. It was believed that by merely being white, police would refrain from attacking them. It would be a tactic that would work for that particular moment but fail the next day. Realising that the police had no intention of releasing their captives, I motioned to Masixole that rather than remaining in front of the police station, we should occupy Main Road, the transport spine of the Southern Suburbs. We swiftly moved the protesters from the gates of the station towards the Southern Suburbs's busiest intersection. Within an hour we received word that the police would be releasing students. Just as had happened at Wits when students marched to Empire Road, the demands of students fell on deaf ears but the calls of disgruntled motorists to radio stations rang true and loud.

It was in the late afternoon that news broke that Higher Education minister Blade Nzimande had reached an agreement with university vice-chancellors and student representatives from SAUS. The agreement was that an increase in fees across the country would be capped at 6%. It was an announcement met with a resounding No from all students across all quarters. The rejection of the proposal had two different rationales, one that was legitimate and the other that was, well, a 'bye Felicia' type of petty. The first reason was that students had begun to warm to the idea of achieving free higher education by demanding a 0% fee increment. Their demand for 0% was simply a stepping-stone to a bigger demand down the road. Accepting the plan laid out by the minister of Higher Education and Training would delay students' efforts. At this point, students were committed to the idea of 0%; it had become the movement's clarion call.

Furthermore, the protest had now become less reliant on the SRC as its representatives. Many students felt that those in attendance did not represent them as students. The petty reason was that Blade Nzimande was caught on camera stating that if students did not accept this offer, they would 'start their own movement called Students Must Fall'.[19] While the comment was made in jest, it riled students, who saw it as a sign that the minister was not taking the situation seriously. They would have to make him aware of how important this moment was for them.

Chapter 13

We Were Sold Dreams in '94 – We Want a Refund

There has to come a time when we as South Africans need to ask ourselves whether we will ever have a generation of young people who won't have to become accustomed to the sound of rubber bullets and stun grenades, inhale the fumes and experience the burning sensation of tear gas and water cannons, or have the knee-jerk reaction to run from rather than towards the police in times of chaos. It seems to me that we have become accustomed to certain forms of history repeating themselves more than others. We allow inequality and injustice to prevail. Then, only once enough people become angry enough with the situation, we let young people fight the battles. We let young people be the release to the pent-up tension in the country. All you have to do is look at the many painful examples: the Sharpeville Massacre in 1960, the youth protests that rocked South Africa in 1976, the school boycotts that created a lost generation in the Western Cape in the 1980s, or the students and young people who became cannon fodder in the forgotten war in the country from 1990 to 1994.

We have become accustomed to dropping the baton just when young people are about to take over. It is the youth who are left to pick up the pieces of the chaos. It should go without saying that South Africa as a society must figure out how to hand over the baton to the next generation without having to start from a standing position, facing the same old objections used in the past for new, ever-evolving problems. The advent of democracy hasn't been able to solve this problem. Children are still dying in pit latrines. Children are still studying under trees or in steel containers. University students are still sleeping in libraries because of a lack of accommodation. We have teachers who refuse to undergo quality assessments, lecturers who never want to undergo curriculum or quality assessment, a two-tier education system of IEB and government schools, a two-tier university system of HBIs and HWIs, poor matric rates and poor graduation rates. Whether it is the basic or the higher education system of the country, the problems that exist in both are intertwined in a fragile web that can't easily be untangled without collapsing the entire system.

Under our education system, we barely produced more university graduates between 2014 and 2015 (344 982) than NEETS between 2015 and 2016 (308 000) between the ages of 15 and 34.[1] So when we marched to parliament on Wednesday, 21 October 2015, it wasn't because we wanted fees to fall or to embarrass the minister of Higher Education. We were just doing what history has repeatedly told us to do. March against those who we feel are creating injustice in the country.

* * *

In the afternoon of Wednesday, 21 October 2015, sitting on the steps of parliament, shoeless and handcuffed to Nathan Taylor, with police officers nervously pacing around us as if they were afraid students would return to free us, I had to wonder: how had it come to this? How did we get here?

Students had started gathering outside the gates of parliament around midday, but events had been building to this moment for some time. The decision to present ourselves at parliament that day was due to a variety of reasons. One was the national call by SASCO to shut down all universities. The call was heeded by most institutions as most universities embarked on protest action. The second reason was the announcement by the minister of Higher Education and Training the day before – and robustly rejected by students – that all fee increments across the country would be capped at 6%. A third reason was the shift in students' anger, away from university management teams and towards the state. No doubt this shift was a welcome reprieve for vice-chancellors, some of whom even joined the protests on that Wednesday. A fourth reason was that the medium-term budget was being delivered to parliament that day and this provided the perfect excuse to throw shade on a gathering of not only parliament but the executive of the country as well.

The chaotic scenes outside parliament of clashes between students and police became a hallmark of #FeesMustFall in 2015. Cape Town, for six hours, became a war zone. Students ducking and diving through side streets and alleyways, then finding strategic locations to stand their ground, and police hunting down anyone who fit the description of a university student, arresting on sight and shooting at will.

Although student leaders in the Western Cape had begun to co-ordinate their activities more effectively, the only real agreement among the various students and student organisations on that Wednesday was that everyone would congregate outside parliament. Political differences were clearly apparent, however. The majority of students outside parliament were not part of any political organisation and there was complete pandemonium as the different political organisations vied for their attention.

SASCO from CPUT and UWC found their corner opposite the main gates and began to sing and chant as each student leader took a turn at leading the chorus of supporters in song. #RhodesMustFall found themselves alongside members of NEHAWU next to the statue of Louis Botha that stood directly in front of the gates. Just beyond them, PASMA from UWC took their positions, gathering their numbers and trying to compete in song with SASCO. Even the EFFSC made an odd appearance, with red berets scattered among the crowd. Their lack of representation in the Western Cape at the time was partially due to SASCO's reluctance to acknowledge them as a registered student organisation at both CPUT and UWC. That chapter at UCT at the time suffered from a stop-start beginning.

By this stage, #FeesMustFall had become more than a political gambit by student parties. It had morphed into a fully fledged non-partisan movement that created the desire among students to not only reimagine how a university could be but work to change it. Thousands of students flooded Plein Street. The first group to arrive came from CPUT as that institution was only a stone's throw away from parliament. Other groups from institutions further away, such as UWC, arrived by train and/or taxi, while many coconuts came in their own vehicles (something that would be important to note later). Some universities bussed their students into town. UCT provided Jammie Shuttles to transport students, though many claimed that these buses were stopped from leaving campus by police officers. Some students were even pepper-sprayed.

Parliament was in full session with the president and his cabinet in attendance, including Blade Nzimande. Students began demanding that the minister come outside and address them. Their pleas were ignored, and agitation accelerated. Attempts to gain the attention of students by students failed. Politics was on display. SASCO refused to listen to PASMA, while PASMA refused to acknowledge SASCO. Students from UCT who looked to #RhodesMustFall leaders for guidance were surprised to see them being shunned by other universities, who didn't view them as legitimate leaders. It would require the members of NEHAWU to get the attention of protesters by collectively sitting on the ground. It was a move that created a crater in the crowd of protesters and shifted focus to a handful of students who stood before them.

There was a debate at that point. Who would hold the megaphone? There is a phrase that is used at the beginning of formal events in South Africa, which I think is unique to our country: 'All protocol observed.' I never quite understood why it always had to be said, but while standing outside in the heat that day watching students fight with one another about who was going to speak first, I realised just how important it was. #RhodesMustFall laid the first claim, but discussions about who from the movement should speak delayed proceedings. When the fight was resolved the #RMF leader who began to speak was largely ignored by the political parties in attendance, who were more concerned about ensuring that those of their national

173

leaders who were there would be given the stage. In the case of PASMA, they had no Western Cape leader and they deferred to Athabile to speak on their behalf. Athabile then did something that would ensure students would trust him later. He donned his #RMF T-shirt, removed his PASMA hat and replaced it with something more non-partisan. He believed that his reputation as a PASMA leader would negate the need for him to wear its colours.

Although students began to congregate around the students who were starting to give speeches, most still weren't paying attention and the speakers weren't loud enough to command it.

At this moment, a group of 60 or so students broke off from the protest and began marching down Plein Street. Curious, I joined the rogue protesters and made my way to the front, thinking to implore them to turn around and return to the main group. When I reached the front, I had my first encounter with Black First Land First (BLF). I had heard about their growing influence within the protests, but they were, by and large, still on the sidelines. So it was to my shock when I found one of the group's national leaders leading the students. When I asked him where he intended to take them, he replied that he wanted them to occupy Adderley Street. Adderley Street can be best described as a major artery road of Cape Town. This BLF leader wanted to shut down Cape Town's CBD.

I thought it was a good idea at the time and I was completely taken over by the adrenalin pumping through me at this point. I knew that standing in front of parliament and giving speeches would get us nowhere, so I joined, and we marched towards Adderley because this felt different. Our route along Spin Street took us past a side road which I'd forgotten about. The road led to the 'back gate' of parliament and provided a second entry point into the country's legislative wing. While the BLF leader and I ignored this gate, the students in tow didn't. They quickly changed direction and marched directly to the gate. For the life of me, I couldn't understand why this gate only had two police officers guarding it. And it was unlocked. I was astounded by the lack of security at one of the country's national key points, especially during a sitting of parliament with thousands of students protesting outside.

When we arrived, we demanded to see Blade Nzimande. We demanded that he come to the gate and leave parliament. I am not quite sure, but it was probably around this time that the EFF stormed out of parliament. It must have been the protest that caused them to do this because we were told that the medium-term budget speech was well under way by then. One of the police officers at the side gate said he would take our message to the minister, but he remained firmly planted in front of us. It was a bizarre moment. We were all taken aback. We asked him when he would go to deliver our message and he replied that he already had. It was comical. But it was also a moment that raised tensions even higher.

I am often asked how we entered parliament that day and I will stand by my word and say that the side gate was not locked. When they realised this, students pushed against it and in a moment I will not soon forget, one of the two police officers on duty grabbed his holster, unbuckled the latch holding his gun and warned us that he would shoot if we persisted. Everything went blank and the next thing I knew, we were inside the precinct of parliament marching towards its doors.

This was when the gravity of the situation hit some of us. In the case of the BLF leader, he seemed intent on storming the doors of parliament and disrupting the session in progress. I knew that such an act would be seen by most as an attempted coup d'état. We stopped at the base of the stairs, only metres away from the doors of parliament, and gathered round, relishing the moment but warning everyone to maintain their positions. Students who had remained outside the front gates began to cheer us on when they saw us. The Public Order Police looked as shocked as we were that we'd managed to get this close to the entrance. They stood behind us looking somewhat dim-witted. By forcing our way through the side gate, we sounded a clarion call that the gates of Jericho had been opened and students began to flood the precinct.

POP used their riot shields to hold the growing group of students back. Students began to kick out at the police officers and some threw bottles in their direction. In retaliation, police pushed out at students and kicked those who came too close. Suddenly, the main gates of parliament opened and the thousands of students on Plein Street stormed inside. Even I was surprised at this development. I couldn't understand how POP had allowed it to happen. During the interviews I conducted while writing this book, I was informed that students simply forced their way through the lock that held the main gates together. Distracted by the students behind them in the precinct, the ones who had come in through the side gate, POP had left their posts at the main gate. Students rushed through the now unarmed main gate and joined the rest of us inside. Lightning had struck twice in just a couple of minutes.

Meanwhile, parliament continued with its session in a business-as-usual manner even though thousands of students were right outside the doors pleading for them to listen to them. I remember thinking to myself that many of those who were inside parliament had once called themselves struggle heroes. So much for that, I guess.

Outside we broke into song as we realised that even if the minister (or any member of parliament for that matter) wasn't going to come out to address us, we had nevertheless achieved something the country had never seen before. For us the feeling was euphoric, but for the police it was a dire situation and we could see they were becoming very unsettled. We urged everyone to sit on the ground to show that we were no threat to anyone. As students began to sit down with their hands in the air at the base of the parliamentary stairs, suddenly six stun grenades were released.

Disorientated by the chaos around them, students began to rush back to the main gate. It seemed to me that POP had laid a trap for us. They had intended for students to enter through the main gate so that they could funnel us out through it. Amidst the chaos, POP targeted those they deemed to be the protest leaders. Chumani Maxwele, who was on the stairs, was charged by police and dragged away. Lindsay Maasdorp, a prominent face in the protest throughout the week and who had confronted police during the protest at UCT on Monday night, found himself right next to a stun grenade when it landed. As he lay on the ground, curled up and grabbing his ears in pain, the police dragged him away too.

I was caught up among the group of protesters who chose not to exit through the main gate but instead ran down the alleyway the breakaway group had initially marched up earlier. Athabile was by my side as we stood our ground around 40 metres away from the initial attack. We were a group of about 30 students. We urged everyone to sit down with our hands in the air in the hope that police would not target us. Some officers looked at us with fear, others with anger. Regardless of the emotions being felt by those seated, a sense of resilience rang true among us; we would not be leaving.

We couldn't see what was taking place at the main gate because our view was blocked by the parliamentary buildings. Looking up at them, we could see the faces of assistants and researchers staring down at us through their windows. When we'd marched up the alley earlier, they had indicated to us that due to our presence, parliament had been locked down. Athabile stood next to me. Or rather, I stood next to him. He had gained the trust of the students that day because he hadn't worn his political colours. I still had my ANC shirt on and I knew that my personality alone wouldn't let students forget which party oversaw the government that had put them in this position. For the students present, most of whom were from UCT and CPUT, Athabile became the symbol of the protest. A fearless student just like them, unaffiliated to any political party at that moment, and ready to throw it all away for the cause they were fighting for.

On the other side of parliament, hundreds remained inside the parliamentary precinct with only a handful of police holding them back. Police stared protesters down as students chanted 'We Want Blade, We Want Blade!' As had happened at Rondebosch police station the day before, white students were told to head to the front of the protest. Dozens of white students proceeded to make their way through the crowd, arms crossed in the air. They stood in front of the POP officers. The logic that had informed this move the day before was that police officers wouldn't dare to attack white students. It was black bodies they were after. Today, however, that plan failed. POP released two stun grenades in front of the white students and students soon retreated. It was at this point that Kevin French, the 63-year-old father of a student in protest but also a member of the Democratic Left Front, found himself detained alongside Nathan Taylor for resisting police while they were assisting students to leave the parliamentary precinct. The students at the main gate made another attempt to stand their ground inside the precinct, knowing that if they were removed, they would probably never get a second opportunity. The second use of stun grenades proved too much for them, however, and police finally managed to push them out. Then the main gates were shut and locked.

Through all this time, parliament stayed in session, listening to a budget speech. Outside their children stood, pleading to be listened to.

After the main gates were locked POP turned their attention to the group I was in. We were still singing and chanting 'We Want Blade!' Again we pleaded with police officers to pass a message on to the minister of Higher Education and Training and tell him that this situation could be ended if he simply showed leadership and addressed the students. There had been a common fear throughout the weeks of protests that students wanted to harm those in authority. It is a fear that I understand, but it exposes how many of the leaders of our country, whether they are in universities or in government, are afraid to be held accountable to the constituencies they claim to represent.

The leader of POP in the Western Cape walked towards our group, which was still seated on the ground, and threw two stun grenades in our direction. One landed in the middle of our group and jolted those around it away from its blast. The second fell at our feet as we scrambled up, giving us little time to get our bearings. Suddenly POP began to beat against us with riot shields while the sound of Tasers rang in the air. Realising that I was partially responsible for leading students into the situation at hand, I knew it would be my responsibility to lead them out. First one in, last one out. I think it was my defiance that triggered the need for the police to detain me at that point.

While the last group of students was finally pushed out of parliament, I found myself sitting next to Chumani, Lindsay, Kevin and Nathan Taylor. We were soon joined by Markus Trengove who – alongside another fellow activist – was waiting by the steps of parliament a few metres from where we were detained. He must have blended into the crowd of journalists who were there because POP initially ignored him. When they realised he was a student and attempted to remove him, his one sign of dissent ended up with him being handcuffed next to me. Our arrests were farcical. At least that is what we thought before we were charged with High Treason and swept away to the Bellville offices of the Directorate for Priority Crime Investigation.

The rest of the afternoon would consist of ongoing clashes between police officers and students, with 30 more students arrested by the day's end. The minister did attempt to address students, but by then the damage had been done and the trust we had in government resolving the situation broken. What had started as a march to remind our public representatives of their responsibility to hundreds of thousands of students across the country, in the end turned into a reminder of the role young people continue to have to play in South Africa – to march against anyone creating or perpetuating injustice.

By Thursday #FeesMustFall had become a fully fledged co-ordinated national movement. Each morning that week student leaders used WhatsApp to communicate and update one another about what had taken place throughout the day and plan for the day ahead. Twitter was utilised to interact with thousands of students at a time, directing them about where to go and when to get there. It also became a platform for students to share their experiences about protest action from the state, police and their universities. In the public's eyes, our narrative changed. Talk radio was flooded with callers phoning in and praising our efforts, saying our protests reminded them of those in 1976. Our bravery dominated newspaper headlines. Wednesday had been a field day for the media: 'STUDENTS MARCH, WHILE POLITICIANS WATCH'. Before the protest at parliament, we had often been described as hooligans, but by Thursday morning we became, almost paradoxically, freedom fighters in a democratic society.

It had been raining on the Wednesday, which had somewhat dulled affairs at Wits, and in any event, the country's attention was firmly fixed on the scenes outside parliament. But Thursday would be different. On Thursday a decision was made to target the elephant in the room.

In the early days of the protest, there were a variety of attempts by national political parties to infiltrate #FeesMustFall. Mmusi Maimane, leader of the DA, embarrassingly attempted to engage with students at UCT where he was swiftly denounced for his attempts to gain easy political points through the protests and was ushered off campus. Helen Zille had been chased away from Stellenbosch by students advocating that the movement would remain non-partisan. Stellenbosch had notoriously fought against any political party seeking any form of influence on campus, let alone their parent bodies. The most significant confrontation, however, would be against the ANC, who had up until this point avoided criticism by students. In fact, the party's spokesperson at the time, Zizi Kodwa, had been on the Wits campus on Monday that week waxing lyrical about the mobilisation efforts of students. The ANC had been protected because SASCO and the PYA had protected it.

Students at the University of Johannesburg placed the ANC firmly in its crosshairs on Thursday morning, having resolved the previous night that they would be marching on Luthuli House, the party's headquarters downtown. Protesters were determined to confront the ANC in their own back yard. A request from UJ was sent to the Wits plenary to join them in the march to Luthuli House, a request that provoked a fierce debate. The tension was palpable. As more and more students found consensus on marching on Luthuli House, the PYA, expectedly so, became more hesitant. It would be a hesitation that set off a series of loud whispers in the corridors of Wits about how far the PYA would stray from its mother body, the ANC. For many students, the march was a no-brainer. If students were to speak truth to power, how could they not speak to the ANC directly? And after all, they were only a stone's throw away.

The EFFSC naturally led the charge in castigating the ANC, with Fallists roaming around and smelling blood. After the events at parliament, the influence of Fallists within the movement grew. Earlier in the protest, the voice of Fallists at Wits had mainly been confined to plenary sessions. Though plenaries are essential, all one can do in a plenary is point students in a particular direction; the final order is still reserved for the 'silent leaders'. Using black pain as an authoritative device, Fallists and independent students began to assert their control of the movement's plenary sessions in the attempt to become 'outspoken leaders'.

At HWIs, the role of Fallists had grown beyond the confines of party politics. The role of #RhodesMustFall at UCT was that of a *de facto* SRC. At Stellenbosch University, #OpenStellenbosch had traditionally been averse to the influence of Fallism in its more radical form but found itself increasingly falling for its whim as protests continued. Because the SRC was much maligned at the university, the Black Student Movement maintained control of the protest alongside independent students. Influencing decisions through plenaries kept the SRC or any other leadership group accountable to the broader student body of protesters. Plenaries thus became a mechanism for the Fallists not only to keep the PYA and any other political party in check but to keep their actions within the bounds of certain parameters.

One could see the anxiety rising among the PYA members. How could a grouping which was aligned to the party, the ANC, march on that very same party? When SASCO had done national marches in the past, these were always directed towards government departments and state institutions, never the national leaders who were only an elevator ride away from them.

The plenary session at Wits became heated. Some questioned why UJ had made the decision to march to Luthuli House in the first place, to which the retort was swift: why should Wits have a monopoly on protest action in the country? It became apparent that students were increasingly feeling the need to place the PYA in a corner and the party finally relinquished their hold on the plenary and acquiesced to its demands.

Students found the journey to Luthuli House easier than their comrades in Cape Town had to parliament the day before. High discipline dominated proceedings and the political uncertainty that was seen at the protest outside of parliament on Wednesday was nowhere to be found between Wits and UJ students. There was a celebratory attitude too. As UJ students marched towards the corner of Jorissen and Bertha streets in Braamfontein, one of the central entrances for Wits University, waiting for them on the corner were hundreds of Wits students. As the UJ contingent neared, the scenes of embracing between the two protesting groups were reminiscent of families reuniting at OR Tambo International Airport's arrivals terminal. EFFSC, PYA, PASMA, Fallists alongside thousands of other independent students made their way to 54 Sauer Street as one.

As students marched, it crossed their minds that while the police had generally been averse to engaging with students over the previous week, the events at parliament had changed this. As they crossed the Nelson Mandela Bridge, they found a police barricade blocking their path. The students approached cautiously. The police force stood firm, primed for action. It was believed at this point that a directive had been given to the police force across the country to shoot first and control crowds later. But students would not be deterred and eventually they found their way through the barricade. Luthuli House, the headquarters of the ANC, had seen its fair share of marches, but never on this scale and certainly not since the end of apartheid. The last march of this size on ANC headquarters (which was called Shell House at that time) fell victim to gunfire and death. Students hoped this would not be their fate today.

When they arrived at Luthuli House, thousands of students sat down on the street while others stood on the pavements and looked on. Mcebo Dlamini led the crowd with songs such as 'Solomon' and 'Azania' while they waited for the leadership of the ANC to address them. A level of discipline was maintained that further entrenched the new public narrative of #FeesMustFall as a modern-day version of the 1976 youth protests in Soweto. At this protest, there was only one microphone and it was firmly in the grip of the fantastic four – Mcebo Dlamini, Vuyani Pambo, Shaeera Kalla and Nompendulo Mkhatshwa.

Mcebo spoke first. His speech roused the crowd as he spoke about the lifestyle of poor black students at Wits, striking a note among students when he chided the university for caring more about parking spaces on campus than residences. (It had been discovered from a protest at the Wits Business School a few days before that there were plans to demolish residential buildings on the campus in favour of a new parking lot.) As Mcebo went on, he implored students to maintain their discipline and not be disrespectful of the secretary-general of the ANC, Gwede Mantashe, when he spoke.

In anticipation of the protest a stage, which was draped in their colours and emboldened with the words 'Celebrating 100 years of the Selfless Struggle', had been set up by the ANC just above where the fantastic four were standing. (I am sure many of the protesting students looked at the words of the slogan with some bemusement.) Mantashe had been watching proceedings from there, looking out over the protesters, together with other ANC and SACP officials. This was something Mcebo clearly didn't miss as he went on at length to describe Mantashe's communist roots. As students demanded that Mantashe leave the stage and address them on the ground, Mantashe stood firm, unwilling to do so. Unlike VCs across the country, Mantashe's initial refusal to leave the stage and meet students on the ground was not because he was afraid of the protesters; it was a flexing of political strength. In his eyes, he would not be told to sit down by a couple of children.

Recognising that an impasse was imminent, Mcebo took the microphone and challenged Mantashe, stating:

> Comrades, when I was growing up, I was told that the ANC respects people. When I was growing up I was inducted in nothing but the ANC. I was told that the ANC is for the people. ANC, come down to the people![2]

His demand was met with loud applause and the students began to sing 'Solomon' again, taunting the secretary-general. Mantashe finally relented. He left the stage, made his way to the students standing in front of him and took his position next to the fantastic four. Students cheered, realising the political importance of bringing the ANC 'down to the people'.

Mcebo ended his speech by stating: 'This is the ANC I know. Which will come to the people and humble itself. We don't want an arrogant ANC ... we want a humbled ANC.'

Nompendulo took over after Mcebo and began to sing 'Amakhomanisi', a further reminder of Mantashe's communist background. She used her platform to highlight the growing antagonism against students from police officers, white students and management, who routinely resorted to violence in response to students' protests. Interestingly, in saying that a revolution had been brewing in the country, she acknowledged movements such as #RhodesMustFall, #OpenStellenbosch and #DecoloniseWits, even though #FeesMustFall had not taken on these movements' ideologies.

During Nompendulo's speech students noticed that, unlike Habib, who had complied with the Wits students' demand that he sit down among them on the floor of Solomon Mahlangu House, Mantashe had remained standing. He had not been told to sit down. What began as murmurs soon became heckles as a small chorus began to demand that Mantashe sit down. For students, it seemed, the ANC was not going to be immune to the politics of humiliation imposed on those who claimed authority or remained gatekeepers to the economic emancipation of young people.

As Shaeera, the third of the ANC trinity at Wits, began to speak the chorus demanding that Mantashe sit down grew from murmurs to chants. The trinity looked on nervously. The 'Father', Mcebo, perched himself beside Mantashe, who was clutching onto a walking stick for support and averting his gaze from the crowd. Nompendulo, the 'Son', looked apprehensively at the crowd like a friend being embarrassed in front of a parent, and Shaeera, the 'Holy Spirit', desperately tried to hand the microphone over to someone she'd described as an 'ordinary student' who was supposed to read out the memorandum to the ANC.

Realising the potential within that moment of hesitation, Vuyani grabbed the microphone and the PYA's worst fears began to play out right in front of them. The #FeesMustFall movement subscribed to democratic practice, he proclaimed, and students had agreed that they would make power, regardless of its form, sit down on the floor when in the presence of students. It was a clear power play. A power play that worked. Students cheered in agreement as Vuyani demanded that the secretary-general take his place on the floor of Sauer Street just as Habib had taken his place on the floor of Solomon Mahlangu House.

Unfazed, the secretary-general of the ANC refused to sit.

A few minutes would pass as students continued to demand that the SG take his seat. The trinity, for the first time, looked weak in the eyes of students and blood was in the water. The student who had been asked to read the memorandum was told by the crowd to refrain from reading out their demands until the SG sat. Then Mantashe made a move to walk away from the protesters, a move that was roundly booed. The ANC was on the defensive. Mantashe, the proud man that he is, refused to let the organisation he represented lose political face by sitting on the floor. Especially if such a demand, as he must have seen it, was coming from the EFF. In comments he made to the media later he stated that his refusal was because he understood there was a balance between complying and being humiliated.[3]

If only Mantashe and the ANC had resisted the urge to disband its Youth League, I couldn't help thinking, maybe they would have had more control of the protest. Perhaps the PYA wouldn't have had to deal with the tug of war for power with the EFF.

The PYA was losing control and losing it quickly. Mcebo, trying to gain control of the situation, took the microphone and attempted to address students. Before the words left his mouth, students began to chant, 'This is not a rally!' It would be a chant that would reverberate through the crowd as an act of defiance against one of its prominent leaders. In response, deferring to his constituency, Mcebo began to sing 'Solomon' to quieten down the loud voices of dissent. Mantashe looked on, resolute, as competing choruses of 'Solomon' and 'Hlala phantsi Mantashe hlala phantsi' echoed through the streets. It was all too clear who was under attack when students began to chant that 'the ANC Must Fall'. These were the words the PYA feared most.

Finally, through a combination of political ingenuity and a bit of doublespeak, Mcebo eventually succeeded in redirecting students' anger away from the ANC and preventing it from reaching its pinnacle. In complete contradiction to the words he'd uttered just half an hour earlier (that Luthuli House was the true place of power and where the country was truly controlled), he exhorted students not to engross and divide themselves in petty politics. The real power, he said, resided in the Union Buildings. A building, he reminded students, they would be shutting down the following day. He further shielded the party by confirming that Mantashe would receive the memorandum but would not be speaking to them.

With a few swift words, Mcebo managed to assert his authority on proceedings and protect the party from embarrassment by calculating that the embarrassment of the state was the lesser of the two evils at a play. It worked. Reluctantly, the crowd allowed the 'ordinary student' to read out the memorandum and remind the ANC of their commitment to free quality education for all, which they had made in 1994. As Mantashe and the

ANC signed the memorandum and walked away from the people, chants in the distance continued: 'ANC Must Fall.'

* * *

On the day of the march to the Union Buildings in Pretoria, I was in Cape Town, where I found myself in another confrontation with police, this time near the University of the Western Cape. I was called to intercept a group of students who had been angered by the comments their vice-chancellor, who had spoken to them earlier in the day, had made when he intimated that his hands were tied regarding the increase in fees. As a result, students chose to march on Cape Town International Airport and shut it down. Madness, I thought to myself, nonsensical madness. By that time the president had made his announcement – that there would be a 0% fee increment – so why would UWC march on the airport? But then again, UWC at that point had been on the receiving end of some of the harshest forms of police aggression in the Western Cape, with most incidents going unreported by media houses.

I thought that maybe if I got myself to the front of the crowd, I could convince them to turn around. Unlike the other locations students had marched on, the airport was protected by legislation which allowed the police force to use live ammunition on a deemed threat. When I arrived, I realised that it was PASMA leading the protest and any chance to talk to them as a publicly known SASCO member would be ignored. Furthermore, they already knew about the president's announcement and were disregarding it. It wasn't that the 0% fee increment was not a win for students, it was a signal to them that more could be gained. For them, we had not achieved Free Quality Education just yet.

We headed down Robert Sobukwe Drive, a name I am sure PASMA found pride in, and neared the corner of Borcherds Quarry Road. From there the airport would be a straight shot away. The police were waiting for us. Standing primed, two Casspirs on hand and a 'just in case of emergency' ambulance in the background, officers stood prepared. As we approached the corner, they released a barrage of rubber bullets and stun grenades, forcing us to flee into the nearby houses. Any attempt to leave a house was met with a shot in our direction by the police. It was a Mexican stand-off. If the impasse was to be resolved and a ceasefire agreed upon, the intervention of the SRC was required. In one of the most bizarre scenes during #FeesMustFall, UWC PASMA leaders and police walked towards each other in a park that separated the police officers and us. A neutral zone of sorts. After a long period of negotiations, eventually we were allowed to return to UWC with a police 'escort'.

What had taken place on the dilapidated park on the corner of Borcherds Quarry Road and Robert Sobukwe Drive in Cape Town was in strange, stark contrast to the events that were taking place at the Union Buildings.

The early hours of the morning were relatively quiet as students slowly made their way to the presidential South Lawns. Some had arrived as early as 6 am from the universities nearby, the University of Pretoria and Tshwane University of Technology. Students from the former had been involved in ongoing protest action throughout the week, with the previous day being dominated by a march on the university library to pull students into the protest and a night vigil held in the evening. At the same time as those in Pretoria began to gather on the South Lawns of the Union Buildings, students at Wits were climbing aboard buses, which were to depart from the university at 7 am and take them to Pretoria. Almost as if in anticipation of conflict, notices began to make the rounds on social media telling students how they should prepare for clashes with police officers. Suggestions such as buying milk to pour in one's eyes and water-soaked cloths to block out teargas were shared, showing students' lack of trust when it came to the police. In response, police began mobilising. Casspirs were positioned on and around the South Lawns.

By this stage, almost all institutions were engaging in solidarity protest actions countrywide. They were all preparing themselves for the announcement by the president, which was scheduled to be made shortly after 10 am. UKZN and DUT marched on West Street towards Durban's City Hall; NMMU continued the shutdown of their university campus and would go on to march towards Port Elizabeth's City Hall as well; UWC and Stellenbosch University continued their discussions with their respective vice-chancellors about fee-related issues on campus; and UCT continued their protest action in solidarity with outsourced workers on campus.[4] It wouldn't only be students mobilising on the day, but labour unions, NGOs, charities and foundations too. All were lending their support to the protest in one way or another. Some people even took off work to march in solidarity with students. Even further afield solidarity marches were taking place in London and New York and messages of support began to flow in from universities across the world. The plan for the day seemed clear. The president would meet with SRC presidents and vice-chancellors from across the country at 10 am, while students from across the province would arrive in time for the president's announcement after the conclusion of the meeting. What could go wrong?

Even before the president's meeting began tensions in the crowd in front of the Union Buildings were building. Many students had still not arrived by the time the first crack in the fencing was made. Police officers stood idly by while the situation in front of them began to unfold. Their calm demeanour was probably due to the up-down nature of the anger students were exhibiting in front of them. In some moments they pressed against the fence, fiercely trying to force their way through, only to have their attention drawn away by the beginning of a song behind them or the arrival of a new group of students. Over the years, the Union Buildings had been the location for a variety of gatherings by citizens and police officers always expect tensions. Their lack of action, at least as I interpreted it, was not due to a reluctance to act, but because they believed there was no need to act at the time. It would be a decision, I believe, they would regret only an hour later.

It is quite difficult to make sense of the events that took place over the next few hours. Most of the student leaders simply couldn't truly account for how and why events played out the way they did because most were not present when things began to go off the rails. SRC presidents were indoors with the president while the Wits SRC would only arrive after midday. Fallists had no political clout and had no chance of managing proceedings. The EFFSC's lack of electoral support at both UP and TUT would have made it difficult for them to gain a semblance of control of the situation either. From burning portable toilets, runaway police Casspirs storming into large groups of students, students climbing the statue of Louis Botha, ongoing battles between police and students in the streets of Pretoria to students using pole vaults to poke, prod and taunt police officers … all of this, mixed with a dangerous combination of heat and dehydration, resulted in an explosion in the country's capital. It was like throwing a Molotov cocktail into a paraffin container. Though it would be a core group of students that would stoke the fire of the protest, they were not the ones who created the conditions for the explosion of violence on the day.

Much of the distress that was vocalised by students was with the violent nature of the clashes that took place in Pretoria. Until that day Wits students had never been at the receiving end of the full force of police brutality as experienced regularly by other institutions around the country. Clashes between students and police tended to be more localised and individualised, rather than against hordes of student groupings. When many of these students climbed back on board their buses heading back to Johannesburg no doubt they would have been wondering how peaceful intent could so quickly turn into vacuous violence.

The go-to excuse that students used was to blame it all on students from TUT because how could a Wits student possibly engage in such action? Whether the small group of students who began the unrest at the Union Buildings were students or not, placing the blame on TUT brought to the surface a long-standing predisposition within #FeesMustFall. A predisposition that would entrench itself within the movement and result in the black elite inside #MustFall movements being vulnerably exposed. The moment we broke ranks and blamed TUT, rather than take collective responsibility for the scenes in Pretoria, became the first sign of why you shouldn't trust a coconut with the revolution. It showed that you couldn't assume (or expect) that the black elite would support you to the bitter end. How could students who earlier in the week refused to have their behaviour 'policed' turn around and, without hesitation, police the anger shown by TUT students?

As I have explained earlier in this book, anyone who believes that #FeesMustFall began in 2015 exhibits either a level of ignorance about the higher education sector in South Africa or has a penchant for rewriting history. The phrase 'the enemy of my enemy is my friend' helps to explain the faux alliance that was created between two separate groups of students who were at war with the state that day. For HBIs such as UWC and TUT, #FeesMustFall was an ongoing state of existence, whereas at HWIs, like Wits and UCT, it was just a new shiny toy that had caught students' interest. The two-tiered higher education system in South Africa created two types of protesting students: those who experienced almost their entire university student body sitting on the edge of financial exclusion each year if NSFAS failed them versus those who represented a group of students bearing the brunt of a university's financial system. The alliance that was created between these two disparate groups functioned like a combination of oil and water.

Where this was most obvious was in the meeting with the president and the various SRC presidents behind closed doors that day at the Union Buildings. In the meeting with the president, they explained that there was a definite difference in opinion between those who came from HWIs and those who came from HBIs. For the HWIs, their best alternative to a negotiated agreement was vastly different from what HBIs required. HWIs were willing to hold out and they even threatened to walk out of the meeting with the president. The Wits SRC had already planned to boycott the meeting altogether, their reason being that they refused to meet the president behind closed doors. Their stance was that the president, too, should come down to the people.

No mass meeting or provincial co-ordination between the various SRCs in the province took place beforehand to brief students about the proceedings for the day. As a result, the differences between student groupings became visceral as clashes in protest ideology came to life. Through a mixture of standing outside in the heat, a group of rogue protesters and the lack of leadership on the ground a tinder was lit. Any attempt to douse the flames that flared up only appeared to escalate the conflict.

The most damning indictment of a government is the erection of walls and fences separating it from the people. When a state actively decides to shut off the public, rather than engage it, then a clear sign is sent to the masses that at some point along the state's journey, the state lost the plot. Tensions increased the longer students remained outside and eventually events boiled over into chaos. Even the announcement of a 0% fee increment from the president would not bring calm to the crowd. Zuma thought that he had brought #FeesMustFall to an end. That he had finally killed off the movement that had been rampaging across the country. Instead, he gave it new life. Phoenix-like, through the fires that erupted across the capital city, a new #FeesMustFall was born. A version that was fiercer in its demeanour and largely unchained from its ANC leanings.

Chapter 14

When Rome Falls: The Fight for the Soul of #FeesMustFall

#FeesMustFall was a complex structure filled with contradictions and competing interests. After the announcement by the president on 21 October 2015 of 0% increase in student fees, the movement became riddled by in-fighting as various structures fought for control. The majority of the subsequent protests ran on the momentum of ending outsourcing on university campuses, but this cause was never a big enough motivator to bring the masses back to the forefront of the protest. Numbers waned as the weeks went by and students prepared for exams. UCT, NMMU and Wits managed to maintain the momentum until their outsourcing demands were met either in part or fully. Eventually, #FeesMustFall 2015 ended, but the search for economic freedom did not.

The new year began with the antagonism between male student leaders and womxn, trans and queer people within the structure of #FMF reaching a zenith. This was not a new conflict; it was just one example of many long-standing disputes in the movement. For example, an exhibit of #RhodesMustFall was disrupted by the Trans Collective at UCT, who stormed the exhibition, bare-breasted and armed with red paint, to protest how the pictures on display had excluded them from the narrative of #RMF. It would be a conflict that spoke to not only the ideological politics that were at play inside the movement but to the vastly more complex nature of people politics.

On 4 April 2016, the first public fight for the soul of #FeesMustFall took place at Wits. Chumani Maxwele alongside Vuyani Pambo and several other prominent student leaders from across the country had gathered inside Solomon Mahlangu House with the intention of shutting down the university. Chumani represented what can be best described as the male cabal of the Fallists, while Vuyani had, at least in popularity, become the Student Commander-in-Chief for the EFF. The latter group of prominent leaders was a mixed bag of PASMA celebrities and male Fallists looking for their time in the limelight.

I was in the library at the Wits Business School when I first got the message that an attempt to shut down Wits had begun. I remember smiling to myself as I realised that I had almost been fooled by Chumani the week before and that this protest stood no chance of succeeding. The shutdown was stopped almost before it began. Its sudden halt was not due to the work of the university management's hired private security or the Public Order Police, as had become commonplace the year before. Instead, the gathering was halted by the womxn leaders of #FeesMustFall who saw the planned protest as a bastardisation of #FeesMustFall because of its exclusion of womxn, queer and trans individuals.

For the womxn leaders such as Thenjiwe Mswane, the organisers of the protest were far from representative of the movement as a whole and she would not allow them to use the name and energy of #FeesMustFall without respecting the ideology it espoused. For her and many others across the country, this was #NotMyFMF. Following the steps of a viral video of a woman going on her morning jog with a sjambok in hand with the intention of beating any man who catcalled her, Thenjiwe proceeded to purchase a sjambok and whip the men who believed they owned the movement. Her concern revolved about who had been excluded from the gathering and who had been included. A concern that met with the response that 'feminists are not allowed, and queer bodies were not allowed'.[1] Thenjiwe was then manhandled by the men in the movement and subsequently beaten by them.

These early bouts of in-fighting in 2016 brought to light all the tensions that had been brewing under the surface. In-fighting between Fallists and political parties led to childish bickering between the groups, with an uneasy truce only taking hold in the face of police violence on campuses. HWIs became battle zones not only for students and police officers but for students against students as well. In Cape Town, SASCO had successfully been moved to the background of #FeesMustFall, while in Gauteng it fought tooth and nail through its SRC position. Fallists went through a period of introspection, cleansing themselves of toxic masculinity and creating greater national bonds and thereby entrenching their role. The EFF saw their electoral support across South Africa's universities increase as it slowly became the legitimate contender for the throne against the incumbent SASCO which, until the end of 2016, was traditionally the dominant student organisation across the country. HBIs turned their backs on HWIs and HWIs realised that without HBIs they simply didn't have the numbers to mount a credible national challenge. Students learned how to use the media more effectively, while the media – excluding *The Daily Vox* – failed to truly understand the protests.

Students were shot in the back while running away from police in scenes eerily reminiscent of the Marikana Massacre; a preacher stood firm as a Casspir barrelled down in his path. Riots escaped the confines of the university and spilt onto the streets of Johannesburg. TUT maintained its reputation as the protest champions but no longer sought to lend their support to Wits. NMMU fought internal battles, some motivated by things as petty as a conflict over a pizza, while the University of Fort Hare found its centenary celebrations halted by disparate protests by students on campus.

PASMA, alongside the Black Solidarity Action group, committed themselves to a national shutdown in August but failed in their attempt because they were unable to garner the requisite support. In all, 2016 was a bizarre year for #FeesMustFall, with most of the conflicts that took place focused on using the name as the vehicle to create change not only within an institution but society at large.

The protest at Wits at the beginning of 2016 was quite unusual for #FMF at the time. During 2015 it had largely been a regionally focused movement with very little, if any, collaboration between different regions. For instance, protests in the Western Cape ignored most of the protest activities of Gauteng; Gauteng ignored the activities of the Eastern Cape. To have such an eclectic gathering of student leaders from across the country leading a protest at a particular university was, therefore, unprecedented. The reason for this gathering was a national conference that had been held the weekend before, which included a variety of stakeholders, all seemingly with similar interests. Significantly, however, certain key parties were excluded.

The 'conference' was funded by Adv Mojanku Gumbi – the former legal advisor to President Thabo Mbeki – and had been organised ostensibly to discuss the future of the movement. In reality, it was more of an 'old boys' club' of the male celebrities of the movement. This pseudo-conference firmly drew a line in the sand on a national level between the various groups in the country who laid claim to #FeesMustFall. The 'true' Fallists, in the main black females who placed emphasis on the role of Black Radical Feminism above the other pillars of Fallism, claimed they had not been invited. And it soon became apparent to many other students across the country that they were not the only exclusions. Prominent figures in the movement such as Alex Hotz, Simamkele Dlavaku and Wanelisa Xaba, publicly stated that they did not recognise the legitimacy of the conference. All three of them played pivotal roles within #FFMF and all arguably had the authority to dismiss such a gathering as frivolous.

At the time the pseudo-conference was being held most of the PYA-aligned student leaders were attending a SAUS meeting at the Birchwood Hotel in Ekurhuleni. This showed that SRC presidents from across the country had not been invited either. The conference was endemic to the in-fighting within #FMF. Its failed attempt at a university shutdown at Wits laid bare, for public scrutiny, the internal politics of the movement. The cracks that had formed the year before between the various student alliances soon became chasms. The fight for the soul of #FeesMustFall grew uglier.

At the beginning of St Gregory of Tours's *A History of the Franks*, a historical account of both the physical and moral chaos that engulfed Europe between AD 455 and 476 with the fall of the Roman Empire, he describes the nature of the period in a manner that for me encapsulates the politics of #FeesMustFall:

> *A great many things keep happening, some of them good, some of them bad. The inhabitants of the different countries keep quarrelling fiercely with each other and kings go on losing their temper in the most furious way. Our churches are attacked by the heretics and then protected by the Catholics; the faith of Christ burns bright in many men, but it remains lukewarm in others; no sooner are church buildings endowed by the faithful that they are stripped again by those who have no faith.*[2]

The period was defined by how allies became enemies and enemies became allies. How the riches of the Roman Empire were laid bare for its conquerors. While most had viewed the Roman Empire as a foreign enemy, many still viewed it as their cultural and political home. The confluence of these two groups had a profound impact on the regeneration of the German Empire but caused a rift between what was left of the Western Roman Empire and Constantinople's Eastern Roman Empire. The story told by St Gregory shares significant similarities with that of #FeesMustFall. Our Rome had been the funding system for higher education. The beginning of the fall came with Zuma's announcement of a 0% increase of student fees. From there on out, however, even though our goal to rid ourselves of Rome altogether had not been completed, our biggest hurdle was not the state, but ourselves.

It is easy to say in hindsight that if we had been able to co-operate more effectively, #FeesMustFall might have been able to achieve the demise of Rome earlier sooner. Be that as it may, it took an extra two years to achieve our goal. Two years characterised by in-fighting and betrayal. Not even Deputy Chief Justice Dikgang Moseneke was immune to the bad blood between students. A conference he held between a variety of student groupings at the beginning of 2017, which was intended to create unity among these disparate groups, lasted only a couple of minutes before in-fighting brought it to a standstill.

Different political parties would regularly quarrel with one another, often resulting in student leaders lashing out angrily against not only their detractors but their supporters as well. Ideological dogmas (non-racialism, for example, or Charterism) often found their fiercest opposition not from gun-wielding police officers, university vice-chancellors, NGOs or the state, but from the movement's heretics: the Fallists.

Faith in the notion of non-racialism or Charterism had managed to burn bright in the days leading up to the announcement by the president, but both would fade under increasing discontent with the content of the announcement. Too many students had seen the reaction of the state to their protest to trust them again. Too many students had realised they could reverse the racialised economic and social inequality status elite institutions perpetuated to turn their backs on change. Too many had seen how the ideals of the Freedom Charter did nothing to reduce sexual violence or the prevalence of patriarchy within the movement. Though the reasons for the protests continuing ranged from the need for completely free education to ending outsourcing and more, the seemingly chaotic nature of #FeesMustFall's politics after 23 October 2015 was not the result of the need to find a new cause but a contestation for the soul of the movement.

The internal politics of #FMF were just as important as the external fights we had with university administrations and the state. The internal political dynamics sometimes changed according to which student party/collective had gained a semblance of control over the movement at a given time. Tracing the ebbs and flows of political control over #FMF allows a better understanding of the movement's changing dynamics. Learning to navigate the alliances made between the PYA, PASMA, EFFSC, BLF or Fallists as well as important independent voices – who would often separate themselves from the broader political coalition – would endow these groups with the necessary skills and social capital to lead the movement.

Yet if you were to navigate too far from your own political home, there was no remorse in removing you from that position of political importance within the movement. Whether it be Fallists, the EFFSC or PYA, each body was constantly striving to control the microphone. Not only to be the face of the movement but its ideological voice. This was not limited to political contestation between parties; this was the politics of contestation between women and men in the movement as well.

Images of Vuyani Pambo of the EFFSC and Mcebo Dlamini of the ANCYL dominated the early images of the #FMF at Wits. Seeing the ANC and EFF marching side by side, even if only through their youth wings, was a sight that many had never believed would ever happen. The animosity between the warring political family members gave the impression that unity between the two would only be achieved if one had conquered the other and yet there they were, leading thousands of students in protests. Regardless of the importance of that moment, it was swiftly rejected by many prominent voices within the movement who believed it created the belief that the movement was led by men.

In response, the faces of women began to dominate the protest across the country. Whether it be Wanelisa Xaba from UCT, Nompendulo Mkhatshwa or Simamkele Dlavaku at Wits, or Faith Pienaar at Stellenbosch University, there was a concerted effort to ensure that women were not only represented but also placed in positions of power. In addition, the transgender community was vocal too, agitating continuously for a change of internal politics. Leading faces such as Sandile Ndlelu and Thato Pule led the charge in this respect, ensuring that representation was not limited to heteronormative forms of opposition. The politics of sex and gender played an equal, if not more important role in #FMF when compared to party politics. Some of what I have described here is just the tip of the iceberg of how the nature of #FMF was often dictated by the manner student leaders would place their relative sense of self-importance against others and where they felt the winds of change blowing.

The internal politics of #FMF used a variety of tactics to gain leverage. WhatsApp groups and screenshots became the modus operandi for the defamation and blackmailing of student leaders. Twitter was utilised as not only a court of public opinion but a co-ordinated mob to attack the character of organisations and students alike. The notion of black pain became an authoritative tool not only against white students and university management but to take power from democratically elected structures that stood in the way of the movement.

Authority is a fascinating device. Its ability to permeate society when deemed legitimate is intoxicating to the holder. It bestows on them a sense of invincibility, even if it's a slight one. During the student protests that shook the country in 2015 and 2016, authority became the most valuable commodity in the student movements. In trying to understand why people join protest movements, the emphasis is generally placed on the ability to recruit individuals willing to sacrifice their 'individual interests in favour of a more collective cause'.[3] In the case of the internal struggle in the #MustFall movements, however, it seemed to be the other way around. The emphasis was placed on controlling the narrative of the collective cause.

Black pain as an authority device was at the heart of many internal #FMF contestations. In conjunction with the politics of humiliation, black pain was often used to delegitimise all other previous governing structures within the university. Images of vice-chancellors being forced to sit on the floor to hear black student lived experiences, the hijacking of university assemblies to provide testimony about the experiences of being a black student at a predominantly white institution became common trade within the student movements. Black pain functioned as their lifeblood, providing students with necessary language to express their relative deprivation.

While chairing the Transformation Assembly at the University of Cape Town in 2015, I could sense the surprise of many at how student and academic testimonies of discrimination gave renewed legitimacy to the efforts of #RhodesMustFall. In addition, there was a genuine level of shock at the experiences of students. Usually, such testimony is utilised to humanise a movement, making what is essentially an abstract movement whose goals and ambitions are difficult to decipher through the white noise, into a tangible co-ordinated group of rational individuals reacting to a harsh reality. For those who had been in the halls of Azania House, the symbolic headquarters of #RMF, during the occupation, we were already exposed to the use of black pain as an authoritative device intended to delegitimise the presence of established university institution such as SRCs, Senate and university Councils.

The idea of black pain is difficult to define as it finds its roots in normative conceptions of a person's own place in society. I believe it encapsulates the struggles faced by black people in the South African context and is demonstrable through individuals' feelings of subjugation, alienation, othering and exploitation unique to the 'black child' due to the presence of whiteness. It is the evocation of lived experiences which bring to light how black people are marginalised, disenfranchised or stripped of their dignity due to the dominance of whiteness – whose gaze perpetuates racial power dynamics in various aspects of a black person's life. The evocative nature of black pain and its widespread resonance often made it an ideal ideology on which to ground students' actions. Students who were usually at cross-purposes when it came to their political agendas were often able to circumvent their differences through the use of black pain, thereby preserving unity.

According to the #MustFall movement, the solution to the struggle of black students, whether financial or social, required a non-partisan collective effort and this collective effort should not be hampered by political differences. Student leaders who could speak to the notion of black pain obtained a level of credibility in the movement regardless of their history or experience as student leaders. It opened the door for certain students to gain prominence within the movement and the student body at large without the experience of student politics. If someone could show a deep theoretical understanding of black pain in conjunction with a symbolic and/or physical representation of how to overcome it, through personal testimony, they could place themselves in a position of power. Black pain functions as an authority that doesn't appeal to any previous form of governance system or traditional form of leadership but still demands a similar form of acquiescence. It evokes what Max Weber commonly understood as a charismatic authority in which 'the prophet is the purest form of authority in that it claims the right to break through all existing normative structures'.[4]

Black pain is an authority that requires an enunciation of one's own culmination of experiences – arguably positive as well as negative – of being black. Thus, the speaker can direct the norms of the movement so long as it resonates with other experiences. It is through using the authority of black pain that student leaders – and by extension the movement as a whole – justify their authority evocatively to call on black students regardless of their socio-economic or political background to advocate for societal change. However, it is this same appeal to black pain as a form of authority which, I believe, has led to the current malaise within the student movements. It is the appeal to black pain as a form of authority – both unjustified and illegitimate – and not the notion of black pain itself that I believe poses several problems for the movement's long-run sustainability.

For me (although I admit there may be other ways of understanding how black pain is used as an authoritative device) Joseph Raz's Service Conception of Authority seems to provide the best theoretical framework to understand the intricacies of the authority of black pain. The service conception argues that the point of political authority is to serve the ruled, who have value in themselves, and thus all political offices, persons and structures are created to benefit the ruled rather than to benefit the officeholders.[5]

I essentialise the term 'value' to our recent conceptions of black pain to understand the motives of the student movement's leaders. As a result, the student leaders serve students who value themselves through the notion of black pain; thus, structures and leadership positions are created to benefit the notion of black pain rather than student leaders themselves.

Raz explains that the Service Conception of Authority is driven by three theses, namely: the Dependence, the Normal Justification and the Pre-emptive thesis. The Dependence thesis explains that any directive made by an authority should be dependent on the deliberations of those whom it seeks to direct. In other words, student leaders cannot utilise the notion of black pain to issue directives if students do not already understand what black pain is/was for them.[6] Black pain as a broad concept is dependent on individuals' personal lived experiences of being black and so to speak on the issue is to draw on the experiences of all those who identify with it.

Normal Justification posits that being under the authority of someone else is the best way for one to achieve one's own independent goals. It claims that to establish that one has authority, you need to show that the subject is better complying with the directives of one's authority rather than following their own rationale.[7] #MustFall movements often require students to believe that if black pain is a result of broader systemic oppression of black people, then it would be better to understand the concept through a more collective perspective brought together by an authority to undo its systemic effects. Black pain thus demands that an individual student relies on a more collective understanding of black pain rather than simply their own personal experience.

Both the Dependence and Normal Justification theses form the foundation for Raz's Pre-emption thesis, which argues: 'The fact that an authority requires performance of an action is a reason for its performance which is not to be added to all other relevant reasons when assessing what to do but should exclude and take the place of some of them.'[8] By appealing to black pain as a justification for action pre-empts people's ability to use their own judgement on a matter. This pre-emption is important because it allows the political leaders of the movement to avoid political/ideological differences impeding the willingness of students to follow their directives. Furthermore, it provides the appropriate means to encourage various forms of civil disobedience that students would ordinarily not undertake. This pre-emption is often the core aspect of the broad-based unity of the various movements. It is also the primary reason for how coconuts not only found prominence within the movement but were often freely allowed to take on leadership roles.

To determine whether black pain should be considered a form of political authority, it must be able to both coerce and justify the coercion of its adherents. #RhodesMustFall relied heavily on black students' experiences of alienation at UCT as a tool for mobilisation and justification for its position as an authority on student matters. The ability of #RMF to speak to the black student's experience was ever present during the attempts to remove the statue of Cecil John Rhodes from campus through various acts, such as storming Council meetings, taking over university Assemblies, occupying student administrative buildings, and denouncing SRCs.

#FeesMustFall was no different, claiming its authority to direct students' actions due to its understanding of the financial struggles faced by black students, a by-product of black pain, at universities. Both used black pain as their justification for claiming authority within the university and maintaining authority within the multi-stakeholder nature of the student movement. Gaining such authority is neither a matter of circumstance nor happenstance, but a calculated process of singing to the tune to which the student mass will be willing to surrender their own judgement to others at the expense of their personal freedom of choice.

There are numerous untold stories of the internal disputes caused by the concern of 'who speaks on whose authority'. The political tension between SRCs, student political parties and the various iterations of the #MustFall movement often came to a head when the question of who got to 'hold the megaphone' arose. The pursuit of the megaphone led to the dismissal of previous 'antiquated' structures of authority. It led to the first salvo of shots fired in the war for the soul of #FeesMustFall.

One such 'antiquated structure' was the Students Representative Council. These organisations across the county, which had predominantly comprised PYA and SASCO, came to be regarded as an impediment to the desired horizontal leadership structure espoused by the movement. University management, through the Higher Education Act of 1998, was mandated to communicate with elected SRCs when it came to student issues. The presence of an SRC thus created was deemed by some to be an arbitrary hierarchy within the movement.

Considering that an SRC's authority is derived from the electoral mandate given to it by the student populace, this democratic form of authority needed to be replaced with another form of authority, one that would enable those who were not democratically elected to still function as proxies for students in university meetings and issue directives to the student body at large. This is a faux form of leadership and it will inevitably fumble at any direct electoral challenge because it requires a similar authority given to SRCs through an electoral mandate without going through the process of electoral politics. No leader of #FeesMustFall across the country was ever democratically elected.

The situation created a crisis for an organisation such as SASCO because it entrenched within the movement the idea that it was necessary to circumvent political organisations in favour of the politics of the individual. The appeal to black pain as a form of authority allowed individuals to surrender their judgement to the narrator of black pain at any given moment in the belief that that narrator was best placed to lead them towards their collective goal. While this tactic put political organisations at a disadvantage, it worked in favour of the charismatic black heterosexual male and the Fallist.

Because of its ubiquitous nature, a narrator could pair their interpretation of black pain with any one of the pillars of Fallism to gain the trust of students. Such an understanding, however, was something political parties often couldn't accomplish because of the constitutional constraints of their individual parties. The circumvention of partisan party politics by black pain, a move spearheaded by Fallists, benefited the student movement in their quest to create a united front and draw on the powerful nature of non-partisan mass mobilisation. Images of students across the political spectrum gave credence and legitimacy to the movement as being representative of students as a whole. In the case of some universities, it allowed the movement to avoid inter-party struggles impeding planned programmes of action. It also allowed for an increase in the prominence of non-partisan students into the politics of the university, something that had rarely been achieved in previous large-scale university-based protests.

PYA structures at HWIs had been blind to the real intentions of this tactic and had even opened their doors to a multi-stakeholder movement; PYA structures at HBIs, on the other hand, who were far more sceptical about the idea of unity, often kept the gates of #FeesMustFall firmly shut to outside interference. I believe there is a definite negative correlation between the number of Fallists (in a more formalised manner) and the presence of Fallism at a university campus with the relative electoral support and strength of the PYA at those institutions. Subsequent SRC elections at Wits and UCT were probably cases in point. The increase in Fallism on both campuses led to the election of the EFFSC on both campuses in 2017 and the complete erasure of SASCO at UCT. Though SASCO exists in name, its presence on campus in terms of electoral support has been largely diminished. The PYA at Wits proved to be a more stubborn foe to remove, but actions to remove the Wits PYA would have significant consequences for the PYA going forward.

The PYA had historically been dominant at Wits. In the years leading up to #FeesMustFall it usually won SRC elections with little competition, apart from an organisation called Project W. Even the EFF failed to gain electoral strength at the institution during the pre-#FMF years. Through the SRC it had been able to maintain its legitimacy during the first week of #FeesMustFall in 2015, fending off numerous attempts to attack its credentials. Led by Shaeera Kalla, Nompendulo Mkwatsha and Mcebo Dlamini, the PYA-led SRC controlled #FMF, ceding power to the EFFSC during plenaries as an optics tactic rather than one of true power-sharing. The decision to include the EFFSC in the protest on 14 October 2015 was meant to create the impression that the movement was non-partisan. I believe the EFFSC were aware of this tactic when they refused the offer by the Wits PYA to chair the first mass meeting of students. In fact, the following day they held a meeting with the SRC as a means of discrediting certain members of the PYA who were influential in the first days of pro-tests and, in addition, asserted that they were colluding with management.

After the announcement of the 0% fee increment and the decision of SAUS and SASCO (through clear pressure from the ANC and ANCYL) to return to class and cease the protests, the doors were opened to delegitimise the Wits SRC. At Wits, as with many other institutions, there was a belief that the protest should not end without securing the end of the outsourc-ing of workers on campus. SASCO was split on this on a national level as many of us felt the mandate given to us would place us in a disadvantaged position within the movement compared to the EFFSC and PASMA.

As I have stated in a previous chapter, #FeesMustFall became a protest of not just students, but academics and workers as well, and the notion of abandoning the fight for workers in favour of a return to class did not sit well with many. The decision ran counter to the belief that the students' struggle ran parallel with the workers' struggle. The accusation was soon laid against the Wits SRC that they were against the black mothers and fathers on campus. Fallists (which at the time included the BLF) on cam-pus, in conjunction with the EFFSC, went on a full offensive against the Wits PYA leaders, seeking to delegitimise their claim to the megaphone and their ability to speak on black pain or the black struggle.

Nompendulo was discredited due to an ill-advised photo of herself on the cover of *Destiny* magazine. She had been the black female face of the movement. Charismatic and domineering in her demeanour, she became the face of the protest on a national level and ensured that women would not be erased from the protest. However, Nompendulo, a loyal comrade of the ANC, was often pictured with her trademark ANC doek and she was not a Fallist. The thinking was that she brought too much publicity to the ANC, the structure all other stakeholders in the movement hated. After the cover photo was released, students rejected her as the face of the movement, calling her opportunistic and accusing her of failing to adhere to the horizontal nature of the movement. Though the issue of the magazine in which she was featured also spoke about the role of other women in the movement, Twitter swiftly worked to discredit her leadership abilities and remove the megaphone from her hand. It was not the last time this happened to Nompendulo. The tactic was used the following year again, in this instance by workers who had been upset with the decision to discontinue the protest.

Shaeera Kalla was next on the list. Shaeera had become president of the SRC after the suspension of Mcebo Dlamini in 2015 for his Hitler-praising comments. Having worked on the '1 Million, 1 Month' campaign earlier in the year – raising money for students on campus who could not afford their registration fee – Shaeera had become prominent in her own right. She was placed at the forefront of #FeesMustFall not only because of her politics but as a response to the popularity of Vuyani Pambo and Mcebo Dlamini. Shaeera would suffer a similar fate to Nompendulo (although not with the same long-term consequences) when she, alongside the leadership of the Wits PYA, was accused of taking a bribe of R40 000 from the ANC to stop the protest.

The accusation came after a clandestine meeting on the Sunday after President Zuma's announcement of a 0% fee increase. The meeting was between PYA leaders at Wits and officials of the ANCYL. The purpose of the meeting (which was also a meeting of national PYA officeholders) was to discuss specific disagreements among PYA members concerning the decision to return to class and the way forward for the PYA in light of the announcement. The meeting was stormed by students under the name Wits #FeesMustFall and led by Lindsay Maasdorp from BLF.

Because of its relationship with the ANC, distrust of the PYA in #FeesMustFall had been growing, a distrust which was not unfounded. This had been clearly put on display the day of the march to Luthuli House when Vuyani Pambo had demanded that Secretary-General Gwede Mantashe sit on the floor and the demand was not echoed by the ANC-aligned student leaders.

The clandestine meeting, however, became the first clear indication of potential collusion between the PYA leaders and the ANC. To Wits #FeesMustFall it was evidence that the ANC was interfering in the protest. Out of that meeting, the idea of selling out came into prominence across the country. PYA and SASCO, overnight, were labelled 'sell-outs' and accused of failing to adhere to the needs of black people because of their commitment to protecting the ANC. The megaphone was firmly stripped from the PYA within #FeesMustFall and the structure has never been welcomed back.

Over the course of the following days, the role of the PYA- and SASCO-led SRCs in #FMF was seriously questioned and the structure by and large remained at odds with the broader movement. This led to the chaotic nature of the 2016 and 2017 protests as contestation for the use of the #FeesMustFall moniker continued. Although the circumvention of SRCs and thus the PYA proved to be effective, it ultimately led to the current problems facing the #FeesMustFall movement.

Black pain places the politics of people above the politics of organisations when determining who wields authority. If the narrator is unable adequately to communicate the broad conception of black pain – maintaining both the Dependence and Pre-emptive theses – their authority is often considered illegitimate and they are swiftly replaced by another narrator. This dependence on a narrator creates a situation in which the individual's strength to speak to black pain is stronger than a political party's ideology because of the limits placed on the party by its own ideologies. For instance, the PYA and SASCO's position on non-racialism is often at odds with the concept of black pain, which results in Fallists and other more black-conscious student organisations using the concept to severely weaken and in some cases revoke SASCO's claim to authority. Throughout the protests SASCO resisted any change to its ideological beliefs and maintained its Charterist undertones, seeking instead to maintain authority through its broad electoral support across universities. Organisations such as PASMA – a traditionally black-conscious movement – on the other hand, were happy to adapt their image in search of achieving authority through black pain, even though it lacked the element of intersectionality, which is key to any appeal to black pain.

Placing political parties or organisations in the position of having to adapt or change their ideology in search of relevance in the long run damages the movement's ability to mobilise. Organisations may choose to abdicate responsibility from the broader movement to run their own programmes or reject the dynamic nature of black pain and seek to reform it into something that represents their own views more. Others may seek to appease notions of black pain without truly seeking to understand it. The ability for black pain to circumvent the need for political parties or organisations eventually makes the political parties the long-term threat to the unity of the movement. The role of PASMA is probably the best example of this.

PASMA, desperate for increased control of the student movement, opened its doors to Fallists and Fallism, believing the ideology to be in unison with its own. PASMA influence within Fallism grew at institutions where the EFFSC did not have a presence. The delegitimisation of SRCs and removal of the PYA within #FeesMustFall played into their hands as they used the movement to spread their message. Recitations of 'Izwe Lethu' and the traditional right-palm salute of PASMA became common within the movement – the right-palm salute symbolising one's commitment to the five aims and objectives of the Pan-Africanist Congress. PASMA leaders grew in popularity in the country's HWIs, institutions where, historically, they had generally failed to find relevance. HWIs became PASMA's celebrity face for the movement. Their rise in popularity, however, was soon seen with disdain within PASMA and it wasn't long before these popular faces were ostracised in favour of students less inclined to support Fallists or be apologetic of the Fallists' attempts to discredit PASMA. PASMA would eventually find itself partnering with the EFFSC (though clashes between the two were not uncommon, especially at TUT) as the EFFSC became the primary political organisation within #FeesMustFall. The EFFSC aligned themselves with Fallists out of convenience rather than necessity. However, Fallists saw through PASMA's façade. They labelled the organisation as patriarchal and anti-women, and in so doing limited the role PASMA would play on a national level.

Although PASMA is just one example, the role of black men in the protest movement indicated a further limitation of the use of black pain as an authoritative device because of its inability to discern the intentions of a narrator – who sings the right tune – because of the narrator's ability to change what one conceptualises as black pain. The intent of the narrator becomes focused on maintaining the Pre-emptive thesis rather than on ensuring that one's authority is only due to one's conception of black pain that remains dependent on students' experiences. By focusing on the Pre-emptive thesis, many black males failed to maintain the Normal Justification thesis as they increasingly used their own deliberations to determine their actions rather than students' deliberations.

Internal fighting among Fallists was driven by the changing dynamic of the interpretation of black pain by students countrywide. The core fault of using black pain as an authoritative device is that it does not give authority to student leaders to lead or issue directives to students, because no one person or organisation can grasp the ubiquitous nature of black pain and maintain the Dependence thesis. Student leaders in PASMA didn't disregard the notion of Black Radical Feminism but would claim that BRF only dealt with the symptoms of society's ills. Of primary concern to PASMA was the land question, while PYA would be of the view that free education should be focused on the working class and poor. All three – Fallists, the EFFSC and PASMA – would argue that education should be free for all students.

As troublesome as the use of black pain as an authoritative device has been, it has not stopped students utilising the experience of being black as the justification for their authority to mobilise, even if it comes at the expense of the long-term unity of the movement. Although there are other reasons to explain the current malaise within the various #MustFall movements, the continued attempts to lead on the authority of black pain continues to tear the movement apart at the seams, unravelling its unity.

Chapter 15

Violent Delights, Violent Ends

There is a peculiar turn of phrase often used by the media to describe the evolving nature of a protest. Peculiar because of the assumptions the media generally make about protest action. It goes along the lines of 'The protest turned violent'. It is a comment which, while trying to explain the evolution of a protest, subdues all the complexities within it. It is an off-hand way to describe how the intensity of a protest evolves from a peaceful gathering into a confrontational interaction with some form of authority without having to explain the power dynamics at play. As such it is misleading. It places the assumption of guilt on the shoulders of protesters, vilifying them while deifying police officers who were 'able to quell' the violence.

The violent and dissociative nature of #FeesMustFall in 2016 was the result of the unlearning and relearning process of understanding the role of violence in a post-Marikana society. In addition to this, violence became an opioid for all involved. Our means of escape and our means of release. Violence between students and police, between institutions, and even among students themselves, all contributed to a cycle in which violence begot violence. This is a vicious cycle unlikely to be halted without one side eventually winning the fight and, even then, never really guaranteed.

Throughout 2016 and 2017, #MustFall movements became enamoured with violence. Sometimes this was righteous, occasionally vindictive and, more often than not, quite ugly.

My dad uses a personal anecdote to describe how violence can intertwine within one's soul, corrupting the incorruptible, strengthening the meek and imbuing cowards with a level of bravery they didn't know they possessed. He harks back to 1985, a different time in the country, when finding out that you were on an apartheid hit list had become a norm in our society. One such hit list, a collection of community organisers and activists all linked as threats to the apartheid state, contained fourteen names. My father's and Archbishop Desmond Tutu's were two of them. My father was under house arrest at the time awaiting his treason trial. The community caught heed of the danger he was in and organised a deployment of individuals to my parents' home to protect them and my brothers. Numerous men would sit outside our home throughout the night and day with the sole purpose of providing the first line of defence. My dad recounts the moment he realised the men were armed to the hilt. When he enquired why they had brought arms onto his premises, they were bemused. 'Moruti,' they replied, 'how else did you think we were protecting you?'

For my father, the mere presence of weapons on the property would have legitimised the apartheid regime's claims that he was a violent risk to their authority. At the time, he remained a proponent of a non-violent approach to change. If apartheid's agents were indeed to storm the property, he alongside many others protecting the home would have been deemed to have 'turned violent' and it would have been the responsibility of the state to 'quell' said violence. The mere act of arming oneself would have been construed as violent in the eyes of the state and the public. Whether you were righteous in your belief about protecting yourself, in the eyes of 'legitimate' authority, your turning to violence, whether in self-defence or otherwise, would be enough proof for your public condemnation.

My dad dismissed those surrounding the house, claiming that he would send his family away instead, placing their safety as his top priority. However, my mother, the monarch of the home, refused to go. She said she would not be intimidated by any government that sought to harm the meek and vulnerable. She insisted that this was her home and neither she nor her children would be forced to run away from it. My father recounts the time as being particularly difficult for him. With two young children in his care, a wife whose immense courage often engulfed his own and an apartheid state threatening his life, he wondered how he would be able to protect his family. He thought to himself that if the apartheid state were to come into his home in the dead of the night with the intent of killing him and his family, then he hoped he would have his own gun in hand. He hoped he would have the courage to fire one shot and bring one person down. Not because he wanted revenge against the state, but because he wanted to leave proof that he had fought back. Proof that he and his family had not been taken away without a fight. Proof to inspire others by showing them that they had resisted until the bitter end.

My father is one of the most peaceful men I have ever encountered, but violent intent fell over his soul that day. His story shows how violence in the hands of the weak and vulnerable, even if only fuelled by intent, is often deemed unacceptable and reprehensible. It's a story that highlights how in the face of looming violence, defending oneself becomes of paramount importance and, in times of violence that threaten one's revolutionary desires, the need to show that you resisted, that you fought back. In the face of impending violence, even the most righteous will consider some form of retaliation. Over the past few years, I have watched the most timid students turn into some of the movement's fiercest foot soldiers. I have watched students turn from 'protest cows' into presidents of SRCs leading the charge against institutional violence and discrimination.

The story of #FeesMustFall between 2016 and 2017 is a story about how violence begets violence and how far people will go to defend their legitimate use of violence. Whether it be students running through the streets of Johannesburg engaging in clashes with police, a university hiring private militia to protect the institution at all costs, or police officers shooting student leaders nine times in the back in the name of quelling the violence, the evidence was everywhere. If 2015 signalled the start of the revolution, the next two years tested our appetite for it. It constantly asked the question:

how willing were we to forgo our humanity to achieve our goal?

The first turn to violence happened in Cape Town on 16 February 2016 and set the tone for the protests over the next few months. The #Shackville protests that rocked UCT were the result of a combination of rage-filled students with good intent acting out their rage with no restraint. The burning of portraits, the torching of a university bus and vehicle and the eventual petrol bombing of the vice-chancellor's office were all entirely avoidable moments of madness that were fuelled by the changing behaviour of the university towards protesters.

The beginning of 2016 was particularly tough for UCT as they were caught in the eye of a perfect storm. Portraying the image of calm to the university community, while in reality the institution was in turmoil, was a challenge. Tensions between #RhodesMustFall and UCT was at an all-time high. #RMF had out-manoeuvred the management team of UCT at every corner throughout 2015. From the occupying of Azania House, storming the Council meeting, hijacking the university Assembly, the removal of the statue of Rhodes, turning public sympathy away from the university, and forcing the university to embark on a process of insourcing, time after time students demonstrated a level of political nuance that UCT and Vice-Chancellor Max Price simply couldn't compete with.

The December break gave the institution a slight reprieve, but at the beginning of 2016 they were forced to contend with #RhodesMustFall once more. This time #RMF set their focus on the residential administration building, Avenue House. Keeping to their modus operandi of occupation and highlighting the plight of black students on campus, #RMF began to voice their concerns about the availability of on-campus accommodation.

Every year UCT embarks on what can best be described as a controlled free-fall when it comes to the provision of on-campus accommodation for students. Each year thousands of would-be applicants to UCT hope and pray for a spot in the residential system, which is chronically short on available beds needed to match the demand. To a potential student who not only lives outside of Cape Town but outside the confines of the city's Southern Suburbs, where UCT is located, securing a place in the residence system provides a variety of benefits when compared to an off-campus living situation. To manage this conundrum, the university over-subscribes the residential system and institutes a set of protocols and mechanisms to regulate the surplus until alternative arrangements are made for the 'vagrant' students. It is an imperfect system and one that disproportionately affects poor black students as one of its unintended consequences.

In 2016 the situation was made markedly worse and unmanageable because of three factors. The first was that #FeesMustFall in 2015 raised the expectancy among university applicants that there would be an increase in available financial aid, as well as the possibility of 'lower' fees for the year. As a result, there had been a boom in applications for residence places, creating a larger than usual over-subscription in the system. Secondly, due to the success of the protests the previous year to not only shut down universities but delay the academic programme, more students were writing deferred exams at the beginning of 2016 than usual. These students, primarily housed by UCT, delayed the subsequent allocation of available beds to new applicants. Lastly, UCT had embarked on a process of clearing the historical debt afflicting certain students, thereby further increasing the number of returning students to UCT and a consequent increase in the demand for beds.[1]

The stand-off at Avenue House was especially odd because of the 'peace treaty' that had been agreed upon by UCT and #RhodesMustFall the previous year. The treaty allowed for #RMF to occupy the unused hall next to Avenue House, with the proviso that the movement would not engage in occupation-politics again. A proviso that would obviously be ignored. This is important to note because it exhibits UCT's willingness to engage with #RMF but also how frequently it succumbed to the demands of the movement. It was frequently negotiating with a gun to its head. The university had constantly been on the back foot and, with the occupation of Avenue House, it was placed in this position once again. UCT implored #RMF to halt their occupation because they were disrupting the work of the administrators designated to solve the crisis. In my opinion, it was a poor choice of tactic by #RMF, something they would realise themselves by the end of the day when they chose to stop the occupation in favour of something more dramatic. The occupation, however, set the tone of the year between student protesters at UCT and the university administration. In addition, and probably most importantly, it forced the university to rethink the diplomatic manner it had engaged with #RhodesMustFall into something more antagonistic.

On Monday, 15 February, #RMF erected a shack on campus as a symbol of the homelessness afflicting students who found themselves without accommodation. The corrugated-iron structure with its compatriot portable toilet alongside struck a jarring image on campus. The ivy-covered walls of UCT provided the backdrop to the poverty-laden imagery of the shack. Located at the base of Jameson Steps, positioned deliberately to disrupt traffic on campus, the structure caused a fair amount of confusion. #RMF used the shack as not only a symbol but a practical space to reside on campus and host plenary meetings for the public to participate in. The whole exercise proved to be an effective tool for highlighting the housing crisis at UCT. It also provoked the university into action.

The university issued a cease-and-desist letter to #RhodesMustFall the day after the shack went up, ordering them to move it a few metres back so as not to disrupt the flow of traffic. #RMF refused and stood firm. The letter elicited a variety of reactions from the movement's disciples. I describe them as disciples because, at this point, the movement had attracted a cult-like following. Dogmatic to a fault and holding onto an idea that they alone could build the society they envisioned, people flocked to the movement. It was this influx that would change the dynamic of the organisation. The political education that had taken place the year before, during the occupation of Azania House, in particular, was replaced with more populist rhetoric. In addition, customs were used to entrench beliefs within the movement rather than challenge notions of oppression not only within society but within the movement as well. A culture had been brewing which shunned the notion of individual accountability, and the use of the notion of black pain had the unintended consequence of permitting a person's actions, if these were in contravention of the spirit of #RhodesMustFall, to avoid having to face internal disciplining. Pleading black pain created a culture in which some students were not just allowed but were implicitly encouraged to act with reckless abandon. One's expression of black pain shouldn't be policed by anyone. Whether strategic or not. #RhodesMustFall had begun to stop creating advocates for change; instead, it attracted disciples of its ideals.

This was best seen through the reclamation of the movement by the womxn earlier in the year, who chose to remove all men in #RhodesMustFall until they'd acknowledged the violence being perpetrated against women in the movement. The claim was that the men in #RMF had created a level of toxicity which stopped any form of discussion about the role of patri-archy in the movement in its tracks and resulted in several instances of sexual assault and the erasure of women within the movement. The advo-cates for change during 2015 had periodically been reflective of their own behaviour as a source of understanding the societal problems they were fighting to change. In 2015, the request by women for #RhodesMustFall to be more reflexive was met with plenary sessions meant to educate men. In 2016, disciples believing their word alone was morally just, would ignore these calls. The hubris that had taken over the organisation percolated even to their lowliest members. #RhodesMustFall could do no wrong in the eyes of its foot soldiers.

The demand by the university for #RMF to shift their shack caused fierce debate. Some believed that to move the structure to a less disruptive location only a few metres away would not take away from students' goals and ambitions. Others, the disciples, argued that moving the shack would be ceding to the university's authority, which was the antithesis of the movement's spirit. In the end, the request, though reasonable, was roundly rejected by #RhodesMustFall, who stood firm, refusing to halt their pro-test action. What took place over the next several hours was in effect a running battle between #RMF and the police force across the university campus. It led to the burning of portraits, torching of university vehicles and student buses, petrol bombing the vice-chancellor's office and the use of rubber bullets and stun grenades on campus in scenes that would have been unimaginable on UCT's campuses even during apartheid. Both #RhodesMustFall and UCT as an institution turned to violence as a means of expression and imposition of their will on the university.

For UCT, the use of private security and police during the previous year's #FeesMustFall protest was already an indicator of their intent to quell protest action. The institution's turn to violence had happened already. What was new this time was their focus on what looked to be the targeting of individual student leaders. In the past, they had used court interdicts to identify who they believed were the true student leaders in #RhodesMustFall's horizontal leadership structure. This became the tool for university management teams to maintain, at least in their eyes, the legal high ground, albeit a high ground built on the ashes of whatever moral authority they had tried to claim during the protests. Interdicts were used publicly to announce the names of those students who they believed were the biggest threats to the institution. While in 2015 this was primarily used as a fear tactic, in 2016 universities chose to use interdicts to turn the spotlight directly on individuals they wanted the police to arrest.

In addition to the use of interdicts, universities across the country markedly began to improve the way they communicated with the broader university community. They had realised that one of the greatest strengths of #RhodesMustFall and #FeesMustFall was their ability to control the narrative of their protest action through social media. Now university communication departments were given carte blanche to control the narrative of the protest from their side. Normal chains of command to disseminate information were replaced with minute-by-minute updates. This was another tool to not only gain control of the war of words between protesters and management but a means of demonstrating universities' authority over students. UCT used this tactic to great effect during #Shackville. 'Between the 16th and 17th of February, UCT issued nine separate updates addressing each event and issue on campus as it unfolded. This included the housing crisis, the shack itself, the burning of the paintings, and information about the university student transport buses, Jammie shuttles, having been set alight. The University made it clear in these web updates that they condemned the actions and would not tolerate such forms of protest.'[2]

For #RhodesMustFall, the events following the erection of #Shackville led to their first public and overt display of violence. The violence, which permeated into the public arena, came about because certain disciples wanted to take matters into their own hands. Riding the wave of group-think, a group of disciples stormed Fuller Hall, one of UCT's oldest residences (built in 1928), demanding that the dining hall feed hungry students. Fuller Hall, draped in ivy and looking out over the same view afforded to Rhodes's statue for decades, stood as a proud monument of UCT's colonial history. Named after Maria Fuller, one of the first women to enrol at UCT, it was built to evoke memories of its distant collegial cousins in Oxford and Cambridge. Its red brick walls, lush yet manicured court-yards and private gardens all paid homage to its Oxbridge roots.

Protesters made their way into the dining hall, feasting on the spoils of conquest. The ominous presence of colonial imagery surrounding them began to hang heavy over their heads. It's unclear who first made the charge, but I can only imagine the fury they must have felt when looking upon the walls of Fuller Hall's dining room. The anger you must feel at pro-testing for an institutional and cultural change of the university and right next to the site of your protest is one of the university's boldest symbols of its colonial history. Soon the hall's paintings were being stripped from the walls, dragged outside, placed in a pile in the middle of the parking lot and set aflame. The glow from the fire was mirrored by students' burning desire to continue the onslaught on all colonial imagery across the univer-sity, and soon students stormed Jan Smuts Hall – the male replica of Fuller Hall – and Jameson Hall, grabbing all the artwork they could. Unlike the year before, when the desire to remove the statue was tempered by some of us, this year tempers were allowed to boil over. Who within the move-ment had the authority to say no? To do so would have been to challenge the other students' notion of black pain and deny their expression. As the flames grew and onlookers watched, #RhodesMustFall turned violent – not violence in a physical sense, but symbolic and psychological.

The event was meant to invoke a level of terror within the university. The burning of portraits, whether #RMF intended to or not, showed the lengths to which the movement was willing to go to achieve its goals. It was a warning shot to the university. The shot was not ignored. Police soon descended on the scene. At first, they stood by idly watching protest-ers singing and dancing around their burning effigy. The 5 pm deadline imposed by the university to move the shack came and went. Students and police watched each other uneasily. Police officers clad in body armour, students equipped with All Star sneakers, all waiting for the other to make the first move.

It would be two hours past the deadline before that first move was made. It came not from students or police officers, but from UCT's private security. The private militia-esque group moved on the shack with the clear intention of removing it. In response, students began to huddle around the structure, with some even trying to dismantle it themselves. Eventually, the police joined the fray and began to assist the private security by releasing a stun grenade to disperse students and move them away from the structure. Attempts to defend the shack were to no avail and it was swiftly toppled. In the confusion of clashes between students and police officers and the private arrests of certain student leaders by UCT's private security firm (Athabile Nonxuba was one), a conservation vehicle was set ablaze. This act would be the first of a variety of arson-related attacks on the university that night.

The importance of the #Shackville moment was that it set the stage for the public crucifixion of #RhodesMustFall. A crucifixion that would set the tone for how the country would view instances of violence – which would continue periodically over the next two years – and affect the public's ability to sympathise with students. Furthermore, the crucifixion allowed for a new movement to be created, one that was markedly different from #FeesMustFall of 2015. Public sympathy, already strained at the time, officially turned against the movement as the destruction of public property and the burning of portraits forced the public into a corner. Either the public would agree with the tactics of #RMF, or they would have to denounce them. The nuance that created the moral ambiguity within the public sphere about the role #RMF in 2015 was all but erased. As Sisonke Msimang eloquently wrote after the events of #Shackville:

[#RhodesMustFall] found a way to demonstrate the symbolism of the colony and to shake the country out of the complacency of accepting the intolerable. They must also know that when you begin to destroy art

(regardless of its quality or who made it) the collateral damage is always,
always far more bloody and self-harming than you can immediately see.
A movement must see beyond the here and now; beyond the catharsis
of immediate disturbance. Catharsis has its own power but it must not
be mistaken for power. What is done in the name of a movement either
build it or haunts it.[3]

#RhodesMustFall incorrectly saw #Shackville as a moment of strength; what it was was a moment of weakness. Some within the movement who had spearheaded the reclamation a few weeks before claimed that it was a weakness driven by the toxic masculinity within the movement. But that would belie the truth of the womxn who were central in the burning of the portraits. Others claimed it was a group of stray students who caused the damage; however, many of the movement's most prominent leaders were present, egging students on, and many of those 'stray' students were the movement's more ardent disciples. #RMF lost control of itself. At that moment it became less concerned with controlling the public narrative of #RMF and more concerned with writing its own. Their narrative, however, was widely rejected and denounced. Rather than placing the judgemental gaze of the public on the university's management team, #RhodesMustFall placed the gaze on themselves, turning many of their ardent supporters into silent detractors. Violence engulfed #RMF on that fateful day and the movement revelled in it.

#RhodesMustFall was not alone in this regard. Students, police, private security, university management teams, academics, and workers across the country all found ways to justify the use of violence. The use of violence became sanguine within the context of the protest. It became the only language that held currency as the political discourse between stakeholders began to break down. For students, it was about the right to protest and access to education, whereas for the university management teams across the country it was about the right to protect their property and the individuals on their property. On each side of the fence, the use of violence had become normalised and in some cases was actively encouraged. Students often feigned ignorance about the less palatable aspects of the movement while simultaneously deploying 'militant groups' with the purpose of organised violence and then claiming that the actions of these groups did not reflect the broader student movement. In turn, police officers hid behind the guise of ensuring the public's safety to justify their actions. University management teams utilised private security as their designated foot soldiers, creating a buffer between themselves and acts of violence deemed necessary to protect the institution. Everyone had a hand in contributing to the violence on campus, but some more than others.

My training is not in the fields of sociology, psychology or anthropology and I would never proclaim/feign to be an expert or authority on something as complex as decolonisation. It would be hubris for me to do so and, frankly, hubris for any young scholar to do so. Simply reading *The Wretched of the Earth* does not make you an expert on decolonisation. Neither will a reading of *I Write What I Like* make you an expert on Black Consciousness. My contention with this positioning aside, throughout the rise of #MustFall politics, the growth of student authorities on these vast and deep concepts mushroomed their way through the movement. I watched students go from barely passing their first-year public administration classes to waxing lyrical about the black condition overnight.

Writers such as Frantz Fanon, Amilcar Cabral, Steve Biko, Maya Angelou, Kimberlé Crenshaw, Robert Sobukwe, Albert Memmi, Walter Mignolo, Toni Morrison – all became common names within the movement. Quoting them became a form of the currency. Without this ability, any exchange of ideas within the movement would not be possible. As a result, the need to gain currency became the primary prerogative of many students. While some embarked on this process better to understand themselves in relation to the world, others embarked on it to gain enough currency to exchange these ideas for influence. Either way, the pursuit of knowledge frequently drove the intensity of student engagements in plenary sessions and would eventually create the logical steps required to justify student violence.

Gaining currency provided you with the ammunition either to scatter-gun your way into prominence, by throwing any and every idea you had out into the open, or become a sniper, waiting for the perfect moment to make your point. Others adopted a more reserved, nuclear-deterrent approach, becoming prominent not because they demonstrated their knowledge, but because others believed they held a large arsenal of it. Academics fell into the pattern as well, each trying to showcase their knowledge of a field to curry favour with students.

The need to become an authority on decolonisation, oppression, Pan-Africanism, Intersectionality, Black Radical Feminism and the history of the apartheid struggle became a sort of arms race within the movement. But as is seen with any arms race throughout human history, the need to arm as a means to influence becomes less important and more of a by-product of the desire to be better armed. It is addictive in nature. Fanon as a catchall for many of the ideas that made their way through the movement became an opioid of the masses. An opiate we all became addicted to in our own ways.

In my case, my opioid was decoloniality. Decoloniality is the undoing of what Walter Mignolo explains as the darker side of modernity, coloniality. I began my Honours year at the University of Cape Town in 2015 focused on understanding how state policy treated Umkhonto weSizwe and South African National Defence Force veterans after the end of apartheid. This was not necessarily my passion at the time, but a useful use of my research skills. Notions of black consciousness and decolonisation had been recreational vices, a way to escape the world for a moment, to damp down the pain of discrimination by creating a means for understanding it. I, like most students at the university, never embarked on the study of decolonisation, oppression, or discrimination as a day-to-day activity. I knew the university was filled with many moral and ethical contradictions, but my experience of the place – and arguably of society as a whole – was not linked to understanding the theoretical minutiae of it. It was experiential in nature, learning by doing and feeling.

With the advent of #RhodesMustFall, however, the notion of decoloniality began to grip my imagination. Suddenly, I found myself keenly discussing issues of how knowledge disseminated in our classes, evaluated in our curriculum and generated by those who claimed to be its custodians, became unreliable sources of truth whose veracity had to be

223

questioned. The occupation of Azania House pushed my understanding of my social environment away from the experiential and into the predictive. I was no longer learning by doing and feeling; I was predicting and acting on these predictions to see the results of my actions. I was no longer trying to understand the university's culture; I was actively testing its existence. I could no longer rely on a simple understanding of my environment. For my experiments, I required the theoretical tools as well.

Unlike the modernist approach, which would see the locus of the experiment as the object of study and my role as the neutral observer of its results, I became the subject of the experiment, actively benefiting from the results of my tests. Benefits that translated into a better understanding of the condition of my blackness within the university. The more I learned, the better I became at understanding my social reality, dampening the pain of feeling that the world arbitrarily treated black people unjustly and changing my response to this pain. Decoloniality became my opioid. The same way that Black Radical Feminism, Fanon, Black Consciousness, Biko, Pan-Africanism and Intersectionality, among other subjects, became the opioids of thousands of students in South Africa.

By understanding the tools to treat it, they became the means for many to lessen the pain of the world. We began to exchange ideas (for example, why would decoloniality be the only way in which I could understand the world and lessen its pain?) and the more we exchanged, the more we equipped ourselves with techniques to better understand and as a result be better placed to translate these ideas to others. It will not work in your favour to limit your ideas to only your social network. To exchange ideas with a broader community opens the doors to new and better insights. Azania House became a hub of knowledge sharing. It was an incubator of ideas and beliefs, all feeding off each other, creating an endless source of feedback to generate new ideas. The space had no perceivable equilibrium point. Soon enough, however, some began to realise that being able to not only disseminate knowledge but also to generate it allowed for you to grow in prominence within the movement. You became the means of easing the pain of being black in a society because you were able to equip people with the tools to lower the number of pain signals our social reality was emitting. By engaging in what is often described as 'oppression Olympics', those with the highest level of layered oppression would eventually become the leaders of the movement. Though this was a butchering of the notion of intersectionality, it still managed to take root within the movement. Thus, if you were a black, transgender, low-income member of the movement, you held greater authority in it than a black, woman, low-income member of the movement. You not only became the authority within the move-ment but through the notion of black pain, you became above critique. You had gained enough currency of ideas to exchange as ideological capital to shield you from critique.

Our quest to deepen our knowledge led to a growing addiction to using Fanon as the opioid to dull the pain of a social and physical reality that made us feel less human than others. Not as an escape but as a tool. Our continued use of this opioid would eventually lead to the misrecognition of the dulling of pain with a feeling of pleasure. We gained pleasure from our sudden enlightenment, a pleasure we would fight tooth and nail to maintain. Soon ideas that challenged our addiction were shut out. The more we perceived the world through a lens of injustice, the more pleasure we gained from it. We marched because we knew we had to fight, but we marched because we enjoyed the feeling of challenging the injustice of the world. We would defend this at all costs not only because we had taught ourselves that what we were doing was righteous, but also because we were addicted to it. Cut us from our opioid of choice, and you cut us from our belief of what makes us feel genuinely human.

Our justification for the use of violence was predicated on the addiction and defence of our use of the opioid of 'Fanon' to understand our society. The rhetoric used to justify the violence that would play out had a vari-ety of forms. One was the belief that our violence was due to the violent environment in which a black child grows up; that to be violent was only a response and a product of the violence that surrounded us all our lives. Coconuts, who would not have lived through the physical violence of pov-erty, embraced the notion of symbolic violence as the justification to be violent ourselves. Another common justification for violence was that we were embarking on a process of decolonisation. Because colonisation was a violent process, its undoing would in turn require a violent act. I could list other ways in which we justified violence in our actions, but most of them were informed by a theoretical idea of what violence is and because it had become something of an addictive reality.

Now, this is not to say that some instances and acts of violence perpetrated by students were not simply done in moments of madness. Or that the torching of vehicles or libraries were not premeditated acts of aggression. Organisations such as Black First Land First willingly engaged in reckless abandon, under the belief that their actions were righteous. Instead I wish to show how the knee-jerk reaction to justify the use of violence by students was primarily borne by our need to extricate ourselves from responsibility, because the theoretical conceptions of our social and physical reality we had become addicted to, and which we used to rationalise our world, dictated that we were victims of violence and never its perpetrators. This last point is crucial because I believe it is why students, bar specific incidences, are often never the first to use violence. Our need to be victims of violence necessitated a use of force against us for us to react and understand our world and circumstances further. It resembles the testing of scientific proofs. The proof in this instance is that black students are treated worse than other groupings by authorities when they advocate for a change in their circumstances. We may have antagonised the police, but we never dared throw the first stone. We left that responsibility to them.

South Africa's police force carries itself with unearned confidence, worn to mask the faults in its ranks. In South Africa's post-Marikana society, the role of the police has been under increased scrutiny. Reverberations from the events that took place on 16 August 2012, which resulted in the death of 34 mineworkers at the hands of South Africa's police force, were far-reaching. They would inform how students perceived the police during the student protests. Reference to the Marikana Massacre became a common trope within the various #MustFall movements. Students understood that the police's need to ensure public safety also meant that it would become open season on them. For many, the police service before Marikana was a symbol of protection and servitude regardless of their inefficiencies, but after Marikana this was no longer the case. The police became a threat to your life.

The police played a vastly different role during the protests in 2016 and 2017 and posed what could and should be regarded as the greatest threat to academic freedom in South Africa since the end of apartheid. The use of the police after 2015 was not to ensure public safety but to censure the political expression of students. It is the only rationale for why police acts of overt aggression in 2015 were limited to sporadic incidents, but over the following years, they became routine. Police Nyalas on campus didn't strike an image of protection, but rather an image of fear. It was a calculated tactic to intimidate students, not to calm tensions. The presence of police on a university campus should never be a norm in our society. Their mere presence goes against the principles of what a university should be. It goes against the cornerstones of academic freedom; with every officer on campus a small piece of that freedom is chipped away. The presence of police on campus doesn't necessarily lead to the censure of academia, but its normalisation opens the door to such an outcome. These attacks against our freedoms in university spaces are never undertaken in big leaps, but small steps in the right direction. This is not to say that students are wholly innocent and should not be accused of denying the expression of academic freedom of others, but students can't use state authority against the university to censure them.

It is under this façade of ensuring the public's safety that police have often been given a get-out-of-jail-free card when it comes to how they act and respond to protest action. I have always wondered how our police force could be so easily antagonised into a physical response by a group of teenagers and 20-something-year-olds. But I think the question I should be asking is how they could justify using violence against unarmed civilians. How could they justify shooting a student nine times in the back, disrupting night vigils with rubber bullets and stun grenades, enforcing apartheid-era curfews, storming residence buildings to make arrests, making priests acceptable collateral damage, throwing stun grenades at seated students, threatening any small gathering of students to disperse immediately or face their wrath, arresting students at will as a deterrent rather than for any probable cause, pepper-spraying a student sitting on the floor reading a Bible ... the list goes on and on. The justification for any form of police action usually falls within some derivative of 'they are ensuring the public safety of others'.

The use of force by the police against students was neither proportional, nor did it meet any of the principles of necessity. I acknowledge that it might be unfair retrospectively to harshly criticise the split-second decisions made by those under intense pressure. I would never want to make the foot soldiers of the war the villains of the tale. After all, many of those who raised arms against us were the same mothers and fathers who lifted us up. By the same token, it would be disingenuous simply to vilify vice-chancellors for allowing the presence of police on campus. In the circumstances, I understand why they would request their assistance. The hostile environment created by students would strike fear into most people. However, the claim that the use of police on campus is to ensure public safety should not be used to justify the assumption that students have a predisposition towards violence. Often just the presence of police on campus further affirms a confirmation bias that's already there in the university: that any gathering of students, and in particular black students, will naturally result in acts of aggression.

It is this confirmation bias that drove many vice-chancellors to employ the services of private security firms. Students saw these as the institutions' private militia on campus. Vice-chancellors and their senior executive teams realised the limitations of their decision-making capabilities on campus when police clashed with students. The imposition of private security was the result. The default position of VCs was to expect the worst, an expectation which informed the way police would subsequently handle students. However, vice-chancellors, as civilians, were not permitted to issue directives to the police (and rightly so) but they bore the brunt of the responsibility for their actions on campus. As a result, often, they became spectators in the ongoing chaos between police and students. With their influence constrained to discussions with liaison officers from SAPS (usually of lieutenant colonel or colonel rank), VCs lost control of the protection of their universities. Liaison officers became on the ground commanders-in-chief and remained focused on ensuring public order and the gathering of any information pertinent to the persecution of students in contravention of the law. The purpose of the police force wasn't to keep the university open but to maintain order. A purpose whose ends didn't match those of the university.

The temptation to invoke a level of violence was not always an all-consuming addiction, however. There were numerous examples where students, police and academics all showed restraint and refrained from using violence as their opioid. The most fascinating of the moments, for me, concerned medical students involved in the protest and their dilemma about whether they should continue with the protest or return to caring for their patients. Final-year medical students had to take into consideration whether, as was claimed, there would indeed be a chronic and damaging effect on South Africa's health care system if they failed to complete their studies and begin their compulsory year of community service. The perception that the health care system would be adversely affected fertilised the ground for a compelling debate on the actual lengths one would go to to achieve the goal of free quality decolonial education.

For the first time, there were tangible consequences to student action directly affecting the worst-off of the country. The dilemma sparked a variety of debates. The first focused on the responsibility of medical students to their patients. This is not to say that university students hold the lives of their patients in their hands; rather it is a question of their moral responsibility towards their patients' well-being. Should you embark on protest action and not tend to your patients or should you tend to your patients at the expense of not protesting alongside your fellow students? All medical students take a version of the Hippocratic Oath when they begin their studies, a commitment to not do harm to their patients. But how do you reconcile this responsibility with what some believe to be the actions that would enable the liberation of a country? I don't wish to exaggerate the circumstances; what I want to do with this example is highlight the thinking behind the debates.

The second debate revolved around the notion that a national shutdown meant that all aspects of all universities would be halted, no exceptions.

No faculty, department or administrative activity would be permitted to continue so long as the demands of students were not met. The debate this 'no exceptions' rule produced was about whether it was morally justified to use medical students as a bargaining chip. A pressure point of sorts. They, compared to most students, represented the most immediate macro-level threat to the functioning of the state. Not in a hypothetical revolution-in-our-lifetime sense, but a real-time, day-to-day threat to the functioning of the country's health care system. At some universities, a sustained national shutdown, without an adequate intervention plan by management teams, meant that final-year medical students would not be able to graduate on time. This delay would have a serious ripple effect across the board with regard to the community service provided to rural clinics and hospitals by new graduates. Students, aware of the repercussions, were forced to reconcile how far they might be willing to push the protest and what exemptions, if any, would be acceptable. Would they be willing to risk the lives of the black bodies they sought to provide with economic freedom by denying them a 'well' functioning health care system?

It should be said that the argument that the entire health care system would be crippled by a decision to continue the protest is both exaggerated and ideologically verbose. This argument is best seen as a scare tactic. It was not an honest assessment of the situation. However, at that moment the threat felt real. It was in this light that the debates played out at UCT and other universities with medical schools and revealed the true strength of students' resolve to embark on protest action. This resolve was not informed by myopic views of revolutions, but through the realist lens that dictated that change of any sort within a society is difficult. Hard choices must be made, and sacrifices to your integrity often have to be incurred. What defines a revolution in the eyes of the public is usually determined by the decisions you make when faced with a conundrum that not only threatens the humanity of others but, more importantly, affects your own humanity as well. What violence will you inflict on yourself to achieve your chimurenga?

Acknowledging that this was not a question you could answer for someone else, that it was something individuals would have to ask of themselves, it was decided that the only people who could decide whether medics should continue with the shutdown would be medics themselves. As such, final-year UCT medics were invited to a plenary meeting. In one of the more memorable plenaries for many of UCT's student leaders, a debate about the morality of #FeesMustFall began. On one side, you had students advocating that if we are willing to harm the people we claim to be fighting for, then what is our purpose? How can we fight for black people, but deny them health care at the same time? What is our role in building a new society when we can so easily discard those we care for the most to achieve our goals? On the other side, you had students advocating that no revolution is without its casualties. It was indeed a romanticism of what a revolution is, but it remained a valid claim none the less. Throughout #FeesMustFall (and to an extent #RhodesMustFall) you were often forced to ask yourself how far you were willing to go to support the cause. The quickest response to this positioning was by one student who stood up and pointedly requested those in defence of the revolution being violent whether they were willing to let their mothers die? Another student responded immediately, saying that South Africa's health care system had already failed his mother (she had apparently died in a failing hospital). The back and forth continued as students grappled with the notion of to what ends were they fighting, and should the means used to achieve these always be just?

Eventually, it was decided that medics should have their own private meeting to come to a common agreement among themselves about their course of action. The morality of the movement was, in essence, deferred to a group of medics. The meeting was closed to all other students to ensure that medics were able to deliberate among themselves. It was a moment that showed how #MustFall movements acknowledged that they could not dictate someone else's humanity. I can only imagine the intensity of the room at that time, the discussions that ensued and the self-reflection that was required of those medical students. They came out of the meeting having taken the decision to continue with the shutdown.

One could go on and on about the various instances of violence bubbling over during the protests. Some were more egregious than others, but all were encompassed within the unrelenting spiral of violence that had gripped the protest. Some found joy in it, while others found despair. Regardless, it held onto our imagination like a vice, often dictating our motivations. No one was immune, but some were better at resisting its consequences than others.

Chapter 16

Should Coconuts be Trusted with the Revolution?

I don't want to give the impression that #FeesMustFall was a coconut revolution. This certainly was never the case and would be an insult to the many students who sacrificed their futures for the belief that they could change the lives of others. #MustFall movements, through the essence of their motives to achieve economic freedom in our lifetime, cannot and should not be considered a coconut revolution. However, to deny the influence of coconuts and the black elite, both political and economic, within the movement would be to pretend that snakes don't hide in tall grass. We don't lie in wait because we want to betray the masses; we lie in wait because we can. We have been trained to do it our entire lives. It protects us from the glare of a post-apartheid society while affording us the opportunity to prowl South Africa's post-1994 society unnoticed. Benefiting from the certain privileges it creates for us, while avoiding most of its worst consequences. That being said, though coconuts have been afforded the privilege to mask ourselves under the guise of being 'not one of those blacks', we still simultaneously face some of the realities of being 'one of those blacks'.

Our proximity to privilege, and whiteness, can also imbue us with a need to preserve it. We have been given a bite of true economic freedom in our lifetime, even though we know it remains a tasteless mirage. A mere illusion of the senses created to numb us from the pain of the reality of our society. From rooftop drinks in Sandton, dinners at the One&Only at the Waterfront in Cape Town, to embracing the gentrification of Maboneng in central Johannesburg, we embrace a world that only a few short decades ago would have been unimaginable. Spaces that provide a window into an existence that was reserved for a few. It would be a mistake to underestimate how much one would do to remain in a fantasy rather than return to reality and take the brunt of it. It is a dilemma not unique to coconuts or the black elite. If you were offered the opportunity to enjoy true freedom and all the fruit it bears, but you knew that failure to grasp it meant to enjoy nothing at all, where does this place you? How badly would you fight to ensure that even if all is lost in your attempts to achieve complete freedom, you could still return to life in your mirage? In fact, would you even know that you were trying to return at all?

Coconuts and the black elite, like any other group within #MustFall movements, will try to steer the movement in a direction that favours them best. But unlike other groups who compete for the soul of the #MustFall movements, we hide in the tall grass, hoping that no one sees us, yet banking on the knowledge that enough people can sense our presence. We unconsciously influence #MustFall politics to protect our self-interest under the impression that our acts are for the greater good. The presence of a bigger villain allows the gaze to turn away from us. We are asked questions we're never truly expected to answer and as a result, in the same way that we traverse our post-apartheid society, coconuts chart the landscape of #MustFall politics; cautious, conniving, curious and always cunning.

It is difficult to see ourselves as the enemy because we barely make it apparent even in our own eyes. During all my years of student activism, the greatest lesson I took with me was: never trust someone who wants to go to jail. Ironic as this might sound coming from me, I believe the urge to be jailed for your cause should undergo some interrogation. This is not to say that being detained for a cause should be a demerit. I am not saying here that those who were jailed were there for the fame and acclaim, although I also wouldn't say it's impossible either. However, people who actively seek to be jailed have either been jailed before and have no qualms about returning, or they have a get-out-of-jail-free card in their back pocket. Either way, their enthusiasm to be jailed should be a warning sign rather than a quality instinctively to be admired.

In my experience, the ones who have the get-out-of-jail-free card are the ones who are the keenest to be arrested. The card comes in various forms. For some, it's the possession of a political surname, knowing that you have the means to pay your bail, understanding how an arrest will or will not affect your future job prospects, scholarships and/or bursaries, or simply knowing that in the event of a trial you will be able to handle the long and arduous process. For others, it is simply not having to truly worry that your personal incarceration will impede the ability for your family to unshackle itself from its economic bondage.

The threat to #MustFall movements by coconuts and the black elite is neither direct nor upfront. It is cerebral. Like any good poker player, we never reveal our cards, unless we intend to. We influence the natural logic of these movements in such a way that their actions will not jeopardise our own ability to achieve economic freedom on our own accord. Our self-interest nurtures a desire to utilise both our access to resources and proximity to whiteness to maintain and grow our endowment of privileges. Whether it is through their ability to take control of plenaries, to provide resources to the movement, or as part of the silent majority of the silent majority, the black elite use their unique position in society to reinforce their need to achieve their own economic advancement. We are subtle in our influence but pervasive in our overall effect.

I came across this subtlety in an interesting conversation I had during #RhodesMustFall in 2015. The conversation brought to light the role of the black elite and coconuts in the movement and the influence they were beginning to have on decisions that were made. It took place during one of the more uneventful plenary sessions in the first few weeks of the occupation of Azania House. The session concerned logistics. I was pulled aside by someone I didn't know at the time who whispered that #RhodesMustFall was classist. Surprised at the blunt nature of her comment, I pressed her to explain. She went on to say that it made absolutely no sense to hold a plenary meeting on a Sunday afternoon. Realising that I was firmly in her crosshairs of criticism, I trod lightly as I let her continue.

In my mind, the only group that should have felt aggrieved by the time and date of plenary that day were the Christians. The role of religion within #RhodesMustFall was often underplayed. The majority of #RMF on-the-ground supporters and protest cows were somewhere along the spectrum of being Christian. They went from Christian in name only to full-on fundamentalists. Most kept their staunchest views to themselves, so long as the movement maintained the veneer of a Christian aesthetic. This would later change due to the utterances by Zizipho Pae, a prominent student leader at the time. She made a Facebook post about the United States Supreme Court's decision to legalise gay marriage. She described the decision as institutionalising and normalising sin. It was a student like her, I thought, who would be the most aggrieved by the scheduling of the plenary on a Sunday. I was wrong in this instance.

It was a sobering moment when my companion explained how it was absurd that those who organised the plenary and knew how these sessions often lasted hours longer than scheduled, still organised them on the day on which Cape Town's public transport system came to a halt. Apparently, the organisers of plenary meetings had either never taken public transport on a Sunday, or they lived in one of the university residences, or they had access to a vehicle. It should be noted that none of the above makes you one of South Africa's black diamonds. Instead, it entails that you enjoy a level of socio-economic leverage not available to most South Africans and in particular most students. Socio-economic leverage that more often than not seems to mimic class – hence my companion's allegation. This conversation forced me to think about how often decisions made by those with socio-economic leverage influenced the logistics, motives and overall direction of the movement. Was there a difference between those students who arrived at a protest with a car and those who travelled there by public transport? Or a difference between a protester from one of South Africa's top private schools and one from a school that still had pit latrines? How do these disparate groups come together to fight the same economic battle? Should they even trust each other? Or is trust a necessity at this point rather than a desire?

I constantly asked myself: how does the average black 20-something-year-old, born in Johannesburg and who spent most of their schooling and university life in the top tier of our educational system find themselves in the heart of a protest focused on economic emancipation? Why do they feel aggrieved with the current situation if their background allows them to avoid the worst ills of our society? What is their definition of economic freedom and is it similar to the definition of those from impoverished backgrounds? What limits are they willing to push to achieve their goals?

I don't trust the black elite and I hope this chapter helps you understand why. I don't trust them because I grew up among them and I have come to the realisation that, once they achieve their goal, they may just become worse than those we currently despise.

Growing up within the private school network and subsequently finding myself at UCT, I was exposed to a lifestyle that has increasingly become common in South Africa. It is a lifestyle where being able to shift from the rural areas of Bushbuckridge on one day and end up in a high-rise all-white party in Sandton the next is a norm. To traverse the globe on family vacations while simultaneously pleading that you are fighting for the economic freedom of others doesn't cause a single moment's pause. I describe it as the 'Pop Mabodlela' phenomenon. My issue with my generation is not that we live the lives that we do, but rather that we allow the world to expect that we would automatically be on the side of black people in the country. It is an odd assumption to make and one I do not believe is fully deserved.

In a variety of situations over the course of the evolution of #MustFall politics, from #RhodesMustFall to #FeesMustFall, this assumption has been shown to be shockingly brittle. How easy was it for students to lay blame on the shoulders of TUT for the events that played out at the Union Buildings and in the streets of Pretoria the day President Zuma announced 0%? To throw them to the wolves and label their actions as 'typical of TUT'? As if the protests against fees that characterised #FMF before 2015 were somehow less righteous than our own. Why was it that in its inception, #RMF paid no heed to the economic plight of students at UCT?

Coconuts and the black elite continuously demonstrate their inherent bias to preserve their privilege yet seem to believe they are the great allies of the revolutionary cause.

However, it is not the way we implicitly stereotype that I believe to be the real issue at hand. Rather it is the use of our socio-economic advantage to gain, maintain and distribute power that entrenches this assumption as a norm.

Take language, for instance. In plenary sessions, English was the predominant language used. Its use was not only a tool to communicate but also one of control. Though some would swap and change between English and vernac, the dominance of English became quite pronounced. It enabled some to gain the trust of the masses by eloquently enunciating elaborate preambles and soliloquies in an elegant and enigmatic manner. Verbose? Yes, indeed. Effective? Most definitely. The purpose was to capture the imagination of the crowd and sway them in your direction. The dominance of English in South Africa is not a historical happenstance. It was a deliberate strategy to gain control of the populace by dictating which language had the greatest authority. An authority one would need if they wanted to move up the social ladder. Hence the use of English became an authority in the protest, although not without a level of pushback.

With the notion of decolonisation taking strong hold, it would become difficult for English to dominate entirely. English often represents an existential threat to most languages in South Africa and the desire to resist such a threat remains strong. One example is the repurposing of the national anthem that completely removes English and Afrikaans from the original. A deliberate act and a protest in and of itself.

Another reason for pushback came from the desire to be able to communicate as broadly as possible with as many students as possible. With English being more of a language of instruction rather than a home language, naturally English would be a mechanism to marginalise in specific instances. There are a variety of reasons why pushback happens, with these two being only the tip of the iceberg.

Some students find indigenous languages – 'indigenous' not being the word I would prefer because it presumes a lack of universality – alienating and English as the best means of communicating with them. The assumption that everyone speaks English fluently because they study in English is also false. It allows certain power relations to take hold and entrench themselves. Yet, for the black elite, for whom both English and another 'indigenous' language come naturally, this dynamic plays directly into their hands. English was often inadvertently used by the elite as a means of gaining authority in the protest, but, simultaneously, employing English as the dominant language was also pushed against. We become masters of English, yet also its most ardent detractors. This can be a dangerous dynamic and it plays out in many other ways too. English is only one site where this dynamic plays out.

Another site is the idea of staying woke rather than being woke – woke being the awareness of society's constraints and impediments which adversely affect historically marginalised groups. Woke politics are interesting. They speak to the gladiator inside all of us. The desire, in situations of risk to one's well-being, to be the greatest protector of yourself and others. Being woke is the state of acknowledging that the world as it seems is often not what it is. To find yourself in this state is frightening yet enlightening at the same time. It is a rush once it is in full swing. Everything feels, smells, tastes and seems different. Relationships you once deemed immovable in your life now seem feeble. Foundations you had built your ideas on now have newly found cracks that quickly turn into chasms. Family members you once deemed cornerstones suddenly feel more like pebbles that need to be skipped away into the distance. With the help of others, through a process of learning and relearning, being woke opens the world to new possibilities and opportunities. However, it also opens you up to new threats as well as the perception of threats, creating a deep desire constantly to stay woke and keep your guard up.

I define staying woke as the ongoing process in which you are constantly seeking out new weapons to not only defend yourself but attack those who you feel are a threat. The more weapons you gain, the more threats you perceive. It is another arms race of sorts, one that I don't believe is necessarily harmful, but which does have unintended consequences. Like any arms race, any new party that seeks to arm itself becomes persona non grata within the community. At least until the moment in which it achieves a level of wokeness that demands the community's respect. Even then, it is still under certain conditions. You see this play out the most when those still in the proverbial dark seek enlightenment and are told they should undergo this process on their own. Staying woke has evolved into being a gatekeeper of enlightenment rather than its torchbearer, bringing those in the dark into the light.

The notion that bringing someone into the light is a tiring task is one that is not unfamiliar to me. It is a frustrating exercise. I wouldn't personally deem it violent, as some may, but it is arduous. When you begin the process with someone, the expectation is raised that you should end the process with them as well. You become, in the eyes of those you are trying to educate, a teacher not for a moment but for a lifetime. It is not a commitment you want to sign up for every single time you try to educate others. As a result, it does become tiring for most. I would never force someone to educate others as they are well within their rights not to. However, what I do believe to be dangerous is the belittlement of those who wish to know more and crave enlightenment. It is a belittlement that is more vindictive than dismissive.

Often, a confrontation between a white person and a coconut is fuelled by an underlying tension historically linked to an experience between said individuals rather than some broader objective. If the coconut didn't come from the same school, they would often project their own experiences onto the random white student. I have done this myself at times and I am not ashamed of it. It became my way of expressing my anger. However, the danger that I pose in doing this is that I mask my own personal anger with my own denial of economic emancipation within the white community in a private school with that of the search for economic freedom for the disenfranchised child living and going to school in Alexandra township. It is obscene to believe that our struggle is one and the same. Similar we may be, but it is our differences that inform our politics towards whiteness and wypipo. Through our socio-economic leverage, we are more than capable of turning the head of the child from Alexandra fighting for economic recognition within their area towards the fight for recognition in a school such as St John's. We disrespect the movement not through our acts, but in our 'true' intentions, intentions that should be but are often not interrogated.

There is a darker side to #MustFall politics. Not its violent delights or its exclusion of wypipo. For all its effort to change our society, its under-belly is riven with untenable relationships. Compromises. The focus on achieving economic freedom in our lifetime by disrupting institu-tions and norms requires certain balances to be achieved because of the nature of inequality in our country. It requires a pact to be agreed upon by disparate socio-economic groups and identities. We learned during #RhodesMustFall that the acceptance of toxic masculinity and chauvinist hoteps (pro-black males with backward views of notions of social pro-gress within society) was often a negotiated compromise between the dominant men who sought out the 'black feminista' as drivers of the ideological umbrella the movement needed to gain broad-based sup-port and the centrists and radical black feminists who realised that these same men were most adept at galvanising the base. #MustFall politics actively excludes 1652s but makes room for certain wypipo to become allies. It accepts religions while acknowledging that these same reli-gions actively work against some of its pillars. #MustFall politics created a bridge between those in HBIs and those in HBWs. It accepted that certain compromises were necessary so that it could carry on with its mission and ideals but interrogated each one and acknowledged the risks they brought to the surface. Yet #MustFall politics turned a blind eye to what I believe is the biggest threat to the movement.

The basic framework and ideology of #MustFall created a blueprint for how a change in our post-1994 society could and, dare I say, should take place under a generation of people temporally detached from our apart-heid history. #MustFall movements work towards de-linking us from the current state of nature that imagines South Africa as a country that is equal for all. They argue that it is just a mythological construct laid over the social and economic truths of the country. We may be resilient as a country, but we are not unbreakable.

#FeesMustFall might be the current iteration of #MustFall politics, but it will not be the last. It was unique in that it was the first to test the blueprint of achieving economic freedom in our lifetime, a blueprint that highlighted how to actively mobilise young people on a sustained day to day programme to both agitate and advocate for change in a post-1994 society. It stands to reason that the success of the movement in eventually achieving its goals will undoubtedly embolden some to improve the process. To highlight its weaknesses and amplify its strengths. To shift the blueprint out of the ivory towers of universities and into spaces broader based and representative of the plight of black people across South Africa.

Eventually, the questions will be asked: what to do with those who have had a glimpse into the world of the economically emancipated, and should they be trusted. Should the revolution include them? In the same breath, those who have glimpsed this supposed utopia should turn the question on themselves: are they willing to risk it all to achieve freedom for all, to give up the proximity to whiteness in order fully to embrace a world no longer dictated by 1652s?

The rainbow nation no longer exists. Its hold on our national consciousness is being taken apart, piece by piece, by a generation of young people no longer enamoured with it nor in awe of it. A generation willing to build a new society that no longer uses the imaginings of a post-apartheid one as its foundation. It is a movement that sees the future of the country as a blank canvas, an opportunity to pick up the baton that was once dropped and start the race for change again.

During the protest at parliament, one image that stuck with me was that of a poster that read 'Our parents were sold dreams in 1994, we are just here for the refund'.

The rules that governed the engagement of young people in politics have begun to be rewritten. The terms of engagement have been altered as we move further away from the end of apartheid in its more formalised and legal state into an apartheid that is more informal yet still visceral. We are far from the beginning of the end game, but our country and our parents need to start thinking deeply about how to chart the future. If they are unwilling, the mission will be taken on by someone else. But just as

#FeesMustFall refused to be told how they should engage in politics, any future iteration of #MustFall politics will most likely take on a similar demeanour. One that I do not believe will be persuaded to stop, even when it achieves its goal.

Notes

Chapter 1

1 Haffajee, F. (2015). 'What if there Were No Whites in South Africa?' *Africa Leadership Initiative*. Available at: https://www.africaleadership.net/what-if-there-were-no-whites-in-sa-ferial-haffajee/ (accessed on 3 April 2018).

2 Lazarus, E and Angelo, V. (1949). *The New Colossus*. Project Gutenberg.

3 Chigumadzi, P. (2015). 'Of Coconuts, Consciousness and Cecil John Rhodes: Disillusionment and Disavowals of the Rainbow Nation'. Ruth First lecture.

4 Steyn Kotze, J and Prevost, G. (2016). 'Born (Un)free: The Construction of Citizenship of South Africa's First Post-Apartheid Generation – Views of University Students'. *Representations* 52, pp 271–294.

5 Jamieson, L, Berry, L and Lake, L. (2017). *South African Child Gauge*. Children's Institute, University of Cape Town.

6 Stats SA. (2018). *Quarterly Labour Force Survey (QLFS), 4th Quarter 2017*. Statistics South Africa.

7 Stats SA. (2016). *Vulnerable Groups Series I: The Social Profile of Youth, 2009–2014 | Statistics South Africa*. Statistics South Africa.

8 Evans, E. (2016). 'Pretoria Girls High School Students are Protesting Racist Hair Policy, Code of Conduct'. *Mic*. Available at: https://mic.com/articles/152924/pretoria-girls-high-school-students-are-protesting-racist-hair-policy-code-of-conduct (accessed on 12 November 2016).

9 Harris, P, Nupen, C and Malebatsi, B. (2016). 'PHSG "Racism" Allegations'. *PoliticsWeb*. Available at: http://www.politicsweb.co.za/documents/phsg-racism-allegations-the-harris-nupen-malebatsi (accessed on 10 June 2018).

10 Keppler, V. (2016). 'Pretoria High: Teachers Called Us "Mmonkeys, Dirty K****rs"'. *The Citizen*. Available at: http://citizen.co.za/news/news-national/1267868/pretoria-high-teacher-called-us-monkeys-with-dirty-hair/ (accessed on 15 November 2016).

11 BBC News. (2016). 'Pretoria Girls High Racism Protest Backed by SA Minister'. *BBC News*.

Chapter 2

1 Lefko-Everett, K. (1998). 'Leaving it to the Children: Non-Racialism, Identity, Socialisation and Generational Change in South Africa'. *Politikon* 39, pp 127–147 (2012).
2 Baines, G. (1998). 'The Rainbow Nation? Identity and Nation Building in Post-Apartheid South Africa'. *Mots pluriels* 7, pp 1–10; Habib, A. (1997). 'South Africa – The Rainbow Nation and Prospects for Consolidating Democracy'. *African Journal of Political Science/Revue Africaine de Science Politique* 2, pp 15–37.
3 Farred, G. (2005). *'Shooting the White Girl First': Race in Post-Apartheid South Africa*. MacMillan Center Council on African Studies.
4 Gqola, P. (2001). 'Defining People: Analysing Power, Language and Representation in Metaphors of the New South Africa'. *Transformation* 47, pp 94–106.
5 Everatt, D. (2012). 'Non-Racialism in South Africa: Status and Prospects'. *Politikon* 39, pp 5–28.
6 Rawls, J. (2009). *A Theory of Justice*. Harvard University Press.
7 Chetty, R. (2014). 'Class Dismissed? Youth Resistance and the Politics of Race and Class in South African Education'. *Critical Arts* 28, pp 88–102.
8 Di Giacomo, J-P. (1980). 'Intergroup Alliances and Rejections within a Protest Movement (Analysis of the Social Representations)'. *European Journal of Social Psychology* 10(1) pp 329–344.
9 Mills, CW. (2009). 'Rawls on Race/Race in Rawls'. *The Southern Journal of Philosophy* 47, pp 161–184.
10 Cumming, G and Collier, J. (2005). 'Change and Identity in Complex Systems'. *Ecology and Society* 10(1).
11 North, DC. (1990). *Institutions, Institutional Change and Economic Performance*. Cambridge University Press.

Chapter 3

1 Stats SA. (2017). *Poverty Trends in South Africa: An Examination of Absolute Poverty between 2006 and 2015*. Statistics South Africa.
2 Swartz, S. (2017). *Another Country: Everyday Social Restitution*. Human Sciences Research Council.
3 Menon, S. (2017). 'SA's Unemployment Rate Hits a 13-year High'. Available at: https://www.timeslive.co.za/news/south-africa/2017-06-01-sas-unemployment-rate-hits-a-13-year-high/ (accessed on 29 December 2017).
4 Stats SA. (2017). *Quarterly Labour Force Survey Quarter 1: 2017*. Statistics South Africa; Department of Higher Education and Training (DHET). (2017). 'FACT SHEET ON "NEETs" (Persons who are Not in Employment, Education or Training)'.
5 Graham, L and De Lannoy, A. 'Youth Unemployment: What Can we do in the Short Run?' Available at: http://www.econ3x3.org/article/youth-unemployment-what-can-we-do-short-run (accessed on 2 January 2018).
6 Stats SA. (2017). *Poverty Trends in South Africa*.
7 Mahadea, D and Simson, R. (2010). 'The Challenge of Low Employment Economic Growth in South Africa: 1994–2008'. *South African Journal of Economic and Management Sciences* 13: 4. Available at: http://www.scielo.org.za/scielo.php?script=sci_arttext&pid=S2222-34362010000400002 (accessed on 2 September 2018).
8 Ibid.; Van der Westhuizen, C. (2012). 'South Africa: Economic Growth, Poverty and Inequality'. *Foresight Africa: Top Priorities for the Continent in 2012*, pp 33–34.
9 Bhorat, H, Van der Westhuizen, C and Jacobs, T. (2009). 'Income and Non-income Inequality in Post-apartheid South Africa: What are the Drivers and Possible Policy Interventions?' Available at: http://www.tips.org.za/files/u65/income_and_non-income_inequality_in_post-apartheid_south_africa_-_bhorat_van_der_westhuizen_jacobs.pdf SSRN 1474271 (accessed on 3 September 2018).

10 Bhorat, H, Naidoo, K, Oosthuizen, M and Pillay, K. (2015). 'Demographic, Employment, and Wage Trends in South Africa'. WIDER Working Paper.

11 Swartz, *Another Country*.

12 Barchiesi, F. (2009). 'That Melancholic Object of Desire'. In University of the Witwatersrand, Johannesburg Workshop on Theory and Criticism, Johannesburg. Available at: http://jwtc.org.za/the_salon/volume_1/franco_barchiesi.htm (accessed on 2 September 2018).

13 African National Congress Youth League. (2010). 'ANCYL Report of the First National General Council – Youth Action for Economic Freedom in Our Lifetime'. African National Congress.

14 Mandela, N. (1956). 'Freedom in Our Lifetime'. Available at: https://www.sahistory.org.za/archive/freedom-our-lifetime-nelson-mandela (accessed on 3 September 2018).

15 Mokoena, HA. (2014). 'Youth: "Born Frees" and the Predicament of Being Young in Post-Apartheid South Africa'. *Ufahamu: A Journal of African Studies* 38.

16 ANC Youth League Manifesto 1944. (2012). *South African History Online* Available at: http://www.sahistory.org.za/archive/anc-youth-league-manifesto-1944 (accessed on 10 June 2018).

17 Bundy, C. (1987). 'Street Sociology and Pavement Politics: Aspects of Youth and Student Resistance in Cape Town, 1985'. *Journal of Southern African Studies* 13, pp 303–330.

18 Edgar, RR and ka Msumza, L. (1966). *Freedom in our Lifetime: The Collected Writings of Anton Muziwakhe Lembede*. Ohio University Press.

19 Biko, S. (2015 [2002]). *I Write What I Like: Selected Writings*. University of Chicago Press.

20 Azania, MW. (2013). 'Why are Young People Buying into Malema's Party?' *Thought Leader*. Available at: http://thoughtleader.co.za/malaikawaazania/2013/07/23/why-is-the-youth-buying-into-malemas-party/ (accessed on 5 January 2018).

21 Nandipha, K. (2013). 'One in Four Youths would Support Malema Party'. *The M&G Online*. Available at: https://mg.co.za/article/2013-06-26-survey-one-in-four-youths-would-support-malema-party (accessed on 6 January 2018).

22 Hurt, SR and Kuisma, M. (2016). 'Undermining the "Rainbow Nation"? The Economic Freedom Fighters and Left-Wing Populism in South Africa'. In 66th Political Studies Association Annual International Conference Hilton Brighton Metropole, Brighton, pp 21–23.

23 Ibid.

Chapter 4

1 Soudien, C. (2008). 'The Intersection of Race and Class in the South African University: Student Experiences'. *South African Journal of Higher Education*, 22, pp 662–678.

2 Ndebele, N. (2013). 'Reflections on Rhodes: A Story of Time'. In *Viewpoints: The University of Cape Town and its Treasures* (edited by Weinberg, P). UCT Press.

3 University of Cape Town (UCT). (2016). *UCT 2015 Teaching and Learning Report*.

4 UCT. (2015). *Employment Equity Plan 2015–2020*.

Chapter 5

1 Gobodo-Madikizela, P. (2007). 'Onwards (or Backwards) into the 21st Century at UCT'. Available at: https://www.news.uct.ac.za/article/-2007-05-07-onwards-or-backwards-into-the-21st-century-at-uct-by-assoc-prof-pumla-gobodo-madikizela (accessed on 5 December 2017).

2 Benatar, D. (2012). 'Racial Admissions at UCT: A Reply to Max Price'. *PoliticsWeb*. Available at: http://www.politicsweb.co.za/news-and-analysis/racial-admissions-at-uct-a-reply-to-max-price (accessed on 11 February 2018).

3 Price, M. (2014). 'Using Historic Disadvantage to Help Gauge Students' Merit'. Available at: https://www.businesslive.co.za/bd/opinion/2014-06-25-using-historic-disadvantage-to-help-gauge-students-merit/ (accessed on 25 November 2017).

4 UCT, *UCT 2015 Teaching and Learning Report*.

5 Soudien, CA. (2013). 'Politics of Intellectual Engagement: Six Key Debates'. *Education as Change*

17, pp 165–179.

6 UCT. (2010). *Admission Policy Debate at UCT* 2010, Part 1 of 8.

7 UCT. (2012). Student Admissions Committee. *Report of the Commission into Student Admissions*. University of Cape Town.

8 Mangcu, X. (2014). 'Ripping the Veil off UCT's Whiter Shades of Pale'. *Sunday Times*, 6 July.

9 Price, M. (2014). 'Staff Transformation at UCT'. Available at: https://www.news.uct.ac.za/article/-2014-07-14-staff-transformation-at-uct (accessed on 13 December 2017).

10 Naicker, C. (2016). 'From Marikana to #FeesMustFall: The Praxis of Popular Politics in South Africa'. *Urban Health News* 1, pp 53–61.

11 Council on Higher Education (CHE). (2016). *South African Higher Education Reviewed – Two Decades of Democracy | Council on Higher Education*.

12 Scott, P. (2004). 'Ethics "in" and "for" Higher Education'. *Higher Education in Europe* 29, pp 439–450.

13 Deem, R and Brehony, KJ. (2005). 'Management as Ideology: The Case of "New Managerialism" in Higher Education'. *Oxford Review of Education* 31, pp 217–235.

14 Winter, R. (2009). 'Academic Manager or Managed Academic? Academic Identity Schisms in Higher Education'. *Journal of Higher Education Policy and Management* 31, pp 121–131.

15 Nash, A. (2006). 'Restructuring South African Universities'. In *Asinamali: University Struggles in Post-Apartheid South Africa* (edited by Pithouse, R). Africa World Press, pp 1–10.

16 Winter, 'Academic Manager or Managed Academic?'

17 Ibid.

18 'Staff Transformation at UCT: A Response'. Available at: https://www.news.uct.ac.za/article/-2014-09-23-staff-transformation-at-uct-a-response (accessed on 13 December 2017).

19 Department of Finance (DoF). (1996). *Growth, Employment and Redistribution: A Macroeconomic Strategy*.

20 Ball, SJ. (2012). 'Performativity, Commodification and Commitment: An I-Spy Guide to the Neoliberal University'. *British Journal of Educational Studies* 60, pp 17–28.

21 Van der Walt, L, Bolsmann, C, Johnson, B and Martin, L. (2002). 'Globalisation and the Outsourced University in South Africa'. *Final Report for CHET*. University of the Witwatersrand.

22 De Nicola, L and Shisana, W. (2010). *Evaluation of Outsourcing at UCT: Project Report and Recommendation*. University of Cape Town.

23 *NEHAWU v University of Cape Town and Others 2002 (4) BLLR 311 (LAC). Ngcobo, J* (2002); Mathekga, JM. (2016). 'The Analyses of Non-Standard Employment and Contemporary Labour Protest in South Africa'. *South African Journal of Labour Relations* 40, pp 139–151.

24 Maree, J and Le Roux, R. (2014). 'Report on Outsourcing at UCT: Findings and Recommendations'.

25 Ibid.

Chapter 6

1 Dlavaku, S. (2014). 'Wits Political Studies Post-Graduate Students: On a Quest to Revolutionalise the Academy'. *Daily Maverick*. Available at: https://www.dailymaverick.co.za/opinionista/2014-12-19-wits-political-studies-post-graduate-students-on-a-quest-to-revolutionalise-the-academy/ (accessed on 10 June 2018).

2 Naicker, 'From Marikana to #FeesMustFall'; Luescher, TM. (2016). 'Frantz Fanon and the #MustFall Movements in South Africa'. *International Higher Education*, pp 22–24.

3 Myers, E. (2017). 'Beyond the Wages of Whiteness: Du Bois on the Irrationality of Antiblack Racism'. *Items*. Available at: http://items.ssrc.org/beyond-the-wages-of-whiteness-du-bois-on-the-irrationality-of-antiblack-racism/ (accessed on 26 February 2018).

4 UCT. (2015). 'From the VC's Desk: Rhodes Statue Protests and Transformation'. Available at: https://www.news.uct.ac.za/

article/-2015-03-18-from-the-vcs-desk-rhodes-statue-protests-and-transformation (accessed on 9 February 2018).

5 Schmahmann, B. (2016). 'The Fall of Rhodes: The Removal of a Sculpture from the University of Cape Town'. *Public Art Dialogue* 6, pp 90–115.

6 Ndebele, 'Reflections on Rhodes'.

7 Hatherley, O. (2016). 'Rewriting the Past: Must Rhodes Fall?' *Apollo Magazine*. Available at: https://www.apollo-magazine.com/rewriting-the-past-must-rhodes-fall/ (accessed on 12 February 2018).

8 Ibid.; Lowry, D. (2016). 'The "Rhodes Must Fall" Campaign: Where Would the Destruction End?' *Round Table* 105, pp 329–331.

9 Knoetze, D. (2014). '"Tokoloshes" Vandalise Rhodes Statue'. *IOL News*. Available at: https://www.iol.co.za/news/crime-courts/tokoloshes-vandalise-rhodes-statue-1692902 (accessed on 12 February 2018).

10 Keet, A. (2014). 'Epistemic "Othering" and the Decolonisation of Knowledge'. *Africa Insight* 44(1), pp 23–37.

11 Rawls, *A Theory of Justice*.

Chapter 7

1 The Collective. (2015). 'FreeTalk – Nelson Mandela: Saviour or Sell Out?' Available at: https://web.facebook.com/events/373622619492457/?active_tab=discussion (accessed on 12 February 2018).

2 Ibid.

3 Ibid.

4 Ibid.

5 BLVCK. (2013). 'Vote BLVCK – About'. Available at: https://www.facebook.com/pg/VoteBLVCK/about/?ref=page_internal (accessed on 12 February 2018).

6 Aluta. (2014). 'VoteAluta – About'. Available at: https://www.facebook.com/pg/VoteAluta/about/?ref=page_internal (accessed on 12 February 2018).

7 Cassim, Y. (2014). 'DASO wins UCT 2014 SRC Election'. *PoliticsWeb*. Available at: http://www.politicsweb.co.za/news-and-analysis/daso-wins-uct-2014-src-election--yusuf-cassim (accessed on 10 February 2018).

Chapter 8

1 News 24. (2010). 'Jogger: Sorry President Zuma. *News24*. Available at: https://www.news24.com/southafrica/news/jogger-sorry-president-zuma-20100218 (accessed on 26 February 2018).

2 Ramphele, L. (2016). 'Is there Trouble in Paradise in the FeesMustFall Movement?' Available at: http://www.702.co.za/articles/12623/is-there-trouble-in-paradise-in-the-feesmustfall-movement (accessed on 26 February 2018); Mthonti, FA. (2016). 'Rapist State's Children: Jacob Zuma and Chumani Maxwele'. *The Con*. Available at: http://www.theconmag.co.za/2016/04/08/a-rapist-states-children-jacob-zuma-chumani-maxwele/ (accessed on 26 February 2018).

3 Amod, T. (2014). 'First Edition'. *Vernac News Cape Town*. Available at: https://vernacnews.co.za/previous-editions/older/first-edition/ (accessed on 26 February 2018).

4 Luckett, T and Mzobe, D. (2016). '#OutsourcingMustFall: The Role of Workers in the 2015 Protest Wave at South African Universities'. *Global Labour Journal* 7.

5 Godsell, G and Chikane, R. (2016). 'The Roots of the Revolution'. In *Fees Must Fall: Student Revolt, Decolonisation and Governance in South Africa* (edited by Booysen, S). Wits University Press, pp 54–73.

6 Ntsebeza, L. (2014). 'The Mafeje and the UCT Saga: Unfinished Business?' *Social Dynamics* 40, pp 274–288.

7 Price, M. (2008). 'UCT Statement and Apology Regarding Professor AB Mafeje'. University of

Cape Town.

8 Jansen, JD. (1998). 'But Our Natives are Different! Race, Knowledge and Power in the Academy'. *Social Dynamics* 24, pp 106–116.

9 UCT. (2015). *University Assembly: The Rhodes Statue and Transformation*. YouTube. Available at: https://www.youtube.com/watch?v=eWVJnBVnyPc (accessed on 3 September 2018).

10 Mugo, K. (2015). 'When Comrades Rape Comrades'. *Mail & Guardian*, 27 November.

Chapter 9

1 Chernick, I. (2015). '"1 Million, 1Month" Officially Launches'. *Wits Vuvuzela*. Available at: http://witsvuvuzela.com/2015/02/20/one-million-one-month-officially-launches/ (accessed on 14 March 2018).

2 Bendile, D. (2015). 'Wits Raises Nearly R2m for Needy Students' Tuition'. Available at: http://ewn.co.za/2015/02/24/Wits-raise-nearly-R2m-for-needy-students-tuition (accessed on 14 March 2018).

3 CHE, 2016, *South African Higher Education Reviewed*.

4 Van der Berg, S. (2014). 'Inequality, Poverty and Prospects for Redistribution'. *Development Southern Africa* 31, pp 197–218.

5 Cloete, N. (2016). 'Free Higher Education: Another Self-Destructive South African Policy'. Centre for Higher Education Trust. Available at: https://www.chet.org.za/papers/free-higher-education (accessed on 2 September 2018); Montenegro, CE and Patrinos, HA. (2014). 'Comparable Estimates of Returns to Schooling around the World'. Available at: https://openknowledge.worldbank.org/handle/10986/20340 (accessed on 2 September 2018).

6 CHE, 2016, *South African Higher Education Reviewed*.

7 Department of Education (DoE). (1997). 'Education White Paper 3: A Programme for the Transformation of Higher Education'. *Government Gazette* 386, 18207.

8 Department of Higher Education and Training (DHET). (2017). *Statistics on Post-School Education and Training in South Africa: 2015*.

9 Ibid.

10 CHE, 2016, *South African Higher Education Reviewed*.

11 Ibid.

12 Cloete, 'Free Higher Education'; UCT. (2016). *University of Cape Town Financial Aid and Fees Department Submission to the Presidential Commission on Funding Higher Education*.

13 CHE, 2016, *South African Higher Education Reviewed*; PricewaterhouseCoopers. (no date). 'Funding of Public Higher Education Institutions in South Africa'. Available at: https://www.pwc.co.za/en/publications/funding-public-higher-education-institutions-sa.html (accessed on 15 March 2018); De Villiers, P. (2017). 'The Poor and Access to Higher Education in South Africa. The NSFAS Contribution'. Available at: https://2017.essa.org.za/fullpaper/essa_3614.pdf (accessed on 3 September 2018); Cloete, N. (2015). 'The Flawed Ideology of "Free Higher Education"'. *University World News* 389.

14 De Villiers, 'The Poor and Access to Higher Education in South Africa'.

15 Ibid.; SALDRU. (2017). *Understanding the National Student Financial Aid Scheme*.

16 SALDRU, 2017, *Understanding the National Student Financial Aid Scheme*.

17 Bhorat, H and Pillay, N. (2017). 'The National Student Financial Aid Scheme (NSFAS) and the Development of the Higher Education System in South Africa'. Available at: http://www.lmip.org.za/document/national-student-financial-aid-schem-nsfas-and-development-higher-education-system-south (accessed on 3 September 2018).

18 Ibid.

19 SALDRU, 2017, *Understanding the National Student Financial Aid Scheme*.

20 DHET. (2010). 'Report of the Ministerial Committee on the Review of the National Student Financial Aid Scheme'.

21 Bhorat and Pillay, 'The National Student Financial Aid Scheme'; DHET, 'Report of the Ministerial Committee on the Review of the National Student Financial Aid Scheme'.

22 DHET, 2010, 'Report of the Ministerial Committee on the Review of the National Student Financial Aid Scheme'.

23 National Student Financial Aid Scheme (NSFAS). (2016). 'Submission by NSFAS on Fee-Free Higher Education'.

24 Ndlazi, S. (2017). 'NSFAS Tweaks its Funding Approach'. *Cape Times*, 20 February. Available at: https://www.iol.co.za/capetimes/news/nsfas-tweaks-its-funding-approach-7842088 (accessed on 15 March 2018).

25 DHET, 2010, 'Report of the Ministerial Committee on the Review of the National Student Financial Aid Scheme'.

26 SALDRU, 2017, *Understanding the National Student Financial Aid Scheme*; Majavu, A. (2011). 'Loan Relief for NSFAS Students'. Available at: https://www.timeslive.co.za/news/south-africa/2011-08-24-loan-relief-for-nsfas-students/ (accessed on 15 March 2018).

27 Cloete, 'The Flawed Ideology of "Free Higher Education"'.

28 Staff Reporter. (2008). 'Durban Students Threaten Further Protests'. *The M&G Online*. Available at: https://mg.co.za/article/2008-02-10-durban-students-threaten-further-protests/ (accessed on 16 March 2018).

29 McGregor, K. (2008). 'SOUTH AFRICA: Student Protests Turn Violent'. *University World News*. Available at: http://www.universityworldnews.com/article.php?story=20080208090147857 (accessed on 16 March 2018).

30 Masombuka, S. (2008). 'Police Open Fire on Protesting Students'. *Sowetan LIVE*. Available at: https://www.sowetanlive.co.za/news/2008-01-30-police-open-fire-on-protesting-students/ (accessed on 16 March 2018).

31 Van Niekerk, L and Venter, Z. (2008). 'TUT Protesters Disrupt Registration'. *IOL News*. Available at: https://www.iol.co.za/news/south-africa/tut-protesters-disrupt-registration-386539 (accessed on 16 March 2018).

32 Gower, P. (2009). 'Student Leaders Arrested at Westville Protest'. *The M&G Online*. Available at: https://mg.co.za/article/2009-02-04-student-leaders-arrested-at-westville-protest/ (accessed on 16 March 2018).

33 Staff Reporter. (2011). 'Tshwane University of Technology under Administration'. *The M&G Online*. Available at: https://mg.co.za/article/2011-08-16-tswane-university-of-technology-under-administration/ (accessed on 14 March 2018); 'CPUT Brought to a Standstill by Student Protests'. *West Cape News*. Available at: http://westcapenews.com/?p=2946 (accessed on 14 March 2018); IOL. (2011). 'UKZN Students Protests in Pictures'. *IOL News*. Available at: https://www.iol.co.za/news/south-africa/kwazulu-natal/ukzn-students-protests-in-pictures-1034387 (accessed on 14 March 2018); *South African History Online*. (2015). 'Student Protests in Democratic South Africa'. Available at: http://www.sahistory.org.za/article/student-protests-democratic-south-africa (accessed on 14 March 2018).

34 News24. (2012). 'Protests Force Closure of TUT Campuses'. Available at: https://www.news24.com/SouthAfrica/News/Protests-force-closure-of-TUT-campuses-20120820 (accessed on 14 March 2018); SAPA. (2012). 'UKZN Classes Suspended'. Available at: https://www.timeslive.co.za/news/south-africa/2012-02-16-ukzn-classes-suspended/ (accessed on 14 March 2018); News24. (2012). 'Students Bring UKZN to Standstill'. Available at: https://www.news24.com/southafrica/news/students-bring-ukzn-to-standstill-20120822 (accessed on 16 March 2018).

35 *South African History Online*, 'Student Protests in Democratic South Africa'; Nyanda, S. (2013). 'Classes Cancelled as DUT Staff Strike'. *Daily News*, 26 February. Available at: https://www.iol.co.za/dailynews/news/classes-cancelled-as-dut-staff-strike-1477351 (accessed on 14 March 2018).

36 Taunyane, O. (2014). 'TUT Shuts Down, Students Evacuated'. Available at: https://www.enca.com/south-africa/tut-shuts-down-evacuates-students (accessed on 14 March 2018); SAPA. (2014). 'Countrywide Protests over NSFAS Funding'. *IOL News*. Available at: https://www.iol.co.za/news/

south-africa/coutrywide-protests-over-nsfas-funding-1637716 (accessed on 14 March 2018);
SAPA. (2014). 'Protest Erupts at Mangosuthu University of Technology'. Available at: https://
www.enca.com/protest-erupts-mangosuthu-university-technology (accessed on 14 March 2018);
SAPA. (2014). 'Sasco Calls for Mass Student Protests'. *The M&G Online*. Available at: https://
mg.co.za/article/2014-01-26-sasco-calls-for-mass-student-protests/ (accessed on 14 March 2018).

Chapter 10

1 Luescher-Mamashela, TM. (2010). 'From University Democratisation to Managerialism: The
Changing Legitimation of University Governance and the Place of Students'. *Tertiary Education
and Management* 16, pp 259–283; Luescher, TM. (2009). 'Racial Desegregation and the
Institutionalisation of "Race" in University Governance: The Case of the University of Cape Town'.
Perspectives in Education 27, pp 415–425.
2 Cele, G and Koen, C. (2003). 'Student Politics in South Africa: An Overview of Key
Developments', *Open Edition Journals*. Available at: https://journals.openedition.org/cres/1517
(accessed on 3 September 2018).
3 Ibid.
4 Letsoalo, M. (2014). 'EFF Takes Limpopo University SRC'. *The M&G Online*. Available at: https://
mg.co.za/article/2014-10-10-eff-takes-limpopo-university-src/ (accessed on 10 March 2018).
5 Nkosi, B. (2015). 'EFF Claims Landslide Victory over Sasco at VUT SRC'. *The M&G Online*.
Available at: https://mg.co.za/article/2015-03-27-eff-claims-landslide-victory-over-sasco-at-vut-
src/ (accessed on 10 March 2018); Mandiwana, N. (2015). 'EFF Wins Univen SRC Elections'.
Capricorn Voice. Available at: https://capricornreview.co.za/65026/eff-wins-univen-src-elections/
(accessed on 10 March 2018); Vilakazi, M. (2017). 'Soshanguve Campus Protests Cannot be
Reduced to #FeesMustFall: An Analysis of the #FeesMustFall Movement at South African
Universities'. Available at: https://csvr.org.za/pdf/An-analysis-of-the-FeesMustFall-Movement-at-
South-African-universities.pdf (accessed on 3 September 2018).
6 EFFSC. (2015). *Economic Freedom Fighters Student Command Constitution.*
7 Cele and Koen, 'Student Politics in South Africa'; Magume, T and Luescher, TM. (2015). 'The
Politics of Student Housing: Student Activism and Representation in the Determination of the
User-price of a Public–Private Partnership Residence on a Public University Campus in South
Africa'. *Journal of Student Affairs in Africa* 3, pp 1–17.
8 Taghavi, D. (2017). 'Exploring Fallism: Student Protests and the Decolonization of Education in
South Africa'. Universität zu Köln. Available at: https://kups.ub.uni-koeln.de/7950/ (accessed on 3
September 2018).

Chapter 11

1 The University of the Witwatersrand (Wits). (2015).'Why Fee Increases are Necessary'. *Wits
University*. Available at: https://www.wits.ac.za/news/latest-news/general-news/2015/2015-10/
why-fee-increases-are-necessary.html (accessed on 22 March 2018).
2 Wits Workers' Solidarity Committee. (2015). 'University Workers' Charter'. Available at: http://
witsworkerssolidaritycommittee.blogspot.co.za/2015/10/ (accessed on 22 March 2018).
3 Nkosi, B. (2015). 'Huge Protest Decries Wits's Outsourcing Practice'. *The M&G Online*. Available
at: https://mg.co.za/article/2015-10-06-huge-protest-decries-witss-outsourcing-practice/
(accessed on 22 March 2018).
4 Naidoo, M. (2012). 'Local Student on Hunger Strike at Wits'. *Sunday Tribune*, 27 May. Available
at: https://www.pressreader.com/south-africa/sunday-tribune/20120527/282699044175253
(accessed on 22 March 2018).
5 Wits. (2013). 'Message from Prof Tawana Kupe'. Available at: https://www.wits.ac.za/news/
latest-news/general-news/2013/2013-06/ (accessed on 22 March 2018); Nkosi, B. (2013).
'Workers Protest at Wits over Job-loss Rumours'. *The M&G Online*. Available at: https://mg.co.za/

article/2013-05-28-workers-protest-at-wits-over-job-loss-rumours/ (accessed on 22 March 2018).

6 Ndlozi, M. (2013). 'Wits University Workers Issue Ultimatum to New Vice Chancellor, Professor Adam Habib'. BDS. Available at: http://www.bdssouthafrica.com/academic-boycott/wits-right-to-protest/wits-university-workers-issue-ultimatum-to-new-vice-chancellor-professor-adam-habib/ (accessed on 22 March 2018).

7 Habib, A. (2015). 'Opening the Conversation: Accelerating Transformation for an Inclusive and Competitive Wits'. Available at: http://blogs.wits.ac.za/vc/2015/05/21/opening-the-conversation-accelerating-transformation-for-an-inclusive-and-competitive-wits/ (accessed on 22 March 2018).

8 Fredericks, I. (2015). 'UCT Protest over Outsourced Labour'. *IOL News*. Available at: https://www.iol.co.za/news/south-africa/western-cape/pics-uct-protest-over-outsourced-labour-1926122 (accessed on 22 March 2018).

9 Petersen, C. (2015). 'UCT Defends Outsourcing Workers Amid Protests'. *Cape Times*, 6 November. Available at: https://www.iol.co.za/capetimes/news/uct-defends-outsourcing-workers-amid-protests-1926033 (accessed on 22 March 2018).

10 Habib, A. (2015). 'South Africa: Approaching a Moment of Reckoning'. Available at: http://blogs.wits.ac.za/vc/2015/09/09/south-africa-approaching-a-moment-of-reckoning/ (accessed on 22 March 2018).

11 It's Happening. (2015). *Wits Fees Must Fall – #WitsFeesMustFall*. YouTube. Available at: https://www.youtube.com/watch?v=Hg0f_FCDEmI (accessed on 3 September 2018).

12 RDM News. (2015). 'Wits Students Clash in Strike Over University Fees'. Available at: https://businesstech.co.za/news/general/101138/watch-wits-students-clash-in-strike-over-university-fees/ (accessed on 23 March 2018).

13 Maimela, D. (2015). 'South African Higher Education Transformation: What is to be Done?' Available at: http://www.dhet.gov.za/summit/Docs/2015Docs/Annex%2016_Maimela_SASCO_HE%20Transformation.pdf (accessed on 3 September 2018).

14 Kalla, S. (2018). Personal communication with Rekgotsofetse Chikane.

15 Habib, A. (2017). Personal communication with Rekgotsofetse Chikane.

16 Wits. (2015). 'Decision to Increase Fees Suspended Pending Negotiations'. *PoliticsWeb*. Available at: http://politicsweb.co.za/documents/decision-to-increase-fees-suspended-pending-negoti (accessed on 23 March 2018).

Chapter 12

1 Lewis, S. (2015). 'Rhodes University Students Join #FeesMustFall Protests'. *The Daily Vox*. Available at: http://www.thedailyvox.co.za/rhodes-university-students-join-feesmustfall-protests/ (accessed on 23 March 2018); Mpulo, M and Pela, N. (2015). '#RhodesMIPmustFall Brings Rhodes University to a Standstill'. *The M&G Online*. Available at: https://mg.co.za/article/2015-10-19-rhodesmipmustfall-brings-rhodes-university-to-a-standstill/ (accessed on 23 March 2018); Van Aardt, T and Dayimani, M. (2015). 'Rhodes Classes Halted as Students Protest over Fees'. *HeraldLIVE*. Available at: http://www.heraldlive.co.za/news/top-news/2015/10/20/rhodes-classes-halted-students-protest-fees/ (accessed on 23 March 2018).

2 Lewis, 'Rhodes University Students Join #FeesMustFall Protests'; Mpulo and Pela, '#RhodesMIPmustFAll Brings Rhodes University to a Standstill'.

3 Concerned Academics at Wits. (2015). 'Statement from Concerned Academics at the University of the Witwatersrand'. Monday, 19 October 2015.

4 Davis, R. (2015). 'Student Protests: UCT Flexes its Muscles'. *Daily Maverick*. Available at: https://www.dailymaverick.co.za/article/2015-10-19-student-protests-uct-flexes-its-muscles/#.WrU8DhuZqM (accessed on 23 March 2018).

5 Ibid.

6 Mpulo and Pela, '#RhodesMIPmustFall Brings Rhodes University to a Standstill'.

7   Van Aardt, T and Dayimani, M. (2015). 'Rhodes Classes Halted as Students Protest over Fees'. Available at: https://www.pressreader.com/south-africa/the-herald-south-africa/20151020/281492160163509 (accessed on 3 September 2018); O'Halloran, P. (2015). 'Grahamstown: Police Action Conceals their Failure of the Community'. *Daily Maverick*. Available at: https://www.dailymaverick.co.za/opinionista/2015-10-21-grahamstown-police-action-conceals-their-failure-of-the-community/#.WrVLaOhuZqM (accessed on 23 March 2018).

8   Davis, 'Student Protests'; Hsu, T. (2015). 'UCT Student Protest: What You Need to Know'. Available at: https://www.news24.com/SouthAfrica/News/UCT-student-protest-What-you-need-to-know-20151020 (accessed on 23 March 2018).

9   Pather, R. (2015). 'A List of #UCTShutdown's Demands #FeesMustFall'. Available at: https://twitter.com/raediology/status/656110039179112448 (accessed on 23 March 2018).

10 Makhafola, G. (2015). 'Wits Management Refuses to Meet with Protesting Students'. *The M&G Online*. Available at: https://mg.co.za/article/2015-10-19-wits-management-refuses-to-meet-with-protesting-students/ (accessed on 23 March 2018).

11 Furlong, A. (2015). 'Students Shut Down UCT'. *Ground Up*. Available at: https://www.groundup.org.za/article/students-shut-down-uct_3412/ (accessed on 23 March 2018).

12 Pather, R. (2015). '#FeesMustFall: UCT Slaps Protesters with Court Interdict'. *The Daily Vox*. Available at: https://www.thedailyvox.co.za/feesmustfall-uct-slaps-protestors-with-court-interdict/ (accessed on 24 March 2018).

13 Kalipa, S. (2015). '#UCTShutdown: Tempers Boil Over'. *IOL News*. Available at: https://www.iol.co.za/news/south-africa/western-cape/uctshutdown-tempers-boil-over-1932536 (accessed on 24 March 2018).

14 Aslam, M. (2015). 'Wits Students Supporting UCT. We May be Miles Apart but We Stand as One. #WitsShutDown #uctshutdown #FeesMustFall'. Available at: https://twitter.com/sayed_095/status/656381185736732672 (accessed on 24 March 2018).

15 Whittles, G and Kekana, M. (2015). '#FeesMustFall: NSFAS Weighs in on Student Protests'. Available at: http://ewn.co.za/2015/10/20/NSFAS-internal-inefficiencies-caused-by-unpaid-loans (accessed on 24 March 2018).

16 eNCA. (2015). 'UFS Joins #FeesMustFall Student Protests'. *eNCA*. Available at: https://www.enca.com/south-africa/ufs-protests-begin-gain-momentum (accessed on 24 March 2018).

17 Charles, L. (2015). 'Fees Must Fall Protest Spreads to UKZN'. *Berea Mail*. Available at: https://bereamail.co.za/65963/fees-must-fall-protest-spreads-to-ukzn/ (accessed on 24 March 2018); Lembethe, K. (2015). 'Westville Campus Joins #FeesMustFall Campaign'. *Highway Mail*. Available at: https://highwaymail.co.za/202524/westville-campus-joins-feesmustfall-campain/ (accessed on 24 March 2018).

18 SABC Digital News. (2015). *Universities across the Country Joined in the 'FeesMustFall' Campaign*. YouTube. Available at: https://www.youtube.com/watch?v=0O7quMgKyMQ (accessed on 3 September 2018).

19 Nzimande, B. (2015). 'Nzimande Jokes that #StudentsMustFall'. *Business Tech*. Available at: https://businesstech.co.za/news/government/101966/watch-nzimande-jokes-that-studentsmustfall/ (accessed on 24 March 2018).

Chapter 13

1   DHET. (2017). 'FACT SHEET ON "NEETs" (Persons who are Not in Employment, Education or Training)'; Sheppard, C. (2016). 'South African Higher Education Performance Indicators 2009–2015': Table 10: Weighted Graduates.

2   Sello, L. (2015). 'Wits, UJ Students March to ANC HQ At Luthuli House'. *eNCA*. Available at: https://www.enca.com/south-africa/wits-uj-students-march-anc-luthuli-house (accessed on 27 March 2018).

3   The Daily Vox. (2015). '#NationalShutDown'. *The Daily Vox*. Live blog 21–22 October. Available

at: http://www.thedailyvox.co.za/nationalshutdown-live-blog/ (accessed on 28 March 2018).

4 Hess, L. (2015). '#FeesHaveFallen: A Victory for Class of 2015 – As It Happened'. Available at: https://www.news24.com/SouthAfrica/News/LIVE-FeesMustFall-students-protest-at-Union-Buildings-20151023 (accessed on 29 March 2018).

Chapter 14

1 Ramphele, L. (2016). 'Is there Trouble in Paradise in the FeesMustFall Movement?' Available at: http://www.702.co.za/articles/12623/is-there-trouble-in-paradise-in-the-feesmustfall-movement (accessed on 26 February 2018).

2 Siedentop, L. (2014). *Inventing the Individual: The Origins of Western Liberalism*. Harvard University Press.

3 Hirsch, EL. (1990). 'Sacrifice for the Cause: Group Processes, Recruitment, and Commitment in a Student Social Movement'. *American Sociological. Review* 55, pp 243–254.

4 Spencer, ME. (1970). 'Weber on Legitimate Norms and Authority'. *The British Journal of Sociology* 21, pp 123–134.

5 Chan, JCW. (2014). *Confucian Perfectionism: A Political Philosophy for Modern Times*. Princeton University Press.

6 Raz, J. (1988). *The Morality of Freedom*. Oxford University Press.

7 Ibid.

8 Ibid., p 46.

Chapter 15

1 Furlong, BA. (2016). 'Rhodes Must Fall Protesters Burn UCT Art'. Available at: https://www.groundup.org.za/article/rhodes-must-fall-protesters-destroy-uct-artworks/ (accessed on 8 April 2018).

2 Taghavi, 'Exploring Fallism'.

3 Msimang, S. (2016). 'The Burning'. Available at: https://africasacountry.com/2016/02/the-burning/ (accessed on 11 April 2018).

Acknowledgements

This book is dedicated to all our modern-day student political prisoners and those still being persecuted for their heroism by the state.

To my dad, whose sparring debates have shaped me into who I am, and to my mother, who has always grounded me in my faith.

To the friends betrayed, I hope to one day find your forgiveness.

To the friends who remained, I have no words to describe the impact you have had on me and the way I viewed the world.

CPSIA information can be obtained
at www.ICGtesting.com
Printed in the USA
LVHW091810200221
679509LV00007B/1602